MODERNISM AND DEMOCRACY

Modernism and Democracy

Literary Culture 1900–1930

RACHEL POTTER

OXFORD
UNIVERSITY PRESS

OXFORD
UNIVERSITY PRESS

Great Clarendon Street, Oxford OX2 6DP

Oxford University Press is a department of the University of Oxford.
It furthers the University's objective of excellence in research, scholarship,
and education by publishing worldwide in

Oxford New York

Auckland Cape Town Dar es Salaam Hong Kong Karachi
Kuala Lumpur Madrid Melbourne Mexico City Nairobi
New Delhi Shanghai Taipei Toronto

With offices in

Argentina Austria Brazil Chile Czech Republic France Greece
Guatemala Hungary Italy Japan Poland Portugal Singapore
South Korea Switzerland Thailand Turkey Ukraine Vietnam

Oxford is a registered trade mark of Oxford University Press
in the UK and in certain other countries

Published in the United States
by Oxford University Press Inc., New York

British Library Cataloguing in Publication Data
Data available

Library of Congress Cataloging in Publication Data
Data available

Typeset by Laserwords Private Limited, Chennai, India
Printed in Great Britain
on acid-free paper by
Biddles Ltd., King's Lynn, Norfolk

ISBN 978-0-19-927393-5

To my Mum and Dad

Acknowledgements

Firstly I would like to thank my PhD superviser Maud Ellmann, for her guidance when this project was at a very early stage. I owe much to her intelligence, humour and generosity. Thanks also to Peter Nicholls, David Trotter, Laura Marcus, Rod Mengham and Morag Shiach, who, at different stages, read chapters of this book, and provided invaluable criticism and support. The librarians at the Beinecke Library at Yale, and at Cambridge University helped me to negotiate around the Mina Loy and H.D. archives, and to conduct my research in its early stages. Thanks to King's College, Cambridge for their financial assistance and, more particularly for the unfailing intellectual support of Pete De Bolla over the years. Thanks also to Queen Mary, University of London and the AHRB, for providing research leave to allow me the time to finish this project. I am also greateful for the help and advice of Sophie Goldsworthy at Oxford University Press who commissioned the book, and later Tom Perridge and Eva Nyika for their patient help with its production. Thanks to Jean Van Altena for her careful editing of the manuscript.

This book was written over a number of years, and many people have helped me with it. Many thanks to the organisers of the London Modernism seminar in its early years, and in particular to Carolyn Burdett, Geoff Gilbert, Lyndsey Stonebridge and Trudi Tate. Our dicussions were crucial to the development of the ideas explored in this book, and to my sense of the excitement of intellectual exchange. Thanks also to Rowan Harris and Tim Armstrong for helping me to understand the work of Mina Loy. At a later stage, my colleagues at Queen Mary have provided a brillant intellectual environment. I would like specifically to thank Michèle Barrett, Paul Hamilton, Cora Kaplan, Javed Majeed and Jacqueline Rose for their support and advice.

Many other people have been important to this project over the years. Thanks, in particular, to Drew Milne, who alone knows how much of this is down to him. I am also grateful to my family, and to Linda Clarke, Mark Currie, Helen Groth, Emer Nolan and Ingrid Scheibler for their friendship. Especial thanks to Henry and Thomas for providing much happiness in the final stages. Finally, and most importantly, thanks to my Mum and Dad, who have provided not only fine editorial advice but have supported me all the way.

Chapter Four, T. S. Eliot, 'T.S. Eliot, women, and democracy', was originally published in Cassandra Laity and Nancy Gish, eds. *Gender, Desire, and Sexuality in T. S. Eliot* (Cambridge: Cambridge University Press, 2004).

The author and publisher also gratefully acknowledge permission to quote from the following: H.D., various extracts from *Collected Poems 1912–1944* (New York: New Directions Press, 1983). H.D., Unpublished material by H.D.: Copyright c (2006) by the Schaffner Family Foundation. Used by kind permission of New Directions Publishing Corporation. T. S. Eliot, various extracts from *The Complete Poems and Plays, Selected Prose of T. S. Eliot, The Letters of T. S. Eliot, vol 1, The Egoist, The Criterion*, and *After Strange Gods*. Copyright, Faber and Faber Ltd. in the UK and Copyright Harcourt Trade in the US. Mina Loy, various extracts from *The Last Lunar Baedeker* and *The Lost Lunar Beadeker* as well as unpublished material by Mina Loy. Used by kind permission of Mina Loy's editor. Roger Conover. D. H. Lawrence, various extracts from *Women in Love, Phoenix: The Posthumous Papers of D. H. Lawrence, The Cambridge Edition of the Works of D. H. Lawrence: Study of Thomas Hardy and other essays, The Complete Poems*. Reproduced by kind permission of Pollinger Limited and the proprietor.

Contents

Introduction

Unacknowledged Legislators: Modernist Poetry and Democracy

The emergence of modernist literature coincided with the birth of the mass democratic state. Yet Anglo-American modernists are notorious for their hostility to democracy and liberalism. As Ezra Pound put it in 1914, 'The artist has been at peace with his oppressors for long enough. He has dabbled in democracy and he is now done with that folly .... The aristocracy of entail and of title has decayed, the aristocracy of commerce is decaying, the aristocracy of the arts is ready again for its service.'[1] Pound's words announce the political terms of a new literary agenda. He debunks the artist's enslavement to democracy and literary commerce, and imagines a new legislative role for the famously 'unacknowledged' poet legislators of Shelley's fancy. Thirty years later, Pound found himself imprisoned and humiliated in Pisa, his visions of a new artistic aristocracy hopelessly dashed. His final humiliation has been seen as a just conclusion, not only for Pound himself, but for the anti-democratic sentiments of modernist writers in general. Michael North sums it up: 'The politics of Yeats, Eliot, and Pound have long been an embarrassment and a scandal. Yeats's authoritarianism, Eliot's prejudices, and Pound's fascist anti-semitism have presented sympathetic critics with insuperable problems of explanation.'[2]

Is modernist poetry, then, tied irrevocably to authoritarian models of poetic authority? Are the poems of Yeats, Eliot, and Pound last-ditch attempts to halt the shift towards a more emancipated political and cultural sphere? Lionel Trilling, writing of the liberal imagination in the 1940s, argued that modernism was simply irreconcilable with democratic beliefs: 'the modern European literature to which we can

---

[1] Ezra Pound, 'The New Sculpture', *Egoist*, 1.4 (1914), 68.
[2] Michael North, *The Political Aesthetic of Modernism: Yeats, Eliot and Pound* (Cambridge: Cambridge University Press, 1991), 1.

have an active, reciprocal relationship ... has been written by men who are indifferent to, or even hostile to, the tradition of democratic liberalism as we know it. Yeats and Eliot, Proust and Joyce, Lawrence and Gide—these men do not seem to confirm us in the social and political ideals which we hold.'[3] Trilling's belief that there was a basic conflict between modernist writing and liberal ideals informed the twentieth-century reception of Anglo-American modernism.

In recent years, however, this picture of modernism has been transformed by extensive work on a much wider literary and cultural landscape. In particular, since the late 1970s more marginal modernist writers have been recovered, particularly women writers. The new modernist landscape, then, includes the work of Virginia Woolf, Gertrude Stein, Marianne Moore, Katherine Mansfield, Dorothy Richardson, H.D., Mina Loy, Djuna Barnes, Nancy Cunard, Mary Butts, Laura Riding, and others. There has often been an assumption that the work of these women modernists forms a more liberal, less élitist literary tradition. Whereas Pound is seen to condemn democratic inclusiveness and literary commerce, Woolf defends a woman's democratic right to education and cultural participation. Their different political and cultural attitudes fuel rather different visions of aesthetic authority.

Andreas Huyssen's influential book *After the Great Divide: Modernism, Mass Culture, and Postmodernism* (1986) is often taken as a reference point for this shift in critical emphasis. It describes the way in which 'high' modernist texts are grounded in a hostility to mass culture, everyday life, and femininity. Huyssen argues that modernist and avant-garde texts are structured around a number of divides: of high modernism and mass culture, individual authority and mass democracy, and male and female. He argues that male modernist writers denigrate mass culture, mass democracy, and the feminine. He reverses the values attached to these categories. The book is thus written from a 'feminist' postmodern position, which he defines by its 'distance from high modernism' and 'the historical avant-garde', which he claims 'was by and large as patriarchal, misogynist, and masculinist as the major trends of modernism'.[4]

---

[3] Lionel Trilling, *The Liberal Imagination: Essays on Literature and Society* (Harmondsworth: Penguin Books, 1970), 299.

[4] Andreas Huyssen, *After the Great Divide: Modernism, Mass Culture, and Postmodernism* (Bloomington, Ind.: Indiana University Press, 1986), 59, 60.

Huyssen's argument relies on a reversal of values which has become dominant in recent accounts of modernism, in which a democratized cultural sphere, women's writing, and the 'feminine' define each other. They are the foundation from which critical analysis begins. The more enlightened critic speaks from the side of modernism's denigrated 'others', whether these are excluded individuals or forms of representation.

However, by reversing the values of these oppositions, ideas have sometimes been forced into problematic new connections. A feminized mass culture, in Huyssen's account, is threatening *because* it challenges the male modernist text which excludes it. A feminized sentimental writing, for Suzanne Clark, is destabilizing *because* male modernist texts eradicate sentimentalism. Popular culture is radical, according to Thomas Strychacz, because it 'gratifies desires', whereas modernist texts block such gratification. The analysis of a modernism focused on the 'Women of 1928' is radical, according to Bonnie Kime Scott, because it destabilizes the 'confining paternal' and 'avuncular' 'Men of 1914' version of modernist writing.[5] The radical force of the feminine, women's writing, and popular culture is produced through its disruption of the élitist male modernist text.

There are two consequences of this critical orientation. First, the male modernist is put in the position of cultural and political authority for which Pound always yearned. The modernist poem or novel, then, becomes the place where women's exclusion is enacted, and the wider political, cultural, and economic sphere recedes from view. As Michael North puts it, 'most of the scholarship that has challenged Kenner's formulation of modernism as the Pound Era has not tried to change his view but rather has begun from it. The result has been the preservation of something called "modernism" in intellectual amber, something whose purported insulation from the cultural world into which it was introduced is now retrospectively accomplished by critical consensus.'[6]

Secondly, the market-place is seen as a democratized and 'feminized' cultural sphere which challenges the autonomy of the male modernist

---

[5] Suzanne Clark, *Sentimental Modernism: Women Writers and the Revolution of the Word* (Bloomington, Ind.: Indiana University Press, 1991); Thomas Strychacz, *Modernism, Mass Culture, and Professionalism* (Cambridge: Cambridge University Press, 1993), 10; Bonnie Kime Scott, *Refiguring Modernism: The Women of 1928* (Bloomington, Ind.: Indiana University Press, 1995), i. p. xxxvi.

[6] Michael North, *Reading 1922: A Return to the Scene of the Modern* (Oxford: Oxford University Press, 1999), 11.

text. In some accounts, the new democratic subjects of modern mass democracies are seen to wield their votes like they wield their bank notes. As Nina Miller puts it, modernist culture is 'a democracy of free, self-fashioning consumers'.[7] Politically, the individual liberal subject is seen as a bearer of rights and choice in a cultural market-place. In the face of this notion of democratic freedom, the claims of modernist writers to literary autonomy are seen as attempts to defend an élite minority culture against the values of a rapidly expanding market-place.

While the attack on democracy is a foundation for high modernist definitions of art, then, a belief in the inherent value of democratization fuels the contemporary critique of high modernism. Women modernist writers tend to be read in relation to this central opposition between democratization and élite modernism. In these accounts, women writers are seen to identify their interests with less authoritarian aesthetic values. In effect, rather than being presented with a 'genealogy of modernism', in Michael Levenson's words, we are presented with two 'genealogies of modernism', in which Eliot defends 'authority not democracy', and Mina Loy, for example, champions a new 'psycho-democracy'.[8] These different attitudes to democracy and authority are seen to provide an interpretative framework for reading the politics of modernist poems: whereas Eliot uses poetic or mythic authority to structure the 'chaos of contemporary history' in *The Waste Land*, Loy's dispersed, witty, free-verse lyrics express the democratic freedoms of the modern woman, and H.D.'s poetic classicism engenders a feminized, modernist counter-tradition.

In this book, I consider the validity of these interpretative frameworks in two ways: first, by providing a historical context for understanding modernist debates about democracy, liberalism, and authority; and second, by considering how ideas of democratization and authority affect the form and content of three very different modernist poets, T.S. Eliot, H.D., and Mina Loy, who hold different attitudes to politics and women's entrance into the cultural sphere.

The first angle is historical, then. It involves asking what modernist writers meant by the terms 'democracy', 'liberalism', and 'authority'. What exactly was Pound attacking in 1914? Why did he believe that

---

[7] Nina Miller, *Making Love Modern: The Intimate Public of New York's Literary Women* (Oxford: Oxford University Press, 1999), 6.

[8] Michael Levenson, *A Genealogy of Modernism: A Study of English Literary Doctrine 1908–1922* (Cambridge: Cambridge University Press, 1984).

democracy and authority were the terms which captured the values of the new literature? Was Pound's object of attack the same as Eliot's when he famously bemoaned a society worm-eaten by liberalism in 1932? Are these gestures as transparent as they at first appear? Were they attacking women's entrance into the political and cultural spheres when they criticized democracy and liberalism? Why did they think that these political ideas were central to their conceptions of modern literature? What had happened in the interim from 1914 to 1932? Certainly, the democracy that Pound had attacked in 1914 had disappeared by 1932, as the pre-war liberal democracies of Europe and America were replaced by the new mass democracies of the post-war period. The liberalism of the pre-war years had also been transformed, as new kinds of political pressures were brought to bear on government. When Eliot discussed the core liberal values which he believed defined society in 1932, the liberalism he had in mind was seen to be in crisis, unable to deal with the new kinds of political pressures of 1930s Europe.

This book takes another look at these attacks on democracy and liberalism, and their significance for the composition of modernist texts. It is a commonplace to argue that in Britain and America nineteenth-century individualist liberalism was supplanted by a new kind of collective liberalism in the early twentieth century. As John Gray puts it, 'The decline of the classical system of liberal thought coincided with, and was in very significant measure occasioned by, the arrival of a mass democracy in which the constitutional order of the free society soon came to be alterable by the processes of political competition.' It was not only that the Reform Act of 1918, which gave the vote to all men and to women over 30, altered the constitutional order of politics in Britain. As Gray argues, one conception of liberal government, as 'the guardian of the framework within which individuals may provide for themselves', was destroyed in 1914, in favour of a 'conception of government as the provider of general welfare'.[9]

Debates about whether liberal values would be undermined by modernity and mass democracy were a key feature of liberal discussion in the nineteenth and early twentieth centuries. Liberal theorists considered whether key liberal beliefs such as the 'moral primacy of the individual person against the claims of any social collectivity' might be destroyed, rather than furthered, by mass democracy. In the early decades of the twentieth century such debates became more acute. In 1911,

[9] John Gray, *Liberalism* (Milton Keynes: Open University Press, 1986), 92.

L. T. Hobhouse, one of the most influential and perceptive political theorists of the period, argued that liberalism was in crisis. He insisted that modern liberals needed to ask whether liberalism could change from being a negative political philosophy, based on the desire to set the individual free from the institutional shackles of church and state. Could modern liberals, he asked, face the new political demands of twentieth-century mass politics, and most importantly, the needs of the newly powerful working classes. Liberalism needed to become what he called a 'constructive' political ideology to compete with the communitarian ideals of the emerging Labour Party.[10]

Self-confessed liberal writers such as E. M. Forster engaged with this sense of political crisis. In *Howards End* (1911) Forster represents the limits of the individualist, humanist, and liberal world-view in the context of Imperial expansion and capitalist conflict in Europe. Forster bases his novel on the experiences of two liberated women, the Schlegel sisters, who embody progressively liberal political and cultural values. Yet their beliefs are in conflict with the real forces of historical change in the novel, the Imperialism and capitalism of the Wilcox men. For Forster, liberalism, humanism, and feminism involve a respect for property rights, land, and locality. They are a bulwark against the devastating, but necessary, 'Wilcox' forces of economic expansion which create British wealth and prosperity. Forster and Hobhouse believe that there is a fundamental contradiction at the heart of modern liberalism, between the expansionist economic forces which drive the British economy and core liberal cultural values.

After the First World War such debates shifted focus. In Britain, the war radically altered the relationship between the individual and the state. Compulsory conscription and repressive policies on freedom of information would have been unthinkable before the war, and many of these pieces of legislation were not revoked once the war ended. At the historical moment when Britain became a genuinely mass democratic state, then, the state's authority over the individual was significantly and permanently extended.

The war speeded up, rather than inaugurated, the belief that modern politics was haunted by this contradiction between political authority and individual liberty. Many intellectuals argued before the war that the individual's theoretical rights were in conflict with his or her actual liberty: while the citizen was the bearer of more rights than ever before,

---

[10] L. T. Hobhouse, *Liberalism* (London: Williams & Norgate, 1911).

in reality he or she had never been more powerless politically. Despite the ongoing nature of such debates, it is nevertheless the case that in the 1920s, with the examples of authoritarian mass politics in Italy and communism in Russia, debates about liberalism and democracy shifted ground. The European example suggested that liberal ideals such as the primacy of individual freedom might be redundant in the context of the new totalitarian democracies of post-war politics. This crisis became far more acutely felt in the 1930s, when the totalitarian states of Europe forced politicians and writers to engage with the prospect of the disintegration of basic liberal beliefs altogether. In Britain, before the First World War, the Liberal Party had dominated parliamentary politics for the previous three decades. By the 1930s, it had 'dwindled to a rump of a mere twenty-one MPs', prompting George Dangerfield famously to claim in 1935 that middle-class English liberalism died a 'strange death' between 1910 and 1913.[11]

These political and cultural shifts informed the bold statements of modernist writers about the status of art in the modern world. Before the war, modernists tended to define art against the liberal principles of equality, legality, and rights. Adopting the terms of the French debate about Rousseau's legacy, T. E. Hulme, Irving Babbitt, Wyndham Lewis, and T. S. Eliot attacked Rousseauistic notions of equality and rights, and defended new models of authority. After the war, writers were more concerned with the way in which mass democracies were controlled by the economic interests of vast, hidden corporations.

In this book I argue that male and female writers shared a sense of unease with the new political mechanism of democracy. What happens to our belief in equality when the masses are 'hypnotized' by the power of a mass media controlled by warmongering capitalists, asks Mina Loy in 1921?

It was not just Loy, Pound, and Eliot who were uncertain of the answers to these questions. As I will discuss in Chapter 1, in the years before the First World War, there was an intense interrogation of the meaning of democracy and liberalism in the period. With mass democracy on the horizon, political commentators considered the future of British and American politics. Many intellectuals, from across the political spectrum, viewed democracy as a cumbersome and dangerous mechanism for defining political, ethical, or literary values. One

---

[11] Quoted in George Searle, *The Liberal Party: Triumph and Disintegration 1886–1929* (Basingstoke: Palgrave, 2001), 1.

important strand of this debate which will feature centrally in this book was the impact of women's emancipation on the democratic process. Politicians and political commentators asked what would happen when women became the majority of the electorate. As the suffragettes ratcheted up the political pressure, modernists wrote obsessively about how the sexual relations between men and women held in embryo wider political questions. Female characters are often the vehicles for ideas of democratic progress and emancipation in modernist novels. In *The Rainbow* and *Women in Love*, for example, D. H. Lawrence presents us with the liberated female characters of Ursula, Gudrun, and Hermione. Yet the connection between democratic progress and women's liberation is rarely simple. In Lawrence's imagination, women pay a price for this emancipation. They become alienated from their natural impulses through their identification with 'abstract' democratic ideals. In his post-war novel *Parade's End*, Ford Madox Ford also gives us a politically complicated account of a liberated woman, in the figure of the suffragette Valentine Wannop. Valentine is spiritually and sexually connected to Tietjens, a landed Tory civil servant, who, we are repeatedly told, is 'pure eighteenth century'. In a Utopian moment in *Parade's End* Tietjens says to Valentine: 'You and I are standing at different angles and though we both look at the same thing we read different messages. Perhaps if we stood side by side we should see yet a third.'[12] Ford, a Tory himself, attempts to bring to life this 'third' perspective, born of the seemingly odd spiritual coupling of the principle of female suffrage and an eighteenth-century sensibility. The real object of attack for Ford is not Valentine, the spirited woman whom he sees as the key to the future, but a debased political legalism. This novel asks how humans can have faith in a political culture in which legalistic argument is privileged over belief?

The subject of this book is modernist poetry, rather than prose. How were the ideas of democracy, authority, and sexual difference played off against each other in modernist poems? Women are often used as political images or instances of the contemporary moment in modernist poems. Eliot, for example, presents us with his image of cultural vacuity in the famous 'women who come and go' in 'The Love Song of J. Alfred Prufrock'. This image fragment is important because of the way it fixes other key ideas in the poem. The history of art is distorted and eroded when it is put into the mouths of these fashionable women. It is important for Eliot that this image of cultural decay is feminized,

---

[12] Ford Madox Ford, *Parade's End* (Harmondsworth: Penguin Books, 1982), 234.

because it makes the line more suggestive, capturing an idea of the loss of artistic authority through cultural inclusion. The task of the poem is somehow to rectify this loss of cohesion through literary authority. For Eliot ideas of cultural democratization, literary tradition, and sexuality are finely balanced, working to define each other.

We might expect women writers, in the face of this denigration of cultural inclusion, to identify their intellectual interests with democratic values. However, their responses are more complicated. Through a close analysis of individual writers, it becomes clear that poets from across the political spectrum and the gender divide are sceptical about aspects of modern democracy, and that this informs their writing in important ways. This scepticism is not necessarily generated out of an élitist vision of poetic authority. At the heart of many modernist texts is the idea that modern democracies become formally inclusive at the historical moment when the state extends its power over the individual citizen. The change from restricted to mass democracy in the period alters the meaning of key political and aesthetic categories. At the moment when the state becomes inclusive, then, the terms of this inclusion become opaque. Many modernist and avant-garde texts, from Kafka's *The Trial*, to Mina Loy's post-war poems, to Auden's poems of the late 1930s, are haunted by this idea. This book suggests that these anxieties feed into the modernist imagination in powerful ways. The following chapters will explore the way that the form and content of modernist texts are responses to these anxieties.

In Chapter 1 I discuss the intellectual context of the years before the war, focusing in particular on the reception of the ideas of Max Stirner and Friedrich Nietzsche in journals such as the *New Age* and the *Egoist* and the ways in which these philosophers were used to attack liberal assumptions about the cultural role of literature. Through the close analysis of these journals, I uncover a significant but hitherto ignored number of anti-liberal feminists. They adopted the ideas of Stirner and Nietzsche to develop a philosophy of politics and culture explicitly hostile to suffragette aims. Literary experiment is placed at the forefront of their visions of anti-liberal political anarchy, a series of ideas that, I will argue, resonated importantly through modernist texts. Chapter 2 considers the diverse range of modernist responses to the political context of the 1910s and 1920s. It analyses in detail the shifting nature of the attack on democracy and liberalism by modernist writers.

Chapters 3, 4, and 5 look at three very different kinds of Anglo-American poets: H.D., Eliot, and Loy, focusing in particular on how they use poetic form to order or control the modern moment. H.D. is a modernist classicist, who studiously avoids reference to contemporary objects, voices, or events, and who sees poetic language as that which is uncontaminated by a sordid modern world. Eliot both incorporates the modern objects, voices, and landscapes of contemporary history and attempts to order this contemporaneity through poetic or mythic authority. Loy's poetry forms part of the European avant-garde. In her poems she embraces the vibrancy of contemporary scenes and voices, and wants to release poetic language from what she calls the 'glass case of tradition'. These different understandings of the legislative role of poetic language produce distinct approaches to the issue of women's position in contemporary culture. In H.D.'s poems gender dynamics are depicted as ahistorical struggles for mastery set in natural or mythical landscapes, and are often about the position of the female poet in relation to a heavily masculine poetic tradition and cultural sphere. Eliot associates women with a debased contemporaneity which needs to be ordered and made meaningful. Loy engages directly with the freedoms and chains of modern women, depicting modern fantasies of freedom as powerful, internalized forms of psychic imprisonment.

While H.D. is the least 'political' of the poets discussed, she has nevertheless been seen as creating an important 'feminist' modernism. The book considers the nature of this poetic feminism. It asks: what are the values which inform her poems? In the context of the discussion in Chapter 1, do her poems constitute a literary version of Stirner's philosophical egoism, a retreat inwards from the political and public sphere? If Pound and Lewis veer between the poles of egoist and authoritarian models of literary agency in the 1910s, does H.D. simply write from an egoist standpoint, an extreme individualism in the absence of civic concepts of morality, rights, and equality? And is this connected to her status as a woman poet? Does she create a gendered landscape in which men occupy the positions of authority which control the fate of individual women? And finally, how is this egoism more 'democratic' than its authoritarian counterpart?

Chapter 4 considers how Eliot's object of attack shifted, from a liberal individualism he connects with Rousseau and the French Revolution in the 1910s to the mass democracy unleashed after the First World War in the early 1920s. In the period generally, as well as for Eliot, these were considered to be rather different political and cultural structures. I argue that despite the shifting nature of his object of attack, however, he consistently depicted women as the key agents and signifiers of contemporaneity, first of the debased solipsistic Romanticism of liberal society and, later, of mass democracy. These connections help explain the construction of 'egoist' linguistic solipsism and poetic authority in the early poems, as well as the depiction of contemporary voices in *The Waste Land*. For Eliot, poetic language has a legislative role which injects significance into a secular and empty modern world.

Chapter 5 analyses the poetry of Mina Loy and includes a discussion of her critical response to the work of Gertrude Stein. Whereas H.D. sees poetry as language which withdraws from a sordid modernity, Loy sees it as language which captures the beauty of the gutter. Like those of H.D., Loy's poems consistently attacked authoritarian male masters and their legislative poetics, particularly that of the Italian Futurists. However, in place of this authoritarian aesthetic, she espoused a dadaist, progressive, free-verse poetics which engaged directly with the reality of modern democracies. She described her idiosyncratic political position as a psycho-democracy, in which she defended internationalism, pacifism, freedom of expression, and democratized individualism, and attacked warmongering, capitalist power, and political authoritarianism. However, her writing is at its most powerful when it engages with the limits of the 'freedoms' of modern democratic societies. Through the close analysis of these three writers, the book aims to re-evaluate our understanding of the relationship between modernist literature, democracy and ideas of sexual difference.[13]

---

[13] A note about my referencing policy: In this book I refer extensively to articles in journals from the early twentieth century. I have not included all of these articles in the bibliography, although they are clearly cited in the footnotes. In an effort to keep the bibliography short, I have included only books and articles of a substantive nature which are referred to directly in my argument.

1

'No artist can ever love democracy': Modernism and Democracy 1907–1914

LIBERALISM BEFORE THE FIRST WORLD WAR

In the period of 1909–14, the arts were significantly reshaped in Britain and the United States. The poetic and prose experiments of Anglo-American modernists would culminate in the publication of *The Waste Land*, *Ulysses*, and the *Later Poems* of Yeats in 1922, and the revised *Cantos* in 1923. In this chapter I will focus on the intellectual context of the pre-war period. In particular, I ask what language was available to writers for understanding the nature of sexual difference during this period when there were wider political debates about the status of liberalism and democracy. Women's enfranchisement, in particular, became a central political and intellectual issue, and pro-suffragists (ranging from pro-suffrage liberal politicians to members of the Women's Social and Political Union (WSPU) in Britain) employed a liberal discourse of rights and equality to argue their case. In the process, they tended to presuppose a highly legalistic and rational account of liberty and female subjectivity.

It was partly this legalism and rationalism which was attacked in the intellectual critique of liberalism and democracy in the pre-war years. In this period the philosophers Friedrich Nietzsche, Max Stirner, and Henri Bergson enjoyed a voguish popularity amongst English avant-garde intellectuals. Their ideas dominated the pages of journals such as the *New Age*, which became a 'Nietzsche' journal after A. R. Orage became editor in 1907, and the *Freewoman*, later the *New Freewoman* and the *Egoist*, which became a sponsor of Stirner's ideas from 1911. These journals also published translations of and articles on the work of Henri Bergson and essays by T. E. Hulme, Ezra Pound, and Wyndham Lewis on poetry and art. Contributors to these journals adopted the categories of Nietzschean 'Sovereign individuality', Stirnerian 'egoism', and Bergsonian 'intuition' to discuss a wide range of issues. In particular, these ideas were used to construct models of identity and liberty in which the individual, amoral will was privileged over legalistic, rational, and moral concepts of subjectivity.

A number of renegade or anti-liberal feminist thinkers in this period adopted the terms of Nietzsche's or Stirner's philosophy to criticize the legalistic and moralistic focus of the suffragette movement. The suffragettes tended to argue their case from the basic liberal idea that each individual is born free and equal, and that a formal political equality such as the right to vote and to freedom of speech should guarantee freedom of action. The seemingly bizarre attacks on 'the vote' by feminists or one-time feminists such as Beatrice Hastings, who helped edit and wrote extensively for the *New Age* from 1907 to 1914, Dora Marsden, who edited and wrote for the *Freewoman* from 1911, and the Russian anarchist Emma Goldman, who edited the American journal *Mother Earth* from 1907, are part of a more general intellectual attack on these juridical notions of liberty which dominated the political debate. Hastings, Marsden, and Goldman discussed the consequences of women's belated attainment of liberal citizenship. They argued that citizenship in the modern democratic state is based on the cohesive ideals of liberty, equality, and rights. Women's citizenship, in particular, is grounded in moral notions of altruism, sentimentalism, and sexual purity. Yet these ideals are 'illusions' which are external to the individual self, and which blind women to the truth of themselves. By identifying selfhood with these external illusions, women experience a damaging split in the psyche.

Reacting against such mental prisons, Hastings and Marsden developed discourses of will and strength to describe female subjectivity. This involved finding words which were free of the external, legalistic discourse of liberal citizenship and the altruistic language of sentimental femininity. Yet their critiques of the idealism of suffragette politics often involved an equally idealistic account of individual liberation, as politicized feminist theory dissolved into theories about the revolutionary potential of individual female strength. Marsden ended up angrily pronouncing the meaninglessness of the 'external' categories of 'woman' and 'man', and insisting that only the sense certainty of the individual body could hold the key to identity. Hastings promoted a 'feminine anti-Suffragist' position, which favoured the 'mental freedom' of the isolated self against the lure of the irrational and 'subconscious' drives of the suffragette 'mob'. Goldman argued that woman needed to emancipate 'herself from emancipation if she really desires to be free', and to recognize the 'internal tyrants', rather than the 'external tyrannies', which keep her in chains.[1]

Hastings, Marsden, and Goldman held very different political beliefs. Hastings and Marsden were one-time British suffragettes who then identified themselves with Nietzsche's and Stirner's ideas. Goldman was a feminist anarchist who moved to the United States and agitated on behalf of a number of political causes. Yet, despite these differences, they shared the belief that feminism needed to shift its focus from the legal and political sphere to the psychological realm. This was no easy task, as it involved trying to write about female selfhood without reverting to the legalistic language of citizenship. For all three writers, then, the burning question for modern feminists was how to develop what Marsden called 'a new language of the self'. The focus on language inevitably led to an interest in literature. Marsden, for example, quickly realized that the London avant-garde was exploring language in a way which went far beyond her own attempts to experiment with new forms: the 'poets and creative thinkers', she stated in 1912, are able to explore the 'positive Ego, sufficiently sure of itself to speak out its wants'.[2]

These feminist figures are interesting because their ideas, both editorially and intellectually, were close to the concerns of a number of modernist Anglo-American writers. Many of the women modernist writers interested in exploring the nature of sexual difference held views closer in spirit to this egoistic feminism than to the liberal presuppositions of the main feminist groups. In fact, where liberal thought makes the rational and moral individual the basis on which to construct politics, ethics, and aesthetics, many writers wanted to dislocate the self from such a foundational position. H.D.'s poems focus on fraught power struggles in an ahistorical landscape, producing images of will and subjection which are inflected with 'natural' and individual, as opposed to social or moral, registers. Mina Loy demands that women ditch their notions of women's moral superiority over men, and prepare for the disintegration of the categories of 'Man' and 'Woman' in the 'humid carnage' of sex.[3] Both foreground a female body whose wilful nature

---

[1] Emma Goldman, 'The Tragedy of Women's Emancipation' (1911), in Alix Kates Shulman, ed., *Red Emma Speaks: The Selected Speeches and Writings of the Anarchist and Feminist Emma Goldman* (London: Wildwood House, 1972), 134, 139.

[2] Dora Marsden, 'The Growing Ego', *Freewoman*, 2.38 (1912), 222.

[3] Mina Loy, 'Songs to Joannes, XII', repr. in Roger Conover, ed., *The Lost Lunar Baedeker* (Manchester: Carcanet Press, 1997), 57.

has been dislodged from moral registers: H.D.'s Eurydice whose face is a 'reflex of the earth', for example, must struggle with the 'arrogant', 'ruthless', 'self-present' Orpheus to be free; Mina Loy's 'Love Songs' depict bodies controlled by sexual impulses which are likened to the carnage of a battlefield.[4] Moral and juridical models of freedom and identity are dissolved in these poems, and categories of individualized will and struggle take their place.

In the process, these writers produce images of the self as an aesthetic, rather than a juridical or moral, unity. It is not whether Orpheus's arrogant consignment of Eurydice to Hades in H.D.'s poem is morally wrong in some abstract sense, but whether she has the strength to assert a coherent language of female beauty in the face of his power over her. Similarly, in Loy's 'Love Songs' there is an absence of moral language. The question posed by the poems is not whether the sexual impulses described are morally wrong, but whether a new kind of aesthetic beauty can be created out of this 'erotic garbage'.[5]

The idea that the self is an aesthetic, rather than a moral, unity is central to their attempts to define what it is to be a 'modern' woman: for H.D., it is a 'tightrope act', a precarious stage performance; for Loy, it is an exuberant linguistic and physical performance in which the artifice of wit and physical beauty dominates over sentimentality and sincerity. Contemporary prose writers such as Katherine Mansfield, Virginia Woolf, Gertrude Stein, and Djuna Barnes shared this sense that, in the face of the disintegration of stable categories of time, morality, and consciousness, artifice could unify a new, modern femininity. The wilful female body lies barely beneath the surface of this modernist artifice. For each of these writers, the will constitutes a slightly different tendency or drive. In Loy's and Barnes's writing, the will is often animalistic in nature. Barnes, in her wonderfully titled 1915 volume of poems, *The Book of Repulsive Women*, isolates an animalistic female body:

> See you sagging down with bulging
> Hair to sip,
> The dappled damp from some vague
> Under lip.
> Your soft saliva, loosed
> With orgy, drip.

---

[4] H.D., 'Eurydice', in H.D., *The Collected Poems, 1912–1944*, ed. Louiz L. Martz (New York: New Directions, 1983), 51–5. Loy, 'Songs to Joannes', 57.

[5] Mina Loy, 'Songs to Joannes, I', 53.

The erotic body is not only in fragments in this poem; the boundaries separating internal and external spaces are blurred, as bodily fluids slowly drip. As in Eliot's 'Love Song of J. Alfred Prufrock', there is an absence of a unified human subject who could connect these body parts together, but Barnes's decadent focus on the body has also dislocated it from moral conventions: women have drawn 'back day by day / From good and bad'.[6] In Loy's poems, stylized female performances barely mask the animal impulses which animate the relationships between individuals: in 'Three Moments in Paris', 'eyes that are full of kohl', trail 'the rest of the animal behind them'.[7] H.D.'s poems and Stein's prose pieces focus on a different kind of will, a will whose strength is measured by whether it is able to master others.

These writers, however, do not simply abandon politics in favour of a literary subjectivism based on the will or the body. They depict the will as a self-legislative tendency which creates and structures models of modern female selfhood. Similar forms of self-legislation are at work in the way in which these modernist texts are put together. These writers want to articulate the darkest recesses of human motivation and desire, whilst also creating a kind of cohesion, or order which can structure these desires.

This book considers the genealogy of ideas which produced the concepts of will, individualism, and artifice in these poems. I focus in particular on the reception of Nietzsche's and Stirner's ideas amongst Anglo-American modernist writers, asking what are the political consequences of this focus. Does this model of selfhood, with its origins in a scepticism about democracy, involve these writers in an identification with authoritarian models of literary agency?

The importance of Nietzsche, Stirner, and Bergson for Anglo-American modernist writing has been analysed extensively before. David Thatcher, John Burt Foster, Michael Levenson, and Michael North, amongst others, have examined the impact of Stirner's and Nietzsche's thought on the work of T. E. Hulme, Ezra Pound, Ford Madox Ford, W. B. Yeats, D. H. Lawrence, and T. S. Eliot.[8] Levenson and North

---

[6] Djuna Barnes, 'From Fifth Avenue Up', 'From Third Avenue On', in *The Book of Repulsive Women* (1915; New York: The Lincoln Press, 1948).

[7] Mina Loy, 'Three Moments in Paris', Hpr. in Conover (ed.), *The Lost Lunar Baedeker*, 15–18.

[8] David Thatcher, *Nietzsche in England, 1890–1914* (Toronto: University of Toronto Press, 1970); John Burt Foster, *Heirs to Dionysus: A Nietzschean Current in Literary Modernism* (Princeton: Princeton University Press, 1981); Michael Levenson, *A Genealogy*

have analysed the political nature of this literary focus, looking at the way in which these writers vacillate between a literary egoism and forms of anti-democratic authority based on tradition, myth, and order. Levenson answers the question 'Why egoism at this pre-war moment?' by invoking wider political developments:

there was a tendency—especially among the artists and intellectuals—to withdraw into individual subjectivity as a refuge for threatened values. Among this group, liberalism decomposed into egoism. And where liberal ideology had made the individual the basis on which to construct religion, politics, ethics and aesthetics, egoism abjured the constructive impulse and was content to remain where it began: in the sceptical self.[9]

Levenson characterizes egoism as a 'decomposed' liberalism. As he goes on to explain, the origins of Anglo-American modernist writing are entangled in two reactions to the sceptical critique of liberalism, either egoism or authoritarianism:

In general, we can say that the modernist apology has embraced one of the two tendencies: either an extreme egoism (in the Stirnerians, in early Hulme, in Ford) or an equally radical absolutism (in Hulme, Worringer). Lewis and Pound veered alternately in both directions, but at any one point, in any one manifesto, the explicit embrace of one tendency precluded the other.[10]

Levenson suggests that writers 'veered' between the two tendencies of egoism and absolutism, but that both reactions emerged from an attack on liberal and democratic values. Vincent Sherry translates 'egoism' and 'absolutism' into the political terms of 'anarchy' and 'authority', and suggests that both political wings used the same language to break with the past: 'the poetic language used on both flanks of the movement—the affective image—is poised ever between those opposite political possibilities of demotic anarchy and antidemocratic authority.'[11]

The importance of such debates for women writers, or for the way in which sexual difference is represented in modernist writing, has not been analysed in any detail. This book argues that such an analysis helps us both to understand the work of women modernists and to

---

of *Modernism: A Study of English Literary Doctrine 1908–1922* (Cambridge: Cambridge University Press, 1984); Michael North, *The Political Aesthetic of Modernism: Yeats, Eliot and Pound* (Cambridge: Cambridge University Press, 1991).

[9] Levenson, *Genealogy of Modernism*, 68.   [10] Ibid. 185.

[11] Vincent Sherry, *Ezra Pound, Wyndham Lewis, and Radical Modernism* (Oxford: Oxford University Press, 1993), 33.

rethink the politics of Eliot, Pound, and Lawrence. Ideas of sexual difference are entangled in concepts of liberalism and democracy. Eliot, Pound, Lewis, and Lawrence, for example, connect democratization and liberalism to women's entrance into the political process and cultural life. Further, they often criticize democracy *because* they claim that it involves women's entrance into politics and culture. They were not alone in making such connections. Democracy was often attacked in this period on the grounds that majority rule would involve a passive, or 'feminine' attitude to politics. Chapter 4 argues, for instance, that Eliot mocks women's participation in cultural life as a kind of shorthand for wider attacks on political democracy and liberalism. He describes women as vacuous users of a cultural language they do not understand, a form of linguistic abuse which creates a dangerous estrangement in which word separates from thing. This is structurally similar to his criticism of the way in which mass democracy enfranchises individuals who have agency in a political process they do not understand.

Eliot's attempt to construct women as the agents of estrangement is similar to the way in which D. H. Lawrence figures women as the sign and symptom of democracy both in his novels and in his essays of the 1910s. In *The Rainbow, Women in Love*, his *Study of Thomas Hardy*, and his 1919 essay, 'Democracy', he attacks the 'abstract' language of liberal democracy: 'Rights of Man, Equality of Man, Social Perfectibility of Man: all these sweet abstractions, once so inspiring, rest upon the fatal little hypothesis of the Average.' 'The Average', he goes on, 'is a pure abstraction.'[12] He argues that modern women such as his characters Hermione and Gudrun in *Women in Love*, in identifying themselves with these abstract ideas, create a damaging form of psychic conflict.

Where do writers such as H.D., Mina Loy, Gertrude Stein, and Djuna Barnes position themselves in these genealogies of ideas? Do they also criticize democracy and cultural democratization? If so, do they attack democracy as an 'abstraction', in the sense that Lawrence uses the term? Are their poems structured around anti-democratic forms of literary authority? Or, alternatively, are they intellectually entangled in the move towards mass democracy? If so, how do the models of selfhood in their poems connect to this intellectual entanglement?

To answer these questions, we must first turn to the intellectual context of the early 1910s, the moment at which Eliot, Pound, H.D.,

---

[12] D. H. Lawrence, 'Democracy', in *Phoenix: The Posthumous Papers, 1936*, i (Harmondsworth: Penguin Books, 1978), 699.

Lawrence, and Loy emerged on to the literary scene. What did the terms 'liberalism', 'democracy', 'abstraction', and 'egoism' mean in this pre-war period? Why were they such loaded and important categories? And in what way were they connected to ideas of sexual difference? Further, how are these categories important for the development of a certain kind of feminist modernism which extends well beyond the pre-war moment?

EGO VOGUES: THE PHILOSOPHICAL ATTACK ON DEMOCRACY

Two German philosophers, Max Stirner and Friedrich Nietzsche, enjoyed a voguish popularity amongst British and American intellectuals, particularly young poets and novelists, in the pre-war period. Stirner, the man that Karl Marx and Frederick Engels dubbed 'Saint Sancho' in *The German Ideology*, wrote a single contribution to post-Hegelian debate in the 1840s, *The Ego and its Own*. It is subjected to a devastating page-by-page critique in *The German Ideology*.[13] Stirner attempts to go beyond Hegel's philosophy by liberating the individual from 'false conceptions' such as 'God', 'spirit', 'law', and 'humanity' and replacing these 'external ideas' with the self-certainties of the individual Ego:

I am *owner* of my might, and I am so when I know myself as *unique*. In the *unique one* the owner himself returns into his creative nothing, of which he is born. Every higher essence above me, be it God, be it man, weakens the feeling of my uniqueness, and pales only before the sun of this consciousness. If I concern myself for myself, the unique one, then my concern rests on its transitory, mortal creator, who consumes himself, and I may say: All things are nothing to me.[14]

Stirner dissolves the theological and humanist conceptions which 'weaken' the individual's autonomy: external ideas are replaced by an individual who 'owns' himself, 'knows' himself, and 'returns into'

[13] Max Stirner, *The Ego and its Own*, ed. D. Leopold, trans. S. T. Byington (Cambridge: Cambridge University Press, 1995). The first English-language translation, by the American translator S. T. Byington, was published in 1907, and in London in 1912. Karl Marx and Frederick Engels, *The German Ideology*, trans. S. Ryazanskaya (London: Lawrence & Wishart, 1965). *The German Ideology* was written during 1845–6, but was not published during Marx's lifetime.

[14] Stirner, *Ego and its Own*, 324.

himself. In some senses Stirner's ego is a corollary to the first phase of Hegel's philosophy of subjectivity, in which the subject withdraws into himself. Marx and Engels criticize Stirner's book on precisely such grounds. Rather than going beyond Hegel, they argue, Stirner's ego merely retreats into itself and dwells there shouting obscenities at religion, morality, and state. They claim that Stirner's 'revolutionary' philosophy relinquishes any belief in the social nature of identity and any hope for the transformation of the state. His philosophy thereby merely takes 'place in the realm of pure thought'.[15]

The Stirner revival in the United States and Britain began in the 1890s, but gained momentum when a new English translation of *The Ego and its Own* was funded and directed by an American anarchist called Benjamin Tucker in 1907.[16] Forty-nine editions of the work appeared between 1900 and 1929. It was a book that appealed to thinkers of very different literary and philosophical persuasions. It was used to forge a genealogy of decadent and nihilistic writing in James Huneker's book *Egoists: A Book of Supermen*, published in 1909.[17] It was also adopted by writers such as Wyndham Lewis and Ezra Pound in order to shape an aesthetic reaction against decadent writing. Perhaps most surprisingly, Stirner's arguments were also harnessed by some feminist thinkers in order to mount a wholesale critique of suffragette feminism.

Why was Stirner's philosophy of the 'unique Ego' and revolution 'in the realm of pure thought' important for some feminist thinkers in the 1900s and 1910s and for literary modernists? Why did both groups find in Stirner's idealistic anti-state ego individualism a resource for conceptions of the modern? Does this common philosophical ground offer a way of understanding the links between pre-war feminism and literary modernism, particularly in writing which attempts to combine the two?

Stirner's philosophy was influential because it offered a way of moving beyond nineteenth century humanism. He argued that modern philosophy is grounded in the claim that it has outgrown religious forms of thought, but that religious categories cling tenaciously to modern ideas. Stirner argues, then, that modern philosophers have

---

[15] Marx and Engels, *German Ideology*, 27.

[16] Tucker wrote extensively for the *New Freewoman*.

[17] James Huneker, an American literature and music critic, collected together his journalism into a book of essays on Stendhal, Baudelaire, Huysmans, and Nietzsche, and ends with a chapter on Stirner. Huneker describes Stirner as 'the most thorough-going Nihilist who ever penned his disbelief in religion, humanity, society, the family': James Huneker, *Egoists: A Book of Supermen* (London: T. Werner Laurie, 1909), 355.

simply transferred religious ideas from the transcendental to the human realm: 'Who is his God? Man with a capital M! What is the divine? The human!' The shift from God to man is 'nothing more or less than a new—*religion*'.[18] This new religion is *the* problem of modernity. All of the secular categories with which we discuss the nature of modern subjectivity, he argues, are religious categories in disguise. Ideas of humanity and politics, for example, tend to rest on notions of the perfectibility of man. The 'illusion' of a 'true' human is set up over and against actual individuals, creating a dangerous split in the psyche.

Stirner argues that the task of modern philosophy is to escape this new 'Man' religion, which relies on a panoply of modern illusions. 'Man', he insists, 'has not really vanquished Shamanism and its spooks until he possesses the strength to lay aside not only the belief in ghosts or in spirits, but also the belief in the spirit.' Christian faith, then, is merely the latest manifestation of the primitive or occult belief in the power of things external to the self. In the modern religious context, however, this belief in the spirit has become all-encompassing. Our world, he suggests, is so populated with ghosts that we are no longer able to engage with material reality: '[T]he whole world is spiritualised, and has become an enigmatical ghost.'[19] In turn, the religious dualism of God and the devil has been replaced by a political opposition: 'Liberalism as a whole has a deadly enemy, an invincible opposite, as God has the devil: by the side of man stands always un-man, the individual, the egoist. State, society, humanity, do not master this devil.'[20] For Stirner, this secular devil is actually man stripped bare of the sacred values which muffle the human response to the world. Real freedom, then, is situated in the individual who is able, through a heroic effort of will, to confront this bare, unhallowed modern world and mould it in his own image. While liberalism is grounded in the political primacy of the economic individual citizen, then, Stirner is at pains to emphasize that he has a very different kind of individuality in mind when he describes the egoist individual. The egoist has freed himself from the illusion of external truth and embraced the freedom to create his own understanding of the world. In this claim to individual independence, the self is redefined as unique, wilful, and aggressive, a secular heroic self fit for the modern world.

Stirner's philosophy was popular among British and American intellectuals because of this vision of the individual's legislative power.

---

[18] Stirner, *Ego and its Own*, 55.   [19] Ibid. 66, 36.   [20] Ibid. 125.

Here is a new picture of human freedom, in which the fantasy of an external, transcendental 'truth' is discarded, and the isolated individual is able to shape the world in his own image. We will see in the next chapter how this focus on the self's legislative role becomes central to Anglo-American modernists in the 1900s and 1910s. There was also another aspect to Stirner's philosophy which chimed with the interests of modernist writers. The ideological battle lines in Stirner's work are drawn up with collective ideas of state, society, and humanity on one side, and the unique individual on the other side. Despite the stated aims of his egoist philosophy, however, his book is often at its most powerful when it describes the difficulties of asserting individual autonomy in the modern world. He presents an extended discussion of how the self is dominated by received political, religious, and moral categories of understanding. In these descriptions, the ego is figured as a fragile entity struggling for independence in the face of powerful external spooks. In fact, rather than emphasizing human uniqueness, Stirner's book is at its most disturbing when it reveals the difficulty of enforcing the boundaries which separate the ego from the world. The most sinister way in which the external world infiltrates the ego is through words. In his discussion of Feuerbach, for example, Stirner argues that Feuerbach fails to rid his critique of religion of the religious ideas which cling to the structure and language of his argument. In a similar vein, Stirner argues that simple words such as 'rights' or 'equality', laden as they are with an ideology of the perfectibility of 'Man with a capital M', split the human psyche in two.

At moments in this book, then, the confident assertion of egoist freedom turns into something very different: a paranoid vision of the total domination of the individual by non-existent ideals. As we will see, this understanding of the individual's place in modern society was also to resonate importantly through modernist writing in the 1910s and 1920s.

Stirner's impact on British and American intellectual life was fuelled by the similarity of his ideas with those of Friedrich Nietzsche. Nietzsche's work had been gaining in influence since 1896, when two of his works, *Thus Spake Zarathustra* and *The Case of Wagner*, which also included *Nietzsche contra Wagner, The Twilight of the Idols*, and *The Antichrist*, were translated into English by Thomas Common and W. A. Hausmann. Alexander Tille had been appointed as editor of the Nietzsche translations in 1895. *A Genealogy of Morals* followed in 1899, but then the project of translating all of Nietzsche's works into English faltered. It was not until 1907, when Oscar Levy undertook the financial risk of translating Nietzsche's works, that the project for a complete edition was begun again. He translated and published *Beyond Good and Evil* in 1907, with *The Birth of Tragedy* quickly following in 1909. Levy oversaw the publication of the complete translation of Nietzsche's works, with the eighteenth and final volume of the complete translation appearing in 1913.

The chronology of these translations is important, because it meant that Nietzsche was imported into English culture in two stages, with the controversial *Thus Spake Zarathustra* defining the first stage, and more sober, and chronologically earlier, works such as *The Birth of Tragedy* controlling the second.

A number of 'Nietzsche' journals sprang up in the first period of his English reception. The first of these was the *Eagle and the Serpent*, which ran from 1898 to 1903, and began the process of popularizing Nietzsche's work for an English audience. In both the early translations and the *Eagle and the Serpent* Nietzsche's ideas were used to engage with the wider political and literary debate about the fate of the individual in the context of modern liberal democracy. In *Thus Spake Zarathustra*, Nietzsche had set out his own version of Stirner's egoist / liberal citizen opposition, focusing on the 'free spirits' or 'sovereign individuals' who stand above and beyond 'the democratic herd'. It was a dualism which was to feature heavily in most of his works.

In the first issue of the *Eagle and the Serpent* the editorial sets out its basic Nietzschean philosophy by emphasizing this central opposition: 'A race of altruists is necessarily a race of slaves.... A race of freemen is necessarily a race of egoists.... The only remedy for social injustice is this: the exploited must save themselves by enlightened self-interest.... Egoism spells justice and freedom as surely as altruism spells charity and slavery.'[21] Altruism and egoism are models of selfhood which have wider social and political consequences, with altruism being consonant with slavery, and egoism producing freedom. As in Stirner's philosophy, the egoist individual, through enlightened self-interest, seizes hold of the material world by disregarding the determining force of external conditions. The opposition of altruism and egoism continued to be central to subsequent English translations of, and articles on, Nietzsche. In the introduction to the 1899 Housmann translation of *A Genealogy of Morals*, Tille claims that Nietzsche's work is timely, because the English

---

[21] 'Editorial', *Eagle and Serpent*, 1 (25 Feb. 1898), 687.

people have intoxicated 'themselves with phrases like altruism, charity, social justice, equality before the law, freedom and right to labour and happiness'. The word 'intoxication' is apt, because he wants to emphasize the way in which individuals are made sluggish and irrational through their blind adherence to the empty phrases of liberal democracy.

It was not only in the realm of politics that the English people were seen to have been intoxicated with non-egoistic beliefs. The dominant avant-garde movement of the 1880s and 1890s was that of French symbolism and literary decadence. The key philosopher of the movement was Arthur Schopenhauer, whose *The World as Will and Idea* (1819) claimed that the world was chaotic and meaningless, controlled by the blind force of the human will. The will, for Schopenhauer, is a negative force, destructive and egotistical. The only palliatives to this egotistical will are either a death-like renunciation or art itself, which is able to change the will into aesthetic form.

By the late 1890s, many writers were interested in moving away from decadent concerns. Nietzsche's work exploded on to the literary scene, because he engaged directly with the problems of Schopenhauer's ideas. In *On the Genealogy of Morals*, then, he begins by setting out how his philosophy moves beyond the pessimism and passivity of Schopenhauer's philosophy: 'At issue was the value of the "unegoistic", the instincts of compassion, self-abnegation, self-sacrifice, those very instincts which Schopenhauer had for so long made golden.' Nietzsche insists that Schopenhauer's valorization of self-renunciation amounts to saying '*no* to life'.[22] In artistic terms, Nietzsche replaces Schopenhauer's nihilistic vision, which tended to see the past as a repository of lost plenitude, with a heroic artist who confronts a secular modernity and creates his own meanings from the chaos.

Nietzsche uses his critique of Schopenhauer as a starting-point from which to dissect the value that has been placed on 'unegoistic actions' in the history of morality, questioning the idea that they are either intrinsically good or good because they have habitually been seen to be good: '[T]here is from the outset absolutely *no* necessary connection between the word "good" and "unegoistic" actions, as the superstition of the genealogists of morals would have it.' He identifies this key metaphysical confusion with the rise of democracy: 'Rather, it is

[22] Friedrich Nietzsche, *On the Genealogy of Morals: A Polemic*, trans. Douglas Smith (Oxford: Oxford University Press, 1996), 7. Note the difference in this translator's title from the 1899 version.

only with the decline of aristocratic value-judgements that this whole opposition between "egoistic" and "unegoistic" comes to impose itself increasingly on the human conscience. To adopt my own terminology, it is the *herd-instinct*, which here finally has its chance to put in a word (and to put itself into *words*).'[23] Nietzsche's genealogy of morality involves carving up history into two main epochs, the aristocratic and the democratic. The differences between these two belief systems would control his philosophy more generally.

Nietzsche's more general critique of modern democracy involves the central claim that there is a fundamental contradiction at the heart of modern democratic societies. He argues that modern liberal democracies seemingly promote an individualist culture, but in fact end up producing social conformity in which there is an absence of truly individual human beings. This central antinomy is one amongst a number in modern political life. The relationships between the individual and society, man and citizen, autonomy and authority, and freedom and necessity are similarly contradictory. Nietzsche sees modern liberal democracies as imposing a spurious universality and equality on human beings through the new 'religious' doctrines of individual rights. Unlike those who see the main achievement of modern politics in terms of its production of the autonomous citizen, then, Nietzsche finds modern humans to be mere isolates and atoms, not full, complete personalities. He argues that modern politics is controlled by the democratic mass who enslave those who are genuinely independent and strong. In rebelling against their masters, the weak and the oppressed have internalized their will to power, but deny that this is their fundamental nature. Modern democracy is characterized by this attitude of moral hypocrisy among those who wield political power. Instead of having the strength and courage to stand up and be independent, to have the will to command and rule, they choose instead to hide their impotence behind slogans such as 'the human average'.

In his Introduction to *A Genealogy of Morals*, Tille labels this modern democratic ideology the 'Christian-democratic neighbour-morality'.[24] In doing so, he repeats Nietzsche's argument that, rather than being a genuinely new epoch in the history of civilization, the modern liberal democratic state is, in fact, merely an episode in the history of Christian

---

[23] Ibid. 13.
[24] Alexander Tille, 'Introduction', in *A Genealogy of Morals*, trans. W. Hausmann (London: Unwin, 1899), p. xiii.

moral culture. Nietzsche carves up recent history into epochs, in which the French Revolution has ushered in a new kind of society and culture. Along with de Tocqueville, he argues that this new historical period has replaced the Christian religion with the new idol of the modern, bureaucratic state. Nietzsche claims, like Stirner, that the modern state is grounded in the illusions of liberty, equality, and the 'rights of man'. However, these idols are simply secular versions of Christian categories, and are as illusory as the existence of God. For example, he argues that the idea of equality is similar to the notion of the equality of all souls before God, and the ideal of liberty is similar to the Christian metaphysical teaching of freedom of the will.

In *On the Genealogy of Morals* Nietzsche argues that the democratic prejudices of the modern epoch dominate all spheres of human activity, including the intellectual sphere. Even in the 'objective sciences', he insists, democratic prejudices lead scientists to privilege reactive over active explanations of human behaviour: 'this represents a failure to recognize the essence of life, its *will to power*'. The shift between aristocratic and democratic culture, then, involves the internalization of actions which were once externalized. The internalization of actions creates a dangerous 'ressentiment': 'The slave revolt in morals begins when *ressentiment* itself becomes creative and ordains values: the *ressentiment* of creatures to whom the real reaction, that of the deed, is denied and who find compensation in an imaginary revenge.'[25] This imaginary revenge masks itself as an unegoistic form of justice. The oppositions of aristocratic and democratic, active and reactive, and externalized and internalized actions, inform the book, and Nietzsche's philosophy, as a whole. They are also central to Nietzsche's claims about modern feminism.

In Nietzsche's texts 'feminism' is seen as an extreme version of the democratic prejudices of the modern epoch. In *The Will to Power*, part of the second wave of Nietzsche's English reception, he characterizes the eighteenth century of Rousseau as the century of 'feminism: Rousseau, rule of feeling, testimony of the sovereignty of the senses, mendacious'. Rousseau feminism has freed women, setting in motion the increasing dominance of the altruistic values of modern society: Rousseau 'unfettered woman who is henceforth represented in an ever more interesting manner—as suffering'. The liberated, yet afflicted, woman is one among a number of weak individuals who has been

---

[25] Nietzsche, *On the Genealogy of Morals*, trans. Smith, 59, 22.

released on to the world stage of politics: 'Then the slaves and Mrs. Beecher-Stowe. Then the poor and the workers.' These individuals embody the sinister values and power of moral *ressentiment*, the assertion of an imaginary revenge in which the weak triumph over the strong: 'next comes the curse of voluptuousness … the most decided conviction that the lust to rule is the greatest vice; the perfect certainty that the morality and disinterestedness are identical concepts and that the "happiness of all" is a goal worth striving for'.[26] Here, Rousseau feminism begins with the sentimental altruistic interest in the welfare of others, proceeds to liberate women and slaves in the interests of equality, and ends with the ideal of mass democracy, in which the interests of the individual are sacrificed in favour of the group.

The idea that feminism was connected to wider shifts towards democracy, and that its ideology was linked to sentimentalism, *ressentiment*, introversion, and literary decadence was central to the early English translators and sponsors of Nietzsche's work. As Edward Garnett put it in 1899, Stirner's and Nietzsche's texts were to 'wage war on Sentimentalism, Pity, Christianity, Decadence in all forms, and Feminism'.[27] This series of connections was also crucial to the construction of sexual difference in Anglo-American modernist writing of the 1900s, 1910s, and 1920s, as we will see in the next chapter.

THE ENGLISH RECEPTION OF STIRNER AND NIETZSCHE: 1907–1914

The English reception of Nietzsche's ideas was coloured by the intellectual climate of the late nineteenth and early twentieth centuries. The focus on 'altruism' and 'egoism' in the early discussion of Nietzsche's ideas is explained by the centrality of these terms within the history of nineteenth-century liberal and socialist political thought. Comte's opposition between egoism and altruism was transposed into mid- to late Victorian political debates about the nature of human motivation. Liberals used 'egoist' arguments to presuppose the selfish rationality of individual agents in claims about the role of the state, but were reluctant

---

[26] Friedrich Nietzsche, *The Will to Power*, trans. Walter Kaufmann and R. J. Hollingdale (New York: Vintage Books, 1968), 59.

[27] Edward Garnett, 'Nietzsche', *Outlook*, 3 (8, July 1899), 747.

to extend the explanatory force of egoism to other spheres of human activity.

Nietzsche's attack on unegoism, or 'altruism', was used for a wide variety of political ends. For example, returning to the opening editorial of the *Eagle and the Serpent*, the phrase 'the exploited must save themselves by enlightened self-interest' actually chimed with the beliefs of sections of the socialist press. This explains why many of Nietzsche's first English readers and sponsors, such as Havelock Ellis, George Bernard Shaw, William Archer, Edmund Gosse, and Edward Garnett, were of a socialist persuasion. At the other end of the political spectrum, however, Nietzsche was also seen as an 'aristocratic radical', as Georg Brandes put it. Nietzsche declared that Brandes's characterization was 'the shrewdest remark that I have read about myself till now'.[28] In accordance with this aristocratic tenor of his thought, he was used by English defenders of a 'true aristocracy', such as Thomas Common, to defend entrenched class positions.

As we will see, the vacillation between egoist and authoritarian intellectual positions is a defining feature of literary polemic and experimentation in the 1910s. From the beginning of Nietzsche's English reception, ten years before the development of Anglo-American modernism, he was being used to defend these contradictory political ends. The reason for this seemingly bizarre connection lies in the construction of a particular kind of enemy: liberal democracy and literary decadence.

During 1906–14 a number of new Nietzsche journals were set up, and the second wave of translations began to appear. The uses to which his philosophy were put were also different, mainly because there were new political and cultural factors in place which meant that the co-ordinates of the debate had shifted. I want to focus on two aspects of this new context: changes in British liberalism and shifts in British feminism.

British liberalism was by no means static or homogeneous during the early twentieth century. Between the two general elections of 1910 and the outbreak of war in 1914, liberalism was significantly reshaped. This reshaping had begun in 1906, when the Liberal Party's landslide victory had included bringing to power a number of influential 'New Liberals' who were interested in transforming liberalism from a politics

---

[28] Friedrich Nietzsche, 'Letter to Brandes', 2 Dec. 1887, in *Selected Letters of Friedrich Nietzsche*, trans. Christopher Middleton (Indianapolis: Hackett, 1996), 279.

of anti-collectivist individualism, towards policies of social reform. The category of political individualism had a particular meaning derived from its vigorous opposition to collectivism, or socialism, in the period of 1880–1918. The ideological battle between an older Gladstonian liberalism and the 'New Liberals' of the immediate pre-war period centred on the question of what would happen to liberal politics in the context of the emerging new mass democratic state. The most influential intellectual members of the New Liberal group were the sociologist L. T. Hobhouse and the economist J. A. Hobson, both of whom identified with socialist, or collectivist, political beliefs in the 1890s, but then argued for a more collectivist liberalism in the 1900s. As Stefan Collini puts it, 'Much which was condemned as "Socialism" in the 1890s was in the vanguard of Liberalism in 1910.'[29] By 1909, for instance, Hobson had rejected his earlier socialism, and argued instead that his view of a collectivist state was continuous with a liberal tradition.

For many older-style liberals, such social reform rested uneasily with the liberal ideal of anti-state individual self-reliance. At stake in the debate between the new liberalism and the old liberalism was how to define central political categories such as liberty and rights. Put very generally, while the older 'individualist' liberalism had tended to define liberty negatively, as freedom from constraint, the collectivists argued for a more positive notion of liberty, in which the state was seen to embody the real will of the people. In accordance with this difference, the individualists and collectivists had rather different ways of defining the category of 'rights': while the individualists tended to focus on negative rights, the right to be free from the interference of others, the collectivists argued for a more positive account of rights, in which the individual would be guaranteed benefits from others through the state. For many individualist liberals, the collectivist new liberals were far too close to socialism for comfort. However, as Hobhouse realized, the move towards mass democracy, significantly spurred on by the Reform Act of 1884, but not fully achieved until 1918, when all men and women over the age of 30 got the vote, meant that all political parties needed to appeal to larger sections of the British electorate. The newly powerful Labour Party threatened to represent the interests of the newly enfranchised classes in a positive way through 'collectivist' policies. For Hobhouse, modern liberalism needed to ask itself whether it could adapt to the

---

[29] Stefan Collini, *Liberalism and Sociology: L. T. Hobhouse and Political Argument in England, 1880–1914* (Cambridge: Cambridge University Press, 1979), 79.

new political pressures produced by mass democracy by being similarly positive and constructive: 'Is Liberalism at bottom a constructive or only a destructive principle? Is it of permanent significance?'[30]

One of the most significant ways in which the modern democratic state changed in the period was the entrance of women into the political process. By 1910, women in Britain and the United States had succeeded in gaining legal rights in a number of spheres: they had won full rights to property ownership and ownership of earnings in the United States in 1860 and in Britain in 1882;[31] the right to marital autonomy had been granted in Britain in 1891;[32] the right to professional employment in specific professions had been granted at different points during the late nineteenth century, although some professions such as the legal profession in Britain did not allow the employment of women until The Sex Disqualification Removal Act of 1919; and the right to higher education was won gradually from the middle of the nineteenth century.[33] These legal rights produced significant changes in the economic and educational status of a minority of women. Many of the women writers of the 1910s and 1920s received some form of higher education.[34] The shift towards women's legal parity with men was facilitated by changes in women's employment and financial independence. During the period 1891–1921 the nature of women's paid work changed away from domestic service and into offices, shops, and assembly work in the new manufacturing industries. From 1901 to 1931 the percentage of women involved in commerce and finance in London rose from 2.8 per cent to 18.1 per cent. The increased

---

[30] L. T. Hobhouse, *Liberalism* (London: Williams & Norgate, 1911), 18.

[31] In the USA, the Act Concerning the Rights and Liabilities of Husband and Wife of 1860 allowed married women to own property and earnings; in Britain the Married Women's Property Act of 1870 allowed women to retain their property and earnings acquired after marriage, and the Married Women's Property Act of 1882 allowed women to retain any property possessed at the time of marriage.

[32] Prior to 1891, legally the husband had a certain kind of ownership of his wife's body in so far as 'it was generally believed that a man could beat his wife, although ... not with a stick thicker than his thumb'. The case of *R* v. *Jackson* of 1891 finally ruled that a husband has no right to coerce his wife or confine her against her will. See Lee Holcombe, *Wives and Property: Reform of the Married Women's Property Law in Nineteenth Century England* (Toronto: University of Toronto Press, 1983), 30, and for a full account, Maeve E. Doggett, *Marriage, Wife-Beating and the Law in Victorian Britain 'Sub Virga Viri'* (London: Weidenfeld & Nicolson, 1992).

[33] Institutions for the education of women had been opening since the middle of the century.

[34] H.D. attended Bryn Mawr College for Women; Mina Loy studied art in Munich in 1899 and in Paris in 1903.

participation of women in the economic market-place was propelled forward by the demand for women workers in the First World War.

Women's citizenship often became a symbol of more general anxieties about the changing nature of political decision making. The close historical and philosophical connections between liberal reform and women's emancipation were severely strained in the period from 1906, the year of the first imprisonment of members of the WSPU for violence, to 1914.[35] In addition to the question of women's violence, all the political parties were worried by the idea that the new female vote was a political unknown. The Labour Party was the most sympathetic to the women's cause, but even it questioned whether it was wise to create voting parity with men, and thereby to move, in one parliamentary act, from an electorate which excluded women to one in which women would be the majority. Further, the women's vote was considered, potentially, to be enfranchising individuals who would be unable to make reasoned political decisions. Asquith complained, for instance, in 1920, that the newly enfranchised women were 'hopelessly ignorant of politics, credulous to the last degree, and flickering with gusts of sentiment like a candle in the wind'.[36] These perceptions of women's political unpredictability, political ignorance, anti-rational sentimentality, and conservatism were constitutive of a more general scepticism about whether mass democracy would actually further liberal ideals of liberty. Hobhouse, for instance, stated in 1911: 'It is perfectly possible that from the point of view of general liberty and social progress a limited franchise might give better results than one that is more extended.'[37] Hobhouse attacked an older liberal 'individualism' in the name of a more collective idea of 'general liberty', but was unsure about whether mass enfranchisement and the entrance of women into the political process would further his political ideals.

The category of democracy is pulled in two directions in such debates, as both a political means, the vote, and a political end, 'general liberty'. The struggle within the Liberal Party to re-define liberalism was partly focused on the question of how these two things connected together. In order to argue that mass democracy would lead to 'general liberty',

[35] In 1906, ten members of the WSPU were arrested and imprisoned in Holloway after an incident outside Parliament, the first of a number of violent clashes and 'stunts' which were to dominate the issue of the women's vote up until the war.

[36] Quoted in G. R. Searle, *The Liberal Party: Trumph and Disintegration 1886–1929* (Basingstoke: Palgrave, 2001), 149.

[37] Hobhouse, *Liberalism*, 45.

it was necessary to presume that the masses would be progressive and enlightened, rather than conservative and reactionary. It was, then, important to explain the causal connections between individual self-interest, individual rights, political and moral self-development, and 'general liberty'. Most political commentators believed that mass democracy could lead to 'general liberty' only in the context of a politically enlightened and morally altruistic citizenship. However, the question of how to create such a citizenship was a vexed one. In a different context, Hobhouse optimistically argued that mass democracy and liberal ideals would enforce each other, because individual enlightenment would produce a collective good: individual self-development will 'not conflict with, but actually stimulate, the development of others'.[38] This liberal argument about the perfectibility of the human individual was deeply contentious. Hobhouse here argues that if the individual is set free from the shackles of external authority, he or she will develop into an enlightened and altruistic human being. Women represented a troubling sticking-point for liberal intellectuals and politicians. Many liberals, like Asquith, believed that there were intrinsic forms of sexual difference which could not be eradicated through education and political equality.

FEMINIST EGOISTS: 1907–1914

In the 1900s and 1910s the dominant feminist group in Britain, the Women's Social and Political Union (WSPU) employed a liberal language of citizenship to agitate for legal reform to represent women's rights to the vote, equal pay, entrance into all professions, equality in higher education, and the rights of working-class women. Liberal thinkers had long argued that women, in their roles as wives and mothers, were intrinsically connected to a natural altruism which was an antidote to egoism. The WSPU, along with a wide range of supportive politicians and women's groups, defended enfranchisement by extending this argument, arguing that women's participation in public affairs would have a general moralizing effect.

From 1907 to 1914 a number of dissonant feminist intellectuals in the United States and Britain began vigorously to question the idea that women were naturally moral, altruistic, and sentimental and

[38] Hobhouse, *Liberalism*, 127.

the identification of women's self-development with the attainment of democratic rights.[39] Might it not be more important, they suggested, to realize women's egoistic drives? Further, do women suffer in a particularly acute way from the contradictions of modern liberal society described by Nietzsche? What if the moralism of existing definitions of femininity actually constitutes one of the most powerful forms of oppression, rather than the route to women's liberation? They claimed that women's attainment of democratic 'rights' and citizenship creates an illusion of female freedom which actually serves to obscure the chains of modern mass society. The most interesting explorations of these questions took place in the pages of the new 'Nietzsche' and 'Stirner' journals.

A. R. Orage became editor of the *New Age* in 1907, and, as David Thatcher argues, 'the *New Age* gained for the work of Nietzsche an intellectual respect and recognition which it had been denied in England up to this time'.[40] The journal is remarkable for the diversity of its articles, which range from pro-suffragist articles by Teresa Billington-Grieg and Gwendolen Bishop to anti-feminist rants by G. K. Chesterton and Belfort Bax, to articles by liberal politicians, to Orage's discussions of Nietzsche. The journal also became a key organ for the dissemination of modernist polemic and writing, publishing important essays by Hulme and Pound, as well as modernist plays, poems, and stories.

Orage had already published two books on Nietzsche, *Friedrich Nietzsche: The Dionysian Spirit of the Age* in 1906 and *Nietzsche in Outline and Aphorism* in 1907, which was a collection of Nietzsche's aphorisms with short introductory sections written by Orage. In 1909, he discussed the possible relevance of Nietzsche's thought for feminism. He published a weekly 'dialogue' under the title 'Unedited Opinions'. In the fifth instalment, subtitled 'Votes for Women', he stated: 'In striving for the vote they [women] are even now obtaining all that the vote could possibly mean. I expect by the time they win the vote (if ever they do), they will be able to do without it.' The vote, in this logic, is less important to women's liberation than the wilful striving which fights for the vote. For Orage, this striving *is* the 'spiritual freedom' that women will obtain, and only a 'spiritual few' are capable of it.[41] Three weeks

---

[39] For the purposes of this book I refer to the identification of emancipation with legal rights as 'liberal' or 'rights' feminism.

[40] Thatcher, *Nietzsche in England*, 228.

[41] A. R. Orage, 'Unedited Opinions, V: Votes for Women', *New Age*, 4.15 (1909), 300–1.

later, however, he retracted his claim about the 'spiritual few': 'There
are no spiritual few and material many; the classification is impossible.'
Instead, he uses this distinction to create a definition of what it is to
be human: 'Doubtless for moments each one of us is spiritually awake,
while most of the rest of us are asleep, but those moments are few and
brief. For the major part of the time all of us are materially minded.'
Here, Orage transfers his claims about an aristocratic few and a 'material
many' from the realm of sociology to the human individual. Everyone
seems to be capable of spiritual freedom, but only a few are in this
state of wilful awakening. In the process he develops what he calls a
more 'vivid form of Democracy' than that currently in circulation, one
that involves destabilizing the idea that individualism is opposed to
democracy: 'What, for example, reduces Mr Chesterton to despair: the
cowardly, supine acquiescence of the many in the tyranny of the few.'
He goes on, 'And what is the cause of this attitude? The absence of a
vigorous spirit of independence and self-respect: in short the absence of
individualism.'[42] Chesterton argued that in the new mass democracies,
the individual is dominated by forms of power which are hidden from
view. Chesterton's complaints were commonplace at the time, as were
his conclusions that it was mass democracy itself which was to blame
for the lack of political accountability in modern societies. Orage, in
contrast, argues from a socialist perspective that we need a more vigorous
spirit of individualism to counter tyranny in all its forms.

Orage argues that this more 'vigorous spirit' of individualism
must also inform the process of interpretation. The sociological
perspective involves adopting a position outside the political process and viewing the individuals involved in it as static, mathematical entities. A form of interpretation which quickly ascribes
explanatory agency to external classifications, such as class and sexual differences, fails to recognize the individual nature of human
responses. Instead, his more 'vivid form of Democracy' involves
seeing the individual as the ground of interpretation. This shift of
ground, captured in Orage's image of 'wilful awakening', also, however, moves beyond the 'materially minded', unconscious standpoint
which most of 'us' occupy most of the time. As I will go on to
argue, the shift of interpretative ground from either an 'abstract'
or a materialist standpoint to an embodied form of understanding

---

[42] Orage, 'Unedited Opinions, VIII: Democracy and Mr Chesterton', *New Age*, 4.18
(1909), 359.

was claimed as an important departure in modernist literature and polemic.

There were other significant philosophical precursors to this kind of shift of emphasis. The 'vitalist' philosophies of Hans Driesch and Henri Bergson, which T. E. Hulme disseminated in the pages of the *New Age* during 1912, for instance, revealed the way in which the intellect works with psychic, linguistic, and social mechanisms to organize reality. Further, Bergson had argued that language does not express our thoughts; rather, it moulds them. He claimed, then, that we are unconscious of the ways in which social conventions determine the way that we feel, think, and act. This scepticism about the legislative dimensions of language was adopted by feminist thinkers to consider the discursive power of gender categories to mould the experiences of the individual body.

Beatrice Hastings, who helped edit the *New Age* from 1907 to 1914 and who wrote for the journal under a wide range of pseudonyms, developed an idiosyncratic feminist philosophy which was grounded in this kind of scepticism. Her perspective altered significantly from 1907, as she changed from a passionate socialist supporter of the suffrage, to become what she called, in March 1910, a 'feminine anti-Suffragist'. Hastings argued that the 'feminine anti-Suffragist' is a new category of person, who has evolved because of the puritanical autocratic moralism of the WSPU. Hastings was particularly angered by the way in which the suffragettes ignored the revolutionary sex revolt which had altered the private relationships between men and women. She rejects the suffragette definition of freedom, since 'Women with the spirit to be free will be free in any era. They will not wait for the vote to certify them free, and they will not make a great deal of noise whether they get the vote now or next century.'[43] The following month, in an article called 'Women and Freedom', she argued that 'Mental freedom must be begotten from within.'[44] Like Orage, her critique of the suffragette focus on democratic rights involved transposing feminist agency from things external to the self to the wilful striving which *is* the self. Unlike Orage, she tried to describe the nature of this 'within', but she struggled to achieve this. The article kept asserting different foundations for individual freedom: she began by claiming that 'personal choice in thought' is the 'starting

43 D. Triformis, 'Lady McLaren's Charter', *New Age*, 6.23 (1910), 533. D. Triformis was one of Beatrice Hastings's many pseudonyms.
44 D. Triformis, 'Women and Freedom', *New Age*, 7.2 (1910), 29.

point of freedom', but went on to state that 'Thought' 'begets' mental freedom, and that 'personal choice' is the 'outward evidence' of thought. She became clearer when she constructed the suffragettes as a 'mob', an irrational and puritanical force which aims to stamp out women's sexual freedom and individualism.

In subsequent articles she attempted to construct a more positive description of the self, but in doing so reverted to dogmatic statements about the biological nature of gender difference. By 1912, for instance, she was asserting that whereas a 'slave freed is a free man, potent to establish and not merely to claim his rights', women should recognize their biological 'limits' in potency.[45] She was not the only writer to use the biological basis of identity to confirm women's weakness and slavish reliance on legal rights to establish power over others. There were a number of writers who contributed to the *New Age* who used such ideas for precisely such ends. Anthony M. Ludovici, for example, an 'aristocratic' Nietzschean who wrote for the *New Age* and was one of the initial translators of Nietzsche's works into English, used Nietzsche's ideas to enforce women's biological weakness and to defend an aristocratic model of political organization.[46] He argued in his book *Nietzsche and Art*, which was published in 1911, that democracy fails because by conferring power on the majority it creates a passive or 'feminine' approach to politics.

Despite the fact that Hastings's feminist scepticism reached a dogmatic dead end, she is interesting because her intellectual career is suggestive of a more general set of shifts in the period. She transferred her politics from the suffragette cause to a Nietzschean feminism, in which the female self is constructed as wilful, active, and dynamic, and is defined by a healthy sensuality. In the United States, the Russian anarchist Emma Goldman also argued that Nietzsche's and Stirner's thought should be harnessed for feminist ends, because of the need to move the ground of feminist debate from the lawcourt to the individual self.[47] Goldman, unlike Hastings, however, explicitly identified her work with a pacifist anarchist politics, and connected anarchism with feminism

---

[45] Beatrice Hastings, 'Pages from an Unpublished Novel, Book XI', *New Age*, 11.21 (1912), 469.

[46] Anthony M. Ludovici, *Who is to be Master of the World? An Introduction to the Philosophy of Friedrich Nietzsche* (London: T. N. Foulis, 1909); idem, *The False Assumptions of "Democracy"* (London: Heath Cranton, 1921).

[47] See Emma Goldman, 'Preface', in *Anarchism and Other Essays* (New York: Mother Earth Publishing Association, 1910), 50.

in articles she published in *Mother Earth*, the journal she co-edited from 1907, and in her enormously successful American lecture tours. In articles such as 'Woman Suffrage' (1910), 'The Tragedy of Women's Emancipation' (1911), 'The Traffic in Women' (1911), 'Marriage and Love' (1911), and 'The Victims of Morality' (1913), she discusses the need for feminism to move beyond its focus on the 'fetich' of liberal rights to an analysis of the 'internal tyrants' which control women's minds.[48] Goldman was interested in the wider social and cultural forces which create these modern tyrannies, viewing these as the cause of women's particular experience of modernity. Women, she argued, have had a belated experience of liberty in liberal terms. In fact, women have attained their political 'rights' at the very moment historically when these rights have ceased to have any real significance. By identifying with these 'external tyrannies', women identify themselves with external illusions. Further, they embrace a feminine artifice which is ultimately damaging: 'Merely external emancipation has made of the modern woman an artificial being.'[49] Women, then, experience, in a particularly acute form, the contradictions of modern liberal society outlined by Stirner and Nietzsche. By focusing her attention on the external tyrannies which control her life, she has become estranged from herself. Goldman states in 1911 that women must learn that 'her freedom will reach as far as her power to achieve her freedom reaches'.[50] Goldman's 'power to achieve ... freedom' is similar to Orage's 'striving' for freedom and Hastings's 'spirit to be free'. All three writers iconoclastically dismantle what Goldman calls, in a Stirnerian flourish, the 'religious and social spooks' and 'monster of Morality' which keep women in chains.[51] By focusing on the present-tense activity of assertion, they try to create a language which avoids reverting either to essentialist accounts of woman's 'nature' or to a focus on what Goldman calls woman's artifice. This present-tense language embodies a dynamic, futuristic energy which these writers see as the key to women's liberation. In a stroke, the historical associations of women with sentimentalism, altruism, and introspection are discarded.

The focus on the liberatory potential of language was also to feature importantly in a new feminist journal launched by a small group of renegade British suffragettes in the autumn of 1911. The journal aimed to offer a forum for ideas in opposition to the suffragette feminism of

---

[48] Emma Goldman, 'Woman Suffrage', in *Anarchism and Other Essays*, 201.
[49] Goldman, 'Tragedy of Women's Emancipation', 134.   [50] Ibid. 142.
[51] Emma Goldman, 'Victims of Morality' (1911), in *Red Emma Speaks*, 127–8.

the WSPU. The *Freewoman: A Weekly Feminist Review* was edited by Mary Gawthorpe and Dora Marsden, a former activist member of the WSPU who had tired of the draconian structure of the party. It first appeared on 23 November 1911, and it was to undergo a number of title changes which reflect the shifting beliefs of its editors.[52] It became the *Freewoman: A Weekly Humanist Review* on 23 May 1912, and then the *New Freewoman: An Individualist Review* on 15 June 1913. Ezra Pound became literary editor in August 1913, and the journal changed its name to the *Egoist* in January 1914. Whilst the *Freewoman* and the *New Freewoman* are more obviously forums for the publication of Dora Marsden's philosophy, she continued to write the weekly unsigned editorial even after she ceased being editor of the *Egoist* due to ill health.[53] These title changes suggest something of the journal's shifting political allegiance from a politicized ego-feminism to a philosophical and aesthetic ego-individualism.

From its inception, the *Freewoman* positioned itself against the feminism of the WSPU organ, *Votes for Women*, which had been founded in 1907, and against the Women's Freedom League's (WFL) journal the *Vote*, which had been started in 1909.[54] A year after the launch of the *Freewoman*, the WSPU established its own official journal, the *Suffragette*, edited by Christabel Pankhurst, and the *New Freewoman* published articles directly critical of articles published in the *Suffragette*.[55] They accused the suffragettes of fetishizing the vote as a means to liberation. James Douglas, for instance, claims in the *Suffragette* that the vote is 'the key to citizenship'.[56] Mrs Tuke also insists that the suffragettes must fight 'to win for women the power to directly influence the legislation in this country through the parliamentary vote'.[57]

[52] The *Freewoman* was criticized by its readers for being expensive. It cost 3*d*.

[53] For a detailed account of Marsden's career in the WSPU, her later differences with the suffragettes, her founding of the *Freewoman*, and her subsequent philosophical interests, see Les Garner, *A Brave and Beautiful Spirit: Dora Marsden, 1882–1960* (Aldershot: Avebury, 1990).

[54] The WFL formed in 1909 as a splinter group of the WSPU. Ray Strachey describes it as 'a society which followed much the same policy as that of the WSPU. though it … conducted its affairs in a more regular and democratic fashion': Ray Strachey, *The Cause* (London: G. Bell & Sons Ltd., 1928; repr. London: Cedric Chivers Ltd., 1974), 310–11.

[55] The *Suffragette* was launched on Friday, 18 Oct. 1912, as a weekly paper at the price of 1*d*.

[56] James Douglas, 'A Word to the Commons', *Suffragette*, 1.1 (1912), 13.

[57] Mrs Tuke, 'Report of a Speech by Mrs Tuke at the Great Meeting in the Albert Hall: Mrs Pankhurst Defies the Government', *Suffragette*, 1.2 (1912), 18.

In the first issue, the *Freewoman* distinguishes its aims from such ideas by prioritizing the evolution of the freewoman's 'becoming' over further legal reform: 'They [the suffragettes] deal with something which women may acquire. We find our chief concern in what they may become. Our interest is in the Freewoman herself, her psychology, philosophy, morality, and achievements, and only in a secondary degree with her politics and economics.'[58] Like Orage, Hastings, and Goldman, Marsden resists identifying female liberation with the acquisition of external ends: the vote, the right to work professionally, and to be educated. This model of freedom, for Marsden, splits the female subject apart, so that freedom is located in something external to the self. She argues that the liberal model of female emancipation merely replaces one kind of subservience to an external law with another: whereas once women were subjected to a patriarchal law, they now confront a legal mechanism of rights. For Marsden, there is something peculiarly sinister about the new state law which tyrannizes the modern female subject. Whereas previously a woman could contemplate the external entity which controlled her, the father/brother/husband, the modern woman has internalized structures of power which are no less 'external' and controlling. By understanding herself through these external categories, the woman creates a powerful but illusory form of modern imprisonment.

Marsden breaks out of this internalized prison by inverting the dynamic of self and world. Freedom, rather than being located in external ends, is instead located firmly in the wilful self who creates the world in her own image. The opening article dismantles existing definitions of the female subject. It discards the 'external' classifications of wife and prostitute, and instead describes two new types of women, 'Freewomen' and 'Bondwomen', against the axis of individual autonomy: 'Bondwomen are the women who are not separate entities—who are not individuals. They are complements merely.'[59] The article calls for women to harness their individual strength in order to break free of their parasitic status: 'Those who are "down" are inferior. When change takes place in the thing itself—i.e., when it becomes equal or superior—by the nature of its own being it rises.' Women can choose between remaining 'as the man's protected female, or, making what may or may not be

---

58 'Notes of the Week', *Freewoman*, 1.1 (1911), 3. Although it is unsigned, 'Notes of the Week' was written by Dora Marsden.
59 Dora Marsden, 'Bondwomen', *Freewoman*, 1.1 (1911), 1.

a successful effort, endeavour to take her place as a master'. The article concludes:

[O]nly Freewomen can be free, or lead the way to freedom. They will learn that their freedom will consist in appraising their own worth, in setting up their own standards and living up to them, and putting behind them for ever their rôle of complacent self-sacrifice. For none can judge of another soul's value. The individual has to record its own.[60]

Marsden's self is a negation of any political or collective register: 'own self' replaces citizenship, 'own worth' replaces the evaluative terms of prostitute and wife, and 'own standards' replace repressive notions of female morality. This article thereby reflects her philosophy as a whole, which sees modern society as hostile and impenetrable to human reason, a battleground of individual wills. The female individual can choose to embrace the will and seize control of her world, or passively to shrink under the weight of a modernity empty of sacred and altruistic values.

Like Orage, Hastings, and Goldman, Marsden uses Stirner's and Nietzsche's ideas to create a new feminist philosophy of dynamism and will. However, she rejects the pacifist register of Goldman's thought, and instead celebrates the inequality of the individual's will-to-power. She writes in December 1913: '[W]e do not "stand for" anything beyond the satisfying of ourselves.'[61] Instead, the ego is an intensified self; a kind of focused embodiment of will and desire:

The only end which it is worth while for the individual to give his attention to, is the increase of his own power, of which he himself is the only one who may be expected to know what is required for its increase. So each man becomes a 'law unto himself', which is a denial of law, since law essentially involves relation and relation is comparison. If the individual is unique, which is a law to himself there can be no law therefore and common life becomes anarchic and disordered.[62]

This legal solipsism reserves no space for structures of social recognition. The ego, rather than the state, is the 'criterion of truth', as Stirner puts it.[63] Marsden splits the individual into her physical nature and her legal person, and claims that it is the former which holds the

---

[60] Dora Marsden, 'Bondwomen', *Freewoman*, 1.1 (1911), 2.
[61] Dora Marsden, 'Views and Comments', *New Freewoman*, 1.13 (1913), 245.
[62] Dora Marsden, 'Views and Comments', *New Freewoman*, 1.4 (1913), 65.
[63] Stirner, *Ego and its Own*, 314.

key to individual identity. Her philosophy of individual strength, autonomy, and freedom echoes the claims of Stirner's and Nietzsche's ego-philosophy. It identifies with the revolution in thought and the liberation from ideas through individual will for which Marx had criticized Stirner half a century earlier.[64]

The radical withdrawal into the sceptical self might seem to be an odd foundation for the development of arguments useful for feminism. Marsden's arguments, however, inject a feminist angle into questions which were central to Anglo-American modernism. She engages directly with the perceived powerlessness of the individual in the context of a newly homogenized twentieth-century world. We will see in the next chapter how modernist writers also believed that the self had become a refuge of artistic integrity in the context of a world become too large and complex to be seen 'whole'.

There was a conscious dissidence to Marsden's polemical pronouncements, particularly as her feminism involved embracing the healthy sensuality of the female body. The established feminist intellectuals reacted immediately. The great liberal campaigner, Millicent Fawcett, who was committed to the limited franchise for property-owning women, for instance, was so offended by the journal that she is reputed to have torn the first issue of the *Freewoman* into little pieces.[65] A furious debate took place on the letter pages of the *Freewoman* over its feminist stance, centred primarily on the journal's attitude to women's sexuality. The WSPU campaigned for women's right to vote by highlighting women's moral superiority over men. Like Hastings before her, Marsden argued that the idea of women's moral superiority circumscribed, rather than furthered, women's freedom. In the fifth issue of the *Freewoman* the new categories of bondwomen and freewomen were transposed on to a discussion of love: 'All love is free. When love is bound it shows the modification of its nature which will soon turn it into something else.'[66] Freedom and love are situated firmly outside the law in this article:

---

[64] While the early feminism of the journal developed its own kind of individualist philosophy prior to any knowledge of Stirner, Dora Marsden instantly identified with his book on its publication in England in 1912. Nearly a year after the first issue, an editorial article states: 'We have just laid aside one of the profoundest of human documents, Max Stirner's 'Ego and His Own'. A correspondent has asked us to examine Stirner's doctrine, and shortly we intend to do so. Just now we are more concerned to overcome its penetrative influence on our own minds': 'The Growing Ego', *Freewoman*, 1.38 (1912), 221.

[65] See Rachel Strachey, *Millicent Garrett Fawcett* (London: John Murray, 1931), 236.

[66] Dora Marsden, 'The Editor's Reply', *Freewoman*, 1.5 (1911), 93.

'[I]n its very nature the development of love-emotion is incapable of subjection to legislative enactment or other artificial coercion.'[67] The journal continued to be a forum for discussions of free love in articles such as 'Modernism in Morality: The Ethics of Sexual Relationships', by Julian Warde; 'The Immorality of the Marriage Contract'; and the four-part editorial series called 'Interpretation of Sex'.[68] These articles prompted W. H. Smith to ban the sale of the *Freewoman* in September 1912 because of the frank discussion of women's sexuality.

Jane Eldridge Miller argues that the impact of the *Freewoman* rested on its role as a forum for women's discussion of their 'private' problems: '[T]he most powerful discussions of marriage in *The Freewoman* were in the letters to the editor, in which women revealed with astonishing honesty and freedom their feelings about sexuality, the indignities of the marriage market, and the frustrations of trying to maintain some kind of personal identity while running a household and raising children.'[69] The journal's interest in articulating women's private problems formed part of a wider focus of interest in the pre-war years. Maggie Humm describes Schreiner's *Woman and Labour* as setting the tone of 'contemporary feminism by arguing that feminism is as much a part of consciousness-raising as of equal rights'.[70]

After the First World War, the idea that consciousness-raising destabilized moral accounts of femininity became more widely accepted. Dora Russell, for instance, looking back on the war years in 1925, insists on the importance of denouncing sex moralism: 'To me the important task of modern feminism is to accept and proclaim sex; to bury for ever the lie that has too long corrupted our society—the lie that the body is a hindrance to the mind, and sex a necessary evil to be endured for the perpetuation of the race.'[71] She argues that the war made such morality look ridiculous:

---

[67] Dora Marsden, 'Concerning Free Love', *New Freewoman*, 1.1 (1913), 12.

[68] Julian Warde, 'The Ethics of Sexual Relationships', *Freewoman*, 1.32 (1912), 110–11; anon., 'The Immorality of the Marriage Contract', *Freewoman*, 1.31 (1912), 81–3; anon., 'Interpretations of Sex', *Freewoman*, 1.24–2.27 (1912), 461–2, 481–2, 501–2, 1–2.

[69] Jane Eldridge Miller, *Rebel Women: Feminism, Modernism and the Edwardian Novel* (London: Virago, 1994), 42.

[70] Maggie Humm, 'Landscape for a Literary Feminism: British Women Writers 1900 to the Present', in Helena Forsäs-Scott, ed., in *Textual Liberation: European Feminist Writing in the Twentieth Century* (London: Routledge, 1991), 14.

[71] Mrs Bertrand Russell, *Hypatia: Or Woman and Knowledge* (London: Kegan Paul, Trench, Trubner & Co., 1925), 24–5.

[D]uring the years of war, young women took the last step towards feminine emancipation by admitting to themselves and their lovers the mutual nature of sex-love between man and woman. It sounds a platitude, but it is, in fact, a revolution. Strange to say, the nearness of death from enemy bombs or enemy fire did not intensify the thought of holiness and heaven. It made the little footrules to measure morality look absurd; it mocked the emptiness of female virtue.[72]

This 'revolution' involves making public what had once been private, or externalizing women's so-called private concerns. But what seems to destabilize this morality is the articulation, as much as the activity, of 'sex-love between man and woman'.

Hastings, Goldman, and Marsden were all aware of and wanted to exploit the disruptive power of women's sexuality. The representation of women's so-called private life was also revolutionary, because it disrupted the sacred illusion of the feminine as unattainable, an idea grounded in ideas of feminine introspection, solipsism, sentimentality, decadence, and deferred desire. As Nietzsche argues in *The Genealogy of Morals*, modernity is defined by an internalization of instincts, an internalization that he classes as 'feminine'. Egoism, for both Nietzsche and Stirner, is an active, wilful individualism opposed to any kind of decadent introspection. The feminist Stirnerians and Nietzscheans looked at in this chapter also separate out egoism from any kind of introspection or sentimentality; but they importantly disrupt the connections between femininity, privacy, and decadent art.

The relationship between sexuality and representation was grounded in arguments about the difference between abstract and embodied language. Stirner's *The Ego and its Own* was centrally concerned with the coercive power of abstract words. When the *New Age* reviewed Byington's translation of Stirner's book in August 1907, for example, the anonymous reviewer suggested that liberalism rests on a meaningless set of abstract categories: 'Stirner was mainly concerned with the two words, Liberty and Man. In essence they may be said to constitute the Alpha and Omega of liberalism in the broadest and narrowest senses. Both words are, strictly speaking, meaningless; or, at least, their meaning is so vague that their use in genuine discussion is extremely perilous.'[73] The dismissal of liberalism by accusing it of a meaningless

---

[72] Ibid. 32.
[73] Anonymous review, 'The Unique Individual, *The Ego and His Own*, by Max Stirner', *New Age*, 1.16 (1907), 250.

verbalism is a powerful tactic, and Marsden does something similar when discussing women's emancipation. She argues that the government's penetration into the private sphere is possible only because of the power of democratic language: ideas of 'humanity', 'justice', and 'mankind' are described as a 'deluge of democratic sentiment' which persuade the individual to agree 'to place the regulating and governing of his life outside his own ordering and under that of the majority of the rest'.[74] She insists that this sinister tyranny of the democratic majority creates a veritable flood of language as well as sentiment: 'Oh Freedom, subtle deceiver! What chains are forged and riveted in thy Name! ... Liberty, Equality, Fraternity, Unity, Justice, Truth, Humanity, Law, Mumbo-Jumbo, Mesopotamia, Abracadabra, Om-Tat-Sat. Intellectual Concepts all—futile products of men who pursue their own shadow.'[75] This bizarre list of ghostly chains fixes individuals in positions of subjection. In a number of articles in 1913 and 1914 Marsden argues that the manipulative might of these 'futile products' structures our very language and beliefs. Both authoritarian regimes and their political opponents use the same idealistic language: 'All who wield authority, do it in the name of an idea: equality, justice, love, right, duty, humanity, god, the Church, the State .... Denying authority, they use the language of authority.' The language which is used both to enforce and to subvert authority has a sinister uniformity which conceals the solidarity of interests at the heart of battles for political power. Marsden's essays reach a truly paranoid vision at this point, as she suggests that such words are the basis of a sinister form of modern surveillance and control. A true denial of authority, she proclaims, can only take place through the abjuration of all ideals, through a radical purification of language: 'The work of purging language is likely to be a slow one even after the battle of argument in its favour shall have been won.' Marsden envisages a future language which will be free of linguistic uniformity: 'When men acquire the ability to make and co-ordinate accurate descriptions, that is, when they learn to think, the empire of mere words, "thoughts" will be broken, the sacred pedestals shattered, and the seats of authority cast down.'[76]

As we will see, Marsden's evocative description of the coercive nature of 'abstract' religious and humanist language and the revolutionary

---

[74] Dora Marsden, 'Views and Comments', *New Freewoman*, 1.1 (1913), 4.
[75] Ibid.
[76] Dora Marsden, 'Thinking and Thought', *New Freewoman*, 1.5 (1913), 82, 83.

potential of 'accurate' or realist description will echo through modernist literary polemic in the pre-war period. Her argument about language also forms an important corollary to her claims about modernity. Linguistic realism is consonant with egoistic sense certainty, both of which are concrete, in contrast to the 'abstract' words and ideologies which claim to have a purchase on the modern world. This world is too large and complex to be seen whole. Democracy is constructed as a powerful linguistic, as well as political, enemy in this essay. Through a kind of linguistic democratization, words have ceased to have any stable meaning. The way of countering this is to move inwards, to pin words to objects or to the individual body. Only language which constitutes an embodiment of the unique self will be free of the terrifyingly coercive power of church and state.

In a number of articles published in the summer of 1913, with the re-launch of the journal under the new title the *New Freewoman*, Marsden uses these arguments to create a series of radical feminist claims:

Accurately speaking, there *is* no 'Woman Movement'. 'Woman' is doing nothing—she has, indeed, no existence. A very limited number of individual women are emphasising the fact that the first thing to be taken into account with regard to them is that they are not a class, sex, or a 'movement'. They—this small number—regard themselves neither as wives, spinsters, women, nor men. They are themselves, each cut off from and differing from the rest. What each is and what each requires she proposes to find by looking into her *own* wants—not 'description by function'.[77]

Marsden here announces the emergence of a kind of feminist avant-garde group committed to the principle of radical isolation. This is perhaps less inherently contradictory than it first appears. She seems to want to describe a set of beliefs which are historically specific, dependent as they are on the negation of existing definitions of feminism. This is primarily a philosophical claim about the way in which language is controlled by ideas of sexual difference. Just as she argues that there will be a political revolution through the power of 'accurate description', so she claims that feminist revolution will happen through a linguistic egoism.

Her claim that 'Woman' has 'no existence' prompted a flurry of response in the letter pages of the *New Freewoman*. In the next issue, she clarified her argument:

[77] Dora Marsden, 'Views and Comments', *New Freewoman*, 1.1 (1913), 4.

[W]e will explain what we meant by saying that "woman", spelt with a capital, Woman-as-type, has no existence; that it is an empty concept and should be banished from language. We meant that there is no definite reality which can be substituted as that to which woman corresponds, which is a thing and not an idea. If we take "female reproductive organs" away from this concept Woman, what have we left? Absolutely nothing, save a mountain of sentimental mush …. It is as nearly related to the first Amoeba as to any particular woman.

Marsden argues that, like law, rights, and citizenship, the language of femininity has no purchase on any 'thing' in the real world. She goes on to claim that the category of woman does not simply mediate the female self; it moulds the lives of 'real' women. She thereby constructs this sentimental, altruistic woman as a metaphysical 'truth' handed down from the previous generation. By reversing the relationship between word and thing, she creates a new definition of female freedom as the ability to create one's own language. The 'Comment' continues by insisting that the truth of this newly created modern woman will rest on a new realism grounded in the female individual:

Is there such a thing even as *a* woman sensed from the inside? If so, we have got to learn what it is. Never in the course of a long life have we felt "There, I felt *that* as a woman." Always things have been felt as individual and unique, as much related to other women as to other men—which is not at all; everything has been sensed as *Ourself*, of which the gender has yet to be learnt: the gender of the self we have yet to learn …. We would soon have heard the last of Man and Woman spelt with capitals, and the day of the individual would be at hand. And the measure of the individual would be not sex, but individual power.[78]

Freedom resides in purging language of the 'sentimental mush' of femininity, and replacing it with a language of sense perception. The 'gender of the self', argues Marsden, will be learnt only through an interrogation which creates its own terms of reference: her 'unique self' is a 'thing' whose nature we are yet to learn to understand. This is a futuristic vision which places linguistic experiment at the heart of modern feminism.

The Stirnerian and Nietzschean feminists writing in this pre-war period argue for the transposition of action from politics to aesthetics; and the trajectory of journals such as the *Freewoman* and the *New Age* conform to this transposition. There has been extensive analysis of the shift from the political feminism of the *Freewoman* to the

[78] Dora Marsden, 'Views and Comments', *New Freewoman*, 1.2 (1913), 24.

almost exclusively literary nature of the *New Freewoman* and the *Egoist*. Whereas Shari Benstock claims that Pound silenced what he saw as unimportant 'women's issues', Linda Kinnahan suggests that Marsden herself participated in 'the polemical silencing of feminism and the related masculinization of a developing modernist aesthetic'.[79] Yet both Benstock and Kinnahan distort the extent to which an individualist philosophy determines both the early feminism and the later literary modernist writing in the journal.[80] As early as 8 August 1912, intellectual freedom is identified with poets: 'So we return to the Ego and its wants. If we wish to learn them, and so learn its nature, we must turn to those persons who have a positive Ego, sufficiently sure of itself to speak out its wants—to the poets and creative thinkers.'[81] The editorial continues by describing the 'positive Ego' as the result of a strong personality and 'the self-conscious sense'. Early in 1913, Rebecca West writes to Dora Marsden about the re-launch of the journal under the title the *New Freewoman* and suggests that 'freedom of expression in literature' might be 'associated with and inspired by your gospel'.[82]

When Pound became literary editor in August 1913, the identification of egoism with the Anglo-American avant-garde was established conclusively. The idea, however, that Marsden was forced to submit to Pound's assertion of authority in the destination of the journal's concerns has been persuasively redressed by Bruce Clark, who has traced ways in which Marsden's individualist philosophy prompted Pound to a similar position. Marsden asked Pound to state his 'philosophical credentials' in 1913, and Pound replied: 'The seven minutes at my disposal is hardly enough to define my philosophical credentials adequately. I suppose I'm individualist, I suppose I believe in the arts as the most effective propaganda for a sort of individual liberty that can

---

[79] Shari Benstock, *Women of the Left Bank: Paris, 1900–1940* (London: Virago Press, 1987), 364; Linda Kinnahan, *Poetics of the Feminine: Authority and Literary Tradition in William Carlos Williams, Mina Loy, Denise Levertov and Kathleen Fraser* (Cambridge: Cambridge University Press, 1994), 23.

[80] The history of the journal has been well documented elsewhere. In particular see Frederick J. Hoffman, Charles Allen, and Carolyn F. Ulrich, *The Little Magazine: A History and Bibliography* (Princeton: Princeton University Press, 1946), 22; Jane Lidderdale and Mary Nicholson, *Dear Miss Weaver, 1876–1961* (New York: Viking, 1970), 75.

[81] Marsden, 'Growing Ego', 222.

[82] Rebecca West, 'Letter to Dora Marsden', n.d. [Feb. 1913], cited in Bruce Clark, 'Dora Marsden and Ezra Pound: The New Freewoman and "The Serious Artist"', *Contemporary Literature*, 33.1 (1992), 97.

be developed without public inconvenience.'[83] Rather than opposing Marsden's views, the individualist aesthetic conformed to Marsden's philosophy and to her increasing identification of egoist expression with writing and art.

Both Marsden's attempt to strip the category of woman of its 'sentimental mush' and the scepticism about all kinds of collective politics leave a critical vacuum. The journal circles in on itself, suggesting that the 'gender of the self' will be learnt in the explorations in psychology and language in the pages of the journal itself. All of the writers considered in this chapter accord the aesthetic a central role in the exploration of the self. It is important, however, that this self is defined as wilful, dynamic, and egotistical, the opposite of any kind of sentimental or introspective understanding of the individual. Literary decadence is replaced by an avant-garde defined by the very ideals of violence, dynamism, and futurism which control Nietzsche's philosophy. The *Freewoman* explores what Billington-Grieg describes as the 'speedier way to full human liberty' in the years preceding the First World War. The journal, in both its feminist and literary forms, identifies this 'speedier way' with writing itself, with a linguistic revolution performed on the level of poetry and art. In the next chapter I will investigate the diverse ways in which Anglo-American writers responded to the challenge to create this linguistic revolution.

---

[83] Ezra Pound, letter to Dora Marsden, n.d. [July 1913?], cited in Lidderdale and Nicholson, *Dear Miss Weaver*, 68.

2

Modernist Literature: Individualism and Authority

Ford Madox Ford, in his 1905 experimental work *The Soul of London*, describes two kinds of city. One is the modern, anonymous metropolis, which he sees as a 'gigantic pantheon of the dead level of democracy'. The other is Ford's London, based on what he calls 'personal impressions'. In *The Soul of London* Ford develops a new 'impressionist' style of writing to capture his personal London. He tries to write without using the 'encyclopaedic, topographical, or archaeological' techniques which he associates with a moribund democracy.[1] Instead, he aims to represent the moment in which the visible world is apprehended. Ford's highly subjective London is produced through a fidelity to the visual world and an ability to endow the visual image with a personal meaning. A strong artistic individuality deliberately intrudes on the writing. He suggests that it is only through this style of writing that he can capture the 'strongly individualised' human beings who live in the city, individuals with 'romantic hopes, romantic fears'.[2]

Ford's book relies on defining the individual against a standardized modern London. In Chapter 1 we considered how the opposition of democracy and individualism was central to philosophical debates in the 1900s. For Ford, as for Marsden, this conflict involves considering the nature of representation. For example, Ford suggests that London's contradictions are modernity's contradictions. The city eludes description, because Ford is unsure where the city really ends: he sees its spirit extending as far as 'the swamps of coastal Africa'. It is not only geographically and spatially that London exceeds its boundaries. It is so large and powerful that it swallows up all who arrive on its streets,

---

[1] Ford Madox Ford, *The Soul of London: A Survey of a Modern City*, ed. Alan G. Hill (London: J. M. Dent, 1995), 12, 3.
[2] Ibid. 5.

eradicating differences of race, religion, and character. The 'Modern Spirit' that creates this surreptitious homogenization is too nebulous and abstract to be visualized or described. London, like modernity, is beyond the reach of language and the imagination.[3]

Ford would continue to explore what he saw as his subjectively 'impressionistic' stylistic techniques as a counter to the homogenizing effects of modernity. In the essay 'Ancient Lights' (1911), for instance, he argues that 'we are standardising ourselves and we are doing away with everything that is outstanding'.[4] Ford blamed the democratic and technological society of the 1900s and 1910s for this standardization. Politically, he was a Tory who was sceptical about the existing Conservative Party and Conservative press. We find him, therefore, attacking the 'opportunism' of contemporary parliamentary politics: about neither the Conservative nor the Liberal Party 'is there a breath of principle or a sign that either has any real comprehension of its traditional significance'.[5] At times his critique of contemporary politics produced a political nostalgia, such as in his essay 'The Passing of the Great Figure' (1909), where he attacks democracy by defending the feudal church. At other times, his views are more intriguing and less easy to place. Democracy, Ford argued, is a poor replacement for the cohesive norms of religion, morality, and class. In the face of the disintegration of these belief systems, the individual is forced to retreat into the self. Ford evocatively describes how this withdrawn individual confronts a confusing array of facts and faces: 'each man by himself ... seeking to make out the pattern of the bewildering carpet that modern life is'. For Ford, modern life is too large and confusing to be seen 'steadily' and 'whole', as Arnold had put it: '[W]e may contemplate life steadily enough to-day; it is impossible to see it whole.'[6]

This picture of the artist's contemplation of modern life threatens to prescribe a more limited role for the writer, one in which the whole is sacrificed to the personal observations of the solitary artist. Ford tried to avoid this by claiming for the modern writer a new role in the face of the 'bewildering' fragmentation of modern life: 'to be brought really into contact with the lives of those around us, this is a thing which grows

---

[3] Ford, *The Soul of London*, 12, 5.
[4] Ford Madox Ford, *Memories and Impressions: A Study in Atmospheres* (London: Harper & Brothers, 1911), 299.
[5] Ford Madox Ford, 'The Critical Attitude', *English Review*, 4 (Jan. 1910), 330.
[6] Ford Madox Ford, *The Critical Attitude* (London: Duckworth, 1911), 28.

daily more difficult in the complexities of modern life. This, vicariously, the artist is more and more needed to supply.[7] For Ford, 'contact' becomes a key critical term, involving a kind of telescopic realism in which the particular stands for the whole.

In an essay called 'The Woman of the Novelists' published in *The Critical Attitude* in 1911, Ford considered the importance of this literary 'contact' for men's understanding of women. In general, he claims, men 'negotiate with great numbers of simulacra in the shape of men'. The artist brings to life a meaningful contact with others which pierces these surface human relations. He or she has a particularly formative role to play in relation to the understanding of women, because 'the conventions of modern life prevent us from really knowing more than two'. However, the 'woman of the novelists' has functioned to obscure further a man's relationship to real women. Men, insists Ford, get to know women through the veil of an ideal literary woman, a 'super-woman heroine', a 'conventional deity'. It is not just novelists who have created this female deity. Women, argues Ford, 'have aided and applauded this setting up of an empty convention'.[8] This fictional female deity is thoroughly idealized, resting on notions of feminine purity, wisdom, and tolerance. She is at odds with the 'bewildering fragments' of the real women in a man's life, who Ford claims have 'the power to bedevil, to irritate, to plague and to madden him'.[9] The contrast between the abstract woman of the novelists and 'real women' rests on the difference between imagination and experience. The experience of the fragmented nature of real women is women's greatest barrier to the vote and to citizenship. Women, like London in *The Soul of London*, embody the contradictions of the modern spirit. For men, they are the ultimate simulacrum of modern life, heavily over-determined by the weight of literary idealizations. In a man's mind, then, they are either too abstract or too fragmented to be seen whole.

Ford's thoughts on the way in which women embody the contradictions of modernity would echo through modernist writing. His desire to foreground a strong authorial subjectivity as an antidote to democratic standardization would also be repeated by a wide range of modernists. D. H. Lawrence, in *The Rainbow* and *Women in Love*, rehearses some of Ford's arguments about the relationship between individualism, democracy, and sexual difference. In *The Rainbow* Ursula Brangwen

---

[7] Ford, *The Critical Attitude*, 66–7.
[8] Ibid. 149, 150, 159, 163, 167.   [9] Ibid. 164.

criticizes modern democracy: ' "Only the greedy and ugly people come to the top in a democracy," she said, "because they're the only people who will push themselves there. Only degenerate races are democratic." ' Ursula suggests that democracy heralds the enervating collapse, rather than progressive advance, of civilization. Lawrence, following Nietzsche, sees democracy as the latest manifestation of the Christian ideology of the equality of all souls before God. For Lawrence, however, the principle of egalitarianism has become connected to the money-based system of advanced capitalism, which reduces humans to standard-ized, mathematical units. ' "I hate equality on a money basis," ' Ursula declares.[10]

In *Women in Love* Lawrence further develops this critique of democracy. Birkin, in an argument with Hermione, proclaims:

'We are all different and unequal in spirit—it is only the *social* differences that are based on accidental material conditions. We are all abstractly and mathematically equal, if you like.... But spiritually, there is pure difference and neither equality nor inequality counts. It is upon these two bits of knowledge that you must found a state. Your democracy is an absolute lie—your brotherhood of man is a pure falsity, if you apply it further than the mathematical abstraction.'[11]

Lawrence, like Ford, characterizes modern democracy as both a form of national economic organization and an ideological principle. Birkin suggests that ideas of democratic equality are based on a materialism and mathematical logic, both of which fail to capture the 'pure difference' of the human spirit. The idea of 'pure difference' does not make much sense without the equality to which it is opposed. Both are a product of the industrialism and historical democratization described in the novel. After all, difference, in *Women in Love*, is a mark of natural human identity severed from class distinctions. Arguably, Birkin's celebration of individualism and difference fetishizes the political and social fragmentation described in the novel.

Lawrence's understanding of equality and difference is more than simply an issue of political belief. It also fuels developments in his literary style. In *The Rainbow* and *Women in Love* Lawrence tries to give expression to the singular self beyond language, law, and 'comprehension'. In *Women in Love*, then, Birkin's intellectual argument against democratic standardization involves thoughts on the nature of

---

[10] D. H. Lawrence, *The Rainbow* (London: Penguin Books, 1981), 512.
[11] D. H. Lawrence, *Women in Love*, ed. David Farmer, Lindeth Vasey, John Worthen (Cambridge: Cambridge University Press, 1987), 103.

language. As Birkin goes on to say a bit later in the novel, it would be hard to capture the 'pure difference' of human identity with the words at our disposal. As he states in relation to the word 'love', 'we hate the word because we have vulgarised it. It ought to be prescribed, tabooed from utterance, for many years, till we get a new, better idea.'[12] Lawrence's own descriptions of women and men in love escape a standardized language by trying to capture the pre-linguistic and unconscious drives of the individual will. In one of the important moments of sexual consummation in the novel, he tries to create a 'better idea' through a highly disorientating prose:

Quenched, inhuman, his fingers upon her unrevealed nudity were the fingers of silence upon silence, the body of mysterious night upon the body of mysterious night, the night masculine and feminine, never to be seen with the eye, or known with the mind, only known as a palpable revelation of living otherness.[13]

This textual moment of groping recognition aims to take the reader beyond the visual language of consciousness. It does this through various forms of linguistic disorientation. If her nudity is unrevealed, the similes of 'silence upon silence' or 'body of mysterious night upon the body of mysterious night' fail to make the image any more concrete. In fact, they function to dislocate further the words from their referents. Yet, the writing avoids collapsing into the kind of abstraction that Lawrence, and other modernists, railed against. There is knowledge here, but it is a form of intuitive, bodily based knowledge which is beyond the reach of consciousness. Lawrence argued more generally that men and women are controlled by forms of will which are antagonistic and polarized, but which are capable of momentary reconciliation: '[W]e start from one side or the other, from the female side or the male, but what we want is always the perfect union of the two.'[14]

We can see in *The Rainbow* and *Women in Love* how far Lawrence has moved away from the visual individualism of Ford's prose. If both writers share a scepticism about the processes of modern standardization and democratization, they disagree about how modern writing should escape these external forms of understanding. Lawrence is interested in a more complex kind of subjectivity than Ford, a subjectivity controlled by unconscious forms of will. His retreat inwards, then, involves

[12] Ibid. 130.   [13] Ibid. 320.
[14] D. H. Lawrence, 'Study of Thomas Hardy', in *Phoenix: The Posthumous Papers, 1936*, i (Harmondsworth: Penguin Books, 1973), 515.

the creation of a language which can represent unconscious processes of thought. For both, however, the modern individual confronts a fragmented social and political world. It is the literary writer who can move beyond the over-used, abstract language of a dead democracy. Their understandings of sexual difference are grounded in these thoughts about democracy, subjectivity, and language: whereas Ford wants his realistic prose to pierce the veil of a fictional female deity, Lawrence strips men and women of the psychic barriers which distort their physical relations.

Ford's impressionism was an important touchstone for a variety of Anglo-American modernist texts, mostly as something to kick against. The place from which he started—that the literary artist must find a way of transforming the standardized prose of modern democratic and technological culture—was shared by modernist writers. There was also a shared sense that the egoist retreat inwards was a response to a modern context which was defined by an absence of shared political, ethical, and cultural norms. These writers disagreed, however, about how this transformation would happen. Lawrence's interest in the unconscious is far removed from the impersonal poetics of T. E. Hulme, Ezra Pound, and T. S. Eliot. In turn, however, Hulme's and Pound's highly visual doctrines of the image are specifically defined against Ford's impressionism. The nature of the new individualism and the stylistic innovations it created would be heavily disputed throughout the 1910s. For Pound, Ford's impressionism was too passive, involving the construction of a mind which 'received impressions' rather than activated new images. By 1912, impressionism had been replaced by Hulme's and Pound's new theories of the image. In turn, by 1914, Imagism had been replaced by the more energetic doctrines of Vorticism. The question of how the modern poem would activate and order new images would trouble these writers throughout the pre-war period. The relationship between egoist retreat and order would also be central to the evolving debate about sexual difference.

T. E. HULME, ROUSSEAU, AND DEMOCRACY

If ideas of political democracy and cultural democratization were central to the prose experiments of Ford and Lawrence in the 1900s and 1910s, they were also important to developments in modern poetry.

T. E. Hulme's famous and influential demand for a new classicism in the arts was grounded in a critique of democratic literary and political values. He was joined by Irving Babbitt, whose book *The Masters of Modern French Criticism* also called for a new classicism in the arts, and Babbitt's student, T. S. Eliot, who declared a similar set of value-judgements in 1916.

Hulme began his writing career as an advocate of the French philosopher Henri Bergson, but then became interested in connecting his theory of poetic language to political questions. Initially, however, in a series of essays written between 1907 and 1911 he advocated a radically egoist account of poetic language. In the first of these essays, he used Bergson's philosophy to move away from the scientific materialism of his youth, arguing that the mechanical language of scientific materialism distorts the world and the self it describes. He argued that materialism is based on the external description of objects, and that any attempt to describe the inner nature of objects always falls back on the language of external description. This is because we are used to thinking about the world in terms of space. However, there is a realm of phenomena, including that of human consciousness and ideas of free will, which exists outside a spatial logic. Bergson calls these non-spatial phenomena 'intensive manifolds', and argues that we need a different kind of language, one which is grounded in intuition, in order to understand them.

In essays such as 'Bergson's Theory of Art' and 'The Philosophy of Intensive Manifolds', which were published in the *New Age*, Hulme explains Bergson's philosophy to an English audience. Hulme argues in these essays that Bergson's philosophy moves beyond the external description of objects and captures an internal realm which is 'absolutely unseizable by the intellect'. Intuition is capable of taking us beyond the intellect: intuition is 'the method of knowledge by which we seize an intensive manifold'.[15] The task Hulme sets himself in 'The Philosophy of Intensive Manifolds' is to describe, through the method of intuition, the nature of this reality beyond rational intellect. As we have seen, Ford had argued a number of years earlier that 'encyclopaedic, topographical, or archaeological' discourses are inadequate because they remain external to the thing they describe. Hulme continues in this

---

[15] T. E. Hulme, *Speculations: Essays on Humanism and the Philosophy of Art*, ed. Herbert Read (London: Routledge & Kegan Paul, 1960), 179.

vein, but his analysis of the 'second method of cognition' with which we apprehend the non-logical and non-spatial realm of reality is more systematic. Whereas Ford was happy to base his new writing on the activating principle of 'personal impressions', Hulme argues that a true account of this non-materialistic cognition must rest on a more subtle theory of mental life. For Bergson, there are two different selves which exist at two different levels. One is the superficial self which interacts with other people. The other is a 'fundamental self' which is buried deep beneath the rational processes of mental life and which is consonant with intuition. Hulme begins by stating that this fundamental self is 'reached at certain moments of tension'.[16] If this is rather vague, in the rest of the essay he tries to develop a more substantial description of the self. He is happier painting a negative picture of the intuitive mind: it is not 'mysterious', 'infinite', or 'ineffable'. In the place of these transcendental categories, he describes a non-rational realm tied to the body: the key words are 'feeling', 'intuition', 'impulse', and 'introspection'. He concludes by claiming that 'in an intuition you place yourself inside the object instead of surveying it from the outside'. This ability to fling yourself empathetically into an object rests on the non-spatial experience of time: 'In that state of mind in which you feel and experience duration, and which we have called intuition, you are actually inside that stream of impulse which constitutes life.'[17]

Hulme's use of Bergson's philosophy of duration and intuition forms the basis of his understanding of the role of the modern artist. It is the artist who is 'able to break through the conventional ways of looking at things which veil reality from us'. This is close to Ford's interest in an artistic piercing of the simulacra which conceal our relationships with other individuals. However, Hulme delves further into the psychic mechanisms which control these mediating structures. It is not that a veil exists only between the self and the world; it also exists between the conscious self and the intuitive self. He argues, like the British Stirnerians and Nietzscheans whom I considered in Chapter 1, that the psychic realm has been invaded by a series of external conventions, or 'spooks' as Stirner would have called them. Within this logic, the 'fundamental self' is figured as a realm of psychic and linguistic freedom which lies beyond the reach of conventional language. Accordingly, the artist's role is to pierce the veil which separates us from reality. This

---

[16] Hulme, *Speculations*, 186. [17] Ibid. 213.

veil is 'dense with the ordinary man', and 'transparent for the artist and the poet'.[18]

Hulme's critique of reason in his essays on Bergson is principally concerned with the way in which language structures the psyche. His next intellectual move was to transfer his focus of interest from the scientific materialism of contemporary philosophy to modern democracy. His Bergsonian analysis of reason is thereby harnessed to a critique of historical and social progress. In his famous essay 'Romanticism and Classicism', written in 1911, Hulme accordingly attacks romanticism as a literature based on ideas of rational progress and democratic emancipation. The terms used in the essay are taken largely from the French debate about the legacy of the French Revolution, in which classicism involves a wide range of antagonisms to the Revolution, and romanticism is connected to democracy and Protestantism. The principal myth of Rousseau-romanticism, as it was called, is that power has been devolved away from the centralized institutions of church and state, and granted to the individual citizen. Charles Maurras, the most influential proponent of the French reactionary classical position in the modern period, connected his political and religious views to an anti-Semitism which he saw as parasitic on Latin culture.

In his essay, Hulme famously claims that the romantic 'had been taught by Rousseau that man was by nature good, that it was only bad laws and customs that had suppressed him'. He continues: the romantic believes that 'man, the individual, is an infinite reservoir of possibilities; and if you can so rearrange society by the destruction of oppressive order then these possibilities will have a chance and you will get progress.'[19] The new classicism is based on an understanding of man as the exact opposite of this, as 'an extraordinarily fixed and limited animal whose nature is absolutely constant. It is only by tradition and organisation that anything decent can be got out of him.'[20] Like Nietzsche, Hulme constructs a rather crude image of Rousseau's political thought as a radical egalitarianism, a secular successor to the Christian teaching of the equality of all souls before God.

Nevertheless, the accuracy or otherwise of Hulme's understanding of Rousseau's thought is less important here than the use to which it was put in arguments about modernist writing. Like Stirner and Nietzsche, Hulme argues that the belief in the human individual as an 'infinite reservoir of possibilities' erects man into a kind of god.

[18] Ibid. 150, 158.   [19] Ibid. 116.   [20] Ibid.

Not only is the idea of the perfectibility of man 'practically a new religion', involving a 'religious enthusiasm', but the shattering of the power of institutional religion involves beginning to 'believe that man is a god'.[21] This 'new religion', as Stirner had labelled it, has a significant impact on the parameters of poetic language. By erecting man into a deity, the romantic poet treats men and women as though their agency were inexhaustible. The language of romantic poetry thus rests on images of human transcendence, and it often relies on 'metaphors of flight'.[22] Further, romantic understandings of the literary imagination are coloured by a religious language. In contrast, classical verse never forgets the finiteness, 'the limit of man'.

Hulme has laid the groundwork for his new definition of modern poetic language. In accordance with the recognition of the limit of man, classical poetry will be realistic: it will rest on 'accurate, precise and definite description', rather than on the mystery gestured towards through the word.[23] The poetic precision of modern poetry will be achieved by avoiding the abstract use of words as 'counters' severed from their referents: poetry 'is not a counter language, but a visual concrete one'. The creation of concrete language will be achieved through the sense certainty of vision: 'It is a compromise for a language of intuition which would hand over sensations bodily.'[24]

In 'Romanticism and Classicism' Hulme politicizes the language with which he discusses modern poetry. Linguistic abstraction is connected to his critiques of the 'abstract' nature of scientific materialism and Rousseau-romanticism. In the face of this twofold philosophical and political abstraction, Hulme defends the concrete and realistic nature of Imagistic poetic language.

In adopting the terms of the French debate about literature and art in which Rousseau is coupled with romanticism, Hulme constructs a particular ideological enemy within an Anglo-American intellectual context. It was a significant target. Lewis attacked a version of it in *Blast*, 1 (1914), and has characters debating its significance in *Tarr*, as we will see below. Irving Babbitt also explored the legacy of Rousseau and romanticism in his work on French culture, *Masters of Modern French Criticism*. Babbitt also incorporates a theory of sexual difference into his argument about romanticism and classicism. He claims that classicism

---

[21] Hulme, *Speculations*, 116, 118.
[22] Ibid. 120.   [23] Ibid. 132.   [24] Ibid. 134.

involves the 'masculine' values of analysis and judgement, in contrast to the 'feminine' values of knowledge and sympathy. He goes on to connect masculinity and femininity to other oppositions: between the scientific and the impressionistic, and between the 'humanistic or aristocratic' and the Rousseauistic or 'pseudo-democratic'. Babbitt's ideas had an important impact on Eliot's work. The 'Rousseau-romanticism' target, with its associated 'feminine' attributes of sympathy and impressionism, was central to the development of Eliot's thoughts on poetry. He addressed the issue in the 'Extension Lectures' he delivered at Oxford University in 1916, and later in the early 1920s. In 1923 he declared that 'There are at least two attitudes towards literature and towards everything and … you cannot hold both.' One attitude is the classical, which is grounded in obedience to outer authority, and the other is the romantic which is based on the principles of the inner voice. We will consider Eliot's understanding of these terms in more detail in Chapter 4.

Hulme's thoughts on the political nature of abstract and imagistic language are, like those of Ford and Lawrence, used to defend a particular set of stylistic developments in the arts. On a social and political level, all three writers believed that experiments in literary style must reflect the changed status of art in the modern world. In the face of a homogenized culture, they propound a turn towards a form of literary 'realism'. Ford's personal 'impressions' are snippets of sense-certain realism; Lawrence's sensory vocabulary captures the unconscious processes of naturally organic bodies; and Hulme's poetic images are 'the very essence of an intuitive language' grounded in objects in the 'real' world. If Ford believed that the self is a refuge of integrity in a debased cultural and political sphere, Hulme also severs the relationship between the individual and 'abstract' ideas such as progress and equality. Hulme delves further than Ford, and his thoughts about the legislative and liberating dimensions of language are accordingly more unsettling. Yet, given the fact that both Ford and Hulme identified with hierarchical forms of social and political organization, it was unclear at this stage how these realistic or naturalistic stylistic experiments were connected to order.

The question of order would be taken up by Hulme in more detail in later essays. It would also become a major preoccupation in essays by Pound, Lewis, and Eliot in the period after 1913. These writers shared Hulme's desire to unpack the ideology which mediates and structures the democratization of politics and the arts. Most significantly, however,

Hulme's construction of Rousseau-romanticism as an ideological enemy combining politics, subjectivity, and style was central to modernist polemic. This enemy would be distorted in accordance with individual preoccupations. Lewis makes Rousseau a sentimentalist in *Blast* and *Tarr*. Eliot connects Rousseau to a general kind of liberalism in his Extension Lectures. Unlike Hulme, however, both writers sexualize the opposition between romanticism and classicism. The tortuous relationships between artistic men and bourgeois women encompass wider ideas of order, fragmentation, and sentimentalism. Rousseau-romanticism, and all it stood for, became marked by sexual difference after 1913.

EZRA POUND, FREEDOM OF EXPRESSION, AND BOURGEOIS WOMEN: 1911–1915

Walt Whitman created the ultimate poetic celebration of American democracy in 1867:

> One's self I sing, a simple separate person,
> Yet utter the word Democratic, the word En-Masse.
>
> Of physiology from top to toe I sing,
> Not physiognomy alone nor brain alone is worthy for the
>   Muse, I say the Form complete is worthier far,
> The female equally with the Male I sing.
> Of life immense in passion, pulse, and power,
> Cheerful, for freest action form'd under the laws divine,
> The modern man I sing.[25]

Whitman sings here of an ideal, rather than achieved, American democracy. Nevertheless, he extols the separate individuals within American democracy, and the political terms of equality, freedom, and religion which allow for their coexistence.

Whitman was *the* important American touchstone for the new generation of American poets which included Pound, Eliot, Moore, H.D., Stevens, and Williams, and for British poets such as Lawrence and John Gould Fletcher. He was the one American poet whom these writers saw as a credible, if troubling, predecessor. During 1909, Pound, newly

[25] Walt Whitman, *Leaves of Grass*, ed. Jerome Loving (Oxford: Oxford University Press, 1990), 9.

arrived in London, took the opportunity to consider Whitman's legacy: 'Mentally I am a Walt Whitman,' declares Pound, 'who has learned to wear a collar and a dress shirt.' According to Pound, Whitman is crude, disgusting, nauseating, and painful to read. Despite this, he is 'America's poet', because he was the 'first great man to write in the language of his people'.[26] Whitman, then, not only sings of democracy; he creates a common poetic language to match American democracy. 'Like Dante', insists Pound, 'he wrote in the "vulgar tongue", in a new metric.' In his poem 'A Pact', Pound reiterates this judgement of Whitman's legacy: 'It was you that broke the new wood, / Now is a time for carving.'

Pound's description of his own poetry as employing Whitmanesque language with formal refinement is interesting. On the surface, it would be hard to imagine a poet more at odds with high modernism than Whitman, both in terms of style and politics. Yet Pound's self-description tells us much about his own early poetry, with its mixture of vernacular language and complicated technical structures. If Whitman's language is 'of the people' in a way which is tied to his democratic political beliefs, however, Pound's use of a 'vulgar tongue' is less easy to place. The use of colloquial language within highly technical poetic structures is a crucial feature of Pound's and Eliot's poetry. In Chapter 4, we will consider the status of a modern 'vulgar tongue' in the poetry of T. S. Eliot.

Like Ford's and Lawrence's, Pound's early writing is grounded in the belief that the writer's scope has become more circumscribed. In accordance with this, the poet is figured as an isolated figure who is a refuge of integrity in the face of redundant collective ideals. For Pound, the poet has access to a past in which meaningful collective ideals were still in place. As Peter Nicholls puts it, Pound produces 'the convergence of stylistic pastiche with a sense of the poet's self not only as estranged and locked in "exquisite loneliness", but as the passive vehicle and conduit for images deriving from "the good old days" '.[27]

In 'I Gather the Limbs of Osiris', a series of essays published in the *New Age* between December 1911 and February 1912, Pound describes in detail this isolated poet. He argues that the individual is the criterion of truth: the poet gets 'his audience the moment he says something so intimate that it proves him the expert: he does not, as a rule, sling

[26] Ezra Pound, *Selected Prose: 1909–1965*, ed. William Cookson (London: Faber & Faber, 1973), 116.
[27] Peter Nicholls, *Modernisms: A Literary Guide* (Basingstoke: Macmillan, 1995), 168.

generalities; he gives the particular case for what it is worth; the truth is the individual'.[28] The 'truth is the individual' in two senses: first, in the sense that it is a form of intimate self-knowledge; and second, in the sense that it resides in linguistic accuracy. Pound defends particularity through an attack on linguistic 'generalities', precisely the kind of argument with which readers of the *New Age* and the *New Freewoman* would have been familiar. But, as with the Stirnerian and Nietzschean thinkers we have looked at, the importance of the particular resides as much in its difference from an unexamined mimeticism, as in its resistance to abstract 'generalities'. Pound goes on, then, to insist that life is 'made up in great part of things indefinite, impalpable; and it is precisely because the arts present us these things that we—humanity—cannot get on without the arts'. The difference between 'generalities' and the 'indefinite' realm is that generalities efface the object to which they ostensibly refer, whereas the indefinite is that which is gestured towards through the concrete image. The 'indefinite' realm, which Pound seems most interested in here, is the poet's own 'intimate' reality as it perceives and engages with the phenomenal realm—what he calls later on in this essay a writer's 'poetic insides'.[29]

In a later instalment of the essay, he clarifies that what makes the poet's intimate reality interesting is not the fact that it is intimate, but its strength of independent vision:

For it is not until poetry lives again "close to the thing" that it will be a vital part of contemporary life. As long as the poet says not what he, at the very crux of a clarified conception, means, but is content to say something ornate and approximate, just so long will serious people, intently alive, consider poetry as balderdash—a sort of embroidery for dilettantes and women.

Pound connects 'generalities', or 'approximate' words, with language which is 'ornate' and demonstrative. The phrase 'embroidery for dilet-tantes and women' is apt because he wants to connect this latter kind of poetry with a form of display and judgement which is feminine and amateurish in nature.

In the next sentence, he goes on to underline the point by identifying this kind of language with 'frilled paper decoration' and 'rhetoric'. As in the previous example, however, Pound immediately clarifies that this departure from generalities does not involve embracing an unexamined verisimilitude. He insists that poetry is beautiful because it

[28] Pound, *Selected Prose*, 33.   [29] Ibid. 33, 35.

imposes a cohesion, or 'arrangement', on 'the thing': the reader must feel that 'he is in contact with something arranged more finely than the commonplace'.[30] We have come closer to clarifying what Pound means by 'individual liberty' in his letter to Marsden. Pound's artistic individualism promotes a strongly realized, rather than a sentimental, artistic self which is able to produce a poetic language which is neither 'abstract' nor unreflectively mimetic.

In February 1912, in his essay 'Prolegomena', Pound shifted the terms of this argument by connecting the development of poetry to historical epochs. He defends the poetic 'precision' of Daniel and Cavalcanti against the 'sentimentalism' of the Victorians: Daniel's and Cavalcanti's 'testimony is of the eyewitness, their symptoms are first hand'. In contrast, the Victorians create poetry which is 'blurry, messy', and 'sentimentalistic'.[31] Armed with this epochal theory of the development of poetic language, Pound was now ready to launch his new theory of modern poetry. Imagism, which he created with the help of H.D. and Richard Aldington during the spring and early summer of 1912, would depart from a blurry, messy, and sentimental nineteenth century. By 1913 he had delivered his famous dos and don'ts: treat the 'thing', whether subjective or objective, directly; avoid superfluous words; avoid abstractions; and 'compose in the sequences of the musical phrase'.[32]

As Pound's thought developed, he came to place more emphasis on the nature of the cohesion, or arrangement, which would take control of the 'thing'. Ideas of democracy and sexual difference were central to his thoughts about the nature of 'blurry and messy' sentimentalism, on the one hand, and cohesion and arrangement, on the other hand. In 'The New Sculpture', another important essay of the pre-war period, published in the *Egoist* in 1914, he develops a more politicized version of the argument about art that he had set out in 'I Gather the Limbs of Osiris'. He continues to vacillate between two poles of thought: this time the democratized mass and the humanism which expresses its intellectual life. He attacks the fact that humanism 'has taken refuge in art', and declares that instead of trying to moralize about the mass of humanity, the modern artist must impose his authority onto his material. The new artist, then, 'knows he is born to rule but he has

[30] Ibid. 41.
[31] Ezra Pound, *Literary Essays of Ezra Pound*, ed. T. S. Eliot (London: Faber & Faber, 1968), 11.
[32] Ibid. 3.

no intention of trying to rule by general franchise'. Again, he rams the point home by equating democracy with dilettantes and women: 'There has been a generation of artists who were content to permit a familiarity with themselves and the "cultured" and, even worse, with the "educated", two horrible classes composed of suburban professors and their gentler relations.'[33] The democratized cultural sphere has produced a debased art which simply mirrors existing humanistic values. Neither this new cultured class nor the art, it is implied, is capable of creating the cohesion, or 'arrangement', which makes the commonplace beautiful.

The task that Pound sets himself, then, is to write poetry which is neither a debased realism nor reliant on the 'abstract generalities' he criticizes in 'I Gather the Limbs of Osiris'. This involves a more constructive, aggressive model of poetic authority than that envisaged by Ford. In his poems after *Ripostes* (1912) he creates a series of rather blunt oppositions between the debased mimeticism of the bourgeoisie and the integrity and intellectual cohesion of the genuine artist. In 'Tenzone', he describes the 'virgin stupidity' of his 'friendly critics'; in 'Salutation', he addresses the 'generation of the thoroughly smug'; in 'Salutation the Second', he greets 'the grave and the stodgy'; in 'Commission', the poet sends his songs to 'the bourgeoise who is dying of her ennuis' and 'the women in suburbs'; and so it goes on.[34] These lines provide a backdrop against which images of artistic integrity are placed. In 'Tenzone', in contrast to this debased readership, the poet mates 'with my free kind upon the crags'; in 'Salutation', he presents an analogy of the poet's self in the lines 'the fish swim in the lake / and do not even own clothing'; in 'Salutation the Second', the 'dance of the phallus' contrasts with the 'grave and stodgy'; and in 'Commission', the poems 'Go with an open speech'.[35]

In the poems of this period, images of individual strength, naked integrity, and direct language are opposed to sentimentality, repetitiveness, and display. Unlike Marsden, however, who used the idea of a strong ego to destabilize static ideas of sexual difference, Pound adopts these oppositions to enforce the differences between men and bourgeois women. Femininity is particularly associated with a vacuous form of cultural display: in 'Simulacra', for example, his image of a woman

---

[33] Ezra Pound, 'The New Sculpture', *Egoist*, 1.4 (1914), 67–8.

[34] Ezra Pound, 'Tenzone', 'Salutation', 'Salutation the Second', 'Commission', in *Selected Poems, 1908–1969* (London: Faber & Faber, 1975), 40, 42, 43, 44.

[35] Ibid.

'reciting Swinburne to herself, inaudibly' is juxtaposed to the image of a 'small child in the soiled-white imitation fur coat'. The connection between Swinburne, femininity, and imitation captures the mixture of literary introspection and feminine mimesis from which Pound's individualist aesthetic is designed to depart.

The connection of femininity with both display and sentimentalism is, of course, by no means particular to Pound's, or to modernist, writing. However, the way in which these ideas are consolidated by means of a series of oppositions which bridge the relationship between language and politics is distinctive. The shift from democracy to a new 'aristocracy of the arts', then, importantly encompasses another key departure: one that discards a 'female' mimeticism, introspection, or sentimentality now classed as 'feminine' and promotes a wilful 'male' artistic creativity.

'WE MAKE YOU A PRESENT OF OUR VOTES. ONLY LEAVE WORKS OF ART ALONE': FUTURISM AND VORTICISM

In the summer of 1914, *Blast* inaugurated what Pound named the 'Great English Vortex'. Pound's desire for a new modernist group was partly animated by the fact that Imagism had, in his view, become diluted by Amy Lowell's editorial policy. She boasted that she had substituted her inclusive editorial policy for what she called Pound's 'despotism'. In contrast to Pound's stern list of 'don'ts', then, she announced a policy of 'pure democracy'. The Vorticists, in contrast, were unashamedly selective. The conflict between Lowell's democratic inclusiveness and Vorticist exclusivity became a way of defining art in *Blast*. At the end of *Blast*, 1, Wyndham Lewis writes a bold word of advice 'To Suffragettes'. He presents them with a special gift: 'We make you a present of our votes. Only leave works of art alone.'[36] Lewis claims to admire the 'energy' and dynamism of the suffragettes, but he insists that the inclusive ideals they are fighting for are without value.

Despite Lewis's and Pound's protestations to the contrary, the typography and violence of *Blast* owes much to the manifestos of Marinetti's Italian Futurists. During 1910–15, Marinetti visited London many

---

[36] Wyndham Lewis, *Blast*, 1 (1914), 151.

times in order to publicize his manifestos and the Futurist exhibitions of paintings. His impact is nowhere more obvious than in Lewis's support for the suffragettes. In his essay 'Against *Amore* and Parliamentarianism', Marinetti defends the suffragettes in a strikingly similar fashion. Ridiculing the 'Amore' and sentimentality attached to 'woman', as well as the debased parliamentarianism which makes politics into a legalistic talking-shop, Marinetti declares that the suffragettes are 'our best allies'. Not only will they destroy 'the woman-poison', the woman as ideal, but they will also destroy parliamentary politics. 'Let us hasten to give women the vote,' he therefore proclaims. It is the 'final and absolutely logical conclusion of the ideal of democracy and universal suffrage as it was conceived by Jean Jacques Rousseau and the other preparers of the French Revolution'.[37] Here women, by being allowed to participate in Parliament, will contaminate and destabilize politics from within.

Lewis and Pound presume a similar historical trajectory in *Blast*, in which Rousseau is the starting-point for a debased nineteenth century which leads inevitably to votes for women. Like Hulme and Marinetti, then, Lewis 'Blasts' Rousseau, but he emphasizes the sentimentalism at the heart of Rousseau's democratic ideals: 'SENTIMENTAL HYGIENICS / ROUSSEAUISMS (wild nature cranks) / FRATERNIZING WITH MONKEYS.' Later on in *Blast*, he again refers to Rousseau by coupling him with sentimentalism: 'The soft stormy flood of Rousseauism, Dickens's sentimental ghoul-like gloating over the death of little Nell, the beastly and ridiculous spirit of Keats' lines'. Here Rousseau's flood, swelling through nineteenth-century verse and prose, swamps all virile artistic expression. Art bows 'the knee to / wild Mother Nature, / her feminine contours, / Unimaginative insult to MAN'.[38] Lewis follows Hulme, then, in erecting Rousseau as a political and literary target, but inflects the terms of mimesis and sentimentalism with vivid images of sexual difference.

Despite the obvious impact of Marinetti's writing techniques on *Blast*, Lewis and Pound were at pains to emphasize their differences from the Futurists. They did so by delivering the ultimate insult to Marinetti. This is that his Futurism is, in fact, only the final expression of the democratic advance he claims to despise: 'The artist of the modern movement is a savage (in no sense an "advanced," perfected, democratic, Futurist

[37] F. T. Marinetti, *Let's Murder the Moonshine: Selected Writings*, ed. R. W. Flint (Los Angeles: Sun & Moon Press, 1991), 82.
[38] Lewis, *Blast*, 1 (1914), 18, 133, 19.

individual of Mr. Marinetti's limited imagination).'³⁹ Here Lewis claims that, not only does Marinetti believe in Rousseau's perfectible man, but that the Futurist is simply the most advanced version of it.

Lewis's insult holds in embryo a number of key differences between Futurism and Vorticism. Marinetti's celebration of dynamism and technology amounts to an 'accelerated impressionism', argue Lewis and Pound, because it involves surrendering art to the present. The basis of the disagreement can be revealed in looking again at Lewis's attack on the suffragettes. Whereas the Futurists would be happy for the suffragettes to help them to burn down the museums, Lewis and Pound are worried by the mindless destruction of artistic tradition. This is because the Futurists and Vorticists have different attitudes to artistic authority. Whereas the Futurists want to discard the past and leap into the future, the Vorticists see the present in terms of the past.

These differences unlock their different conceptions of the modern artist. In 'The Founding Manifesto of Futurism', Marinetti presents us with artists who escape the past through the Nietzschean, wilful assertion of 'immense pride'.⁴⁰ Marinetti's individual, Lewis counters, is actually a modern version of Rousseau's idea that the individual 'is an infinite reservoir of possibilities', as Hulme had put it. It is simply that Marinetti constructs history and tradition as the shackles that keep men in chains.

In 'Long Live the Vortex', accordingly, Lewis announces the values of his new art movement by opposing Marinetti's advanced, democratic Futurist to his Vorticist 'savage'. He sheds the 'civilised and academic vision' which veils the artist's response to the world and the wider response to art. This involves stripping bare the artifice of democratic culture. Lewis connects this veil to the pseudo-democratic rhetoric which controls discussions of modern art. He insists that the ideas of 'the Man on the Street', 'the People', 'perfectibility', and 'standardization' obscure our intuitive response to artworks. Here, Ford's critique of 'standardisation', Hulme's attack on 'human perfectibility' and Pound's attack on linguistic 'generalities' are collected together and politicized. These pseudo-democratic phrases are the discursive blocks which hold together the powerful and insidious veils of modern intellectual life.

We are on familiar territory here: a programme for modern art is launched through an attack on the democratic abstractions which veil the individual's self-understanding. Lewis puts in the place of these

³⁹ Ibid. 33.　　⁴⁰ Marinetti, *Let's Murder the Moonshine*, 47.

abstractions some familiar ideas focused on the body: 'the Reality of the Present', the untimely nature of the artist, crude energy, and 'vivid and violent ideas'. Yet, the Vorticists also develop a new set of avant-garde ideas which take us in a surprising direction. In contrast to the democratic language which mediates our relationship to art, *Blast* will blast the class hierarchy which controls the production and reception of art: it will 'not appeal to any particular class, but to the fundamental and popular instincts in every class and description of people'.[41] The popular instincts are here the foundation for an inclusive theory of art: *Blast* is created for the 'timeless, fundamental Artist that exists in everybody'. Lewis connects the timeless human instinct to the unconscious: 'WE NEED THE UNCONSCIOUSNESS OF HUMANITY.'[42] This amounts to a kind of radically inclusive theory of the reception of art, in which the art instinct is a basic element of what it is to be human.

Lewis adopts Orage's distinction between sleepy and awake individuals, in order to recast the language with which we discuss art. Artistic instinct, which is described as 'permanently primitive', is contrasted to the 'civilised' vision of the advanced individual. Lewis clarifies that by the words 'savage' and 'primitive' he means the intuitive response to modern life. Lewis's anti-democratic statements are specifically aimed at the mechanisms of democratic control: Parliament, the franchise, the rhetoric of 'the man on the street'. This is anti-democracy in the name of the destabilization of class hierarchies. It is in this sense, then, that the suffragettes can be commended for their vital energy, while being criticized for their pointless pursuit of the franchise.

We have seen in Chapter 1 how a range of different thinkers attempted to separate out the wilful energy which 'strives' for the vote, from the vote itself. These thinkers set themselves the task of finding a new kind of language for describing a self set free from the 'external' categories of politics, religion, and morality. In *Blast*, Lewis and his Vorticist allies do precisely that. The consequences of stripping bare the human mind, however, are unsettling. At one moment in *Blast* we are asked to 'BLESS this hysterical WALL built round the EGO'. Like Stirner, Lewis is often at his most powerful when he describes the difficulties of building the egoistic defence against the encroachment of external 'spooks'. The idea of a hysterical wall, for instance, could hardly suggest a more fragile barrier. Later in *Blast*, Lewis insists that artists need 'a course of egotistic hardening'. The need to enforce the ego's boundaries is not

41 Lewis, *Blast*, 1 (1914), 7.   42 Ibid.

just important for artists. In his manifesto called 'The New Egos', he describes the modern town-dweller as erecting an 'impersonal' defence against the encroachment of the world. For every modern individual, the 'frontiers' which separate his ego from life 'interpenetrate, individual demarcations are confused'. The 'blurry, messy' nineteenth-century Pound attacked in 'Prolegomena' is catapulted right into the heart of the modern world by Lewis. This is precisely the substance of modern life that the artist must bend to his will. In *Tarr*, these ideas are brought to life in the tortuous relationships between men and women.

SKEWING ART AND SEX: *TARR* AND THE CRITIQUE OF MIMESIS

'Rare and cheap, fine and poor, these contrasts are the male and female, the principle of creation to-day.'[43] In this comment from *Blast* Lewis announces the polarized sexual principles of creation. In his novel *Tarr* he explores these principles in more detail. *Tarr* was serialized in the *Egoist* from April 1916 to November 1917. In the novel's preface, written in 1915, Lewis considers the influence of Nietzsche's 'gospel of the beyond-law-man' on the Parisian, Italian, and Russian avant-gardes. The influence is not an entirely beneficial one. 'Nietzsche's books are full of seductions and sugar-plums,' he declares. 'They have made "aristocrats" of people who would otherwise have been only mild snobs or meddlesome prigs ... and they have made an Over-man of every vulgarly energetic grocer in Europe.'[44] The novel describes a cultural milieu in which every mild snob in Europe seems to have drifted on to the streets of Paris to try their hand at art. Art, then, becomes the means by which 'energetic grocers' fancy themselves as the 'unacknowledged legislators' of the world.

The task of the novel is to create the criteria by which we can distinguish between the genuine and the non-genuine artist. At the centre of the novel is Kreisler, the German 'artist' who managed to 'lose' a painting once, but really just roams the streets of Paris in search of money, violence, and sex. The descriptions of Kreisler's antics, however,

---

[43] Ibid. 145.
[44] Wyndham Lewis, *Tarr: The 1918 Version*, ed. Paul O'Keefe (Santa Rosa, Calif.: Black Sparrow Press, 1996), 13.

are framed by the thoughts and actions of Tarr, the novel's other chief male protagonist. The novel begins with a number of discussions between Tarr and three other male characters, about the nature of art, love, marriage, and women. It ends with discussions between Tarr and Anastasya Vasek about similar topics. These discussions are like a picture frame of the main events of the novel: Kreisler's descent into madness, rape of Bertha Lunken, duel with Soltyk, and final suicide.

The novel also follows Tarr's relationships with the two polarized female characters, Bertha and Anastasya. Bertha is a stupid, sentimental, bourgeois German. Anastasya is an intelligent, beautiful, aristocratic Russian-German. It is through his relationships with these two women that Tarr's thoughts about art are clarified. Sex, declares Tarr at both the beginning and the end of the novel, is opposed to art. For most people, 'the finer part of their vitality goes into sex'.[45] In Kreisler's case, his madness is the result of his sex instincts being diverted into art, which is 'a silly false channel'. For Kreisler, and for others like him with no genuine artistic talent, their 'art-spirits should be kept firmly embedded in sex, in *fighting*, and in *affairs*'.[46] Lewis's 'art-spirits' help clarify the statement in *Blast* that there is a 'timeless, fundamental Artist that exists in everybody'. The fundamental artist is an instinct of creativity which produces action. Tarr, in contrast to Kreisler, successfully directs his vitality into art. The art he produces, significantly, is 'ascetic' and 'divorced from immediate life', rather than sensuous: he avoids depicting the naked human form.[47]

Tarr's artistic creativity and sense of self, however, are weirdly precarious. His ego depends on Bertha's 'wistful, democratic face, full of effort and sentiment'. In turn, it is threatened by Anastasya, who stands outside the democratic crowd and is powerfully egotistical, cerebral, and sensual: 'None of his ego was required by his new woman. She possessed plenty of her own.—This, he realized later, was the cause of his lack of attachment. He needed an empty vessel to flood with his vitality, and not an equal and foreign vitality to coldly exist side by side with.'[48] These two women are representative of the two opposed principles of bourgeois democratic banality and a natural superiority. Yet Tarr requires the former, rather than the latter, for the production of his 'ascetic' art.

---

[45] Lewis, *Tarr*, 29.
[46] Ibid. 302.   [47] Ibid. 30.   [48] Ibid. 316, 314.

Lewis conflates a number of things through his gendered dichotomy. On one level, Anastasya's egoistic independence threatens Tarr's own egoistic sense of self. At another level, Lewis is trying to make a more sustained point about sexual desire and the production of modern art. An earlier conversation with Anastasya about Rousseau revealingly unveils Tarr's thoughts. She accuses him of being a fan of 'Jean-Jacques'. He disagrees. Where Rousseau sentimentalizes nature, Tarr recognizes and values its chaotic ugliness: '[T]he birth of a work of art is dirty and messy,' declares Tarr. It involves 'chaos and filth' and dung. Here, the 'blurry, messy' modernity, so central to Hulme's and Pound's call for classicism, order, and authority, is lauded as the essential bedrock of modern art. Earlier, Tarr underscores this point by insisting that the vitality of the crowd is essential to art: '[I]n Latin countries you have a democracy of vitality, the best things of the earth are in everybody's mouth and nerves. *The artist has to go and find them in the crowd.*' Tarr, and, by implication, art, vacillates back and forth between this feminized democratic chaos and asceticism. In contact with the 'clean and solid' Anastasya, for example, Tarr finds himself 'revolted' in a new way by the 'ugliness and foolishness' of the 'bourgeois' Bertha. Yet, the artistic necessity of mess is sustained until the end of the novel. ' "I'm the new animal," ' declares Tarr towards the end of the novel, ' "we haven't found a name for it yet. It will succeed the Superman. Back to earth!" '[49] Here, the Nietzschean superman is a stage in the trajectory towards a vital art that adopts the energies of modern democracy and moulds them into organic form.

Eliot, in a short prose piece of 1915 called 'Hysteria', presents us with his own version of the Bertha Lunken–Tarr relationship: a man attempts to escape from the engulfing power of a woman's body. A rhetoric of disgust and fragmentation is central to the man's struggle. We will consider this piece in more detail in Chapter 4. Suffice it to say for the moment that from now on, the modern male artist will often set himself the task of imposing a form onto the mess of modern life, and that the mess will be connected to democracy and bourgeois femininity. What is notable about *Tarr*, however, is that Lewis, in characteristic fashion, tries to take us beyond the very dichotomy of chaos and asceticism in which he grounds his theory of art. Anastasya has some of the attributes of a female 'principle' or character type which will feature in other modernist novels and poems. Her egoism, 'cleanliness', and

---

[49] Ibid. 236, 234, 301, 307.

independence will be revisited in the characters of Valentine Wannop and Sylvia Tietjens in Ford's *Parade's End*, as we will see below, and in Lawrence's Gudrun in *Women in Love*. Importantly, then, two female principles emerge from the shifting identifications of this period: one is associated with liberal democracy and is connected to a fragmented or blurry modernity; the other is a new egoistic femininity which is a site of ascetic withdrawal from these democratic principles.

THE WAR, MASS DEMOCRACY, AND THE INDIVIDUAL: 1917–1924

During the First World War the nature of the British state altered significantly. The war transformed state regulation of the economy. As soon as war was declared, the government seized control of the railways, the Bank of England and finance, overseas trade, and the labour force. By the end of the war, this state control had been extended to coal, shipping, food, textiles, and rents. The war speeded up a transformation in the British economy which had begun at the end of the Great Depression of the 1890s. From the 1890s until the outbreak of the war, companies began to amalgamate into huge firms. During the economic boom of the 1920s, companies continued to merge at an extraordinary rate. By the time of the world economic crisis of 1929–31, Britain had become a system of monopoly capitalism. The war also altered significantly state control over the individual. In 1916, the Military Conscription Act was passed, which meant that all able-bodied men had to go to the front. In addition, the Defence of the Realm Act was extended significantly, leading to tight state control over freedom of information.

In 1918 the extension of the franchise meant that all men over the age of 21 and all women over the age of 30 were able to vote. Despite the fact that women would not achieve full voting parity with men until 1928, it is nevertheless generally true that for the first time in history, Britain became a genuinely mass democratic state. At the historical moment when the state became genuinely democratic, then, it also significantly increased its power over the economy and the individual. This contradiction had an immediate impact on developments in the arts. It also altered the tone and parameters of critical essays about the relationship between writing and politics.

A new spectre began to haunt the essays of a number of modernist writers during the latter parts of the war and immediately after the war: that of a secretly tyrannical modern bureaucratic state. As we have seen, before the war, liberal democracy was attacked on a number of key fronts: first, as presupposing a progressive and rights-based notion of the perfectibility of the individual subject; second, as an abstract discourse of equality, based on a mathematical logic; third, as resting on ideas of human standardization. Essays and poems of the post-war period are marked by a different kind of political enemy. This is a form of power which is hidden, sinister, and unidentifiable.

In 1917, Pound published a series of essays in the *New Age* called 'Provincialism the Enemy'. There are a number of enemies in these essays: the Germany of 'Deutschland über Alles', German scholarship, and socialism. Pound repeats his attack on democracy, but also passionately defends individual liberty in the context of this tyrannical German state. He repeats the familiar claim that institutional religion has declined, and that a new 'idol' has emerged in its place. However, rather than being the new idol of 'Man with a capital M', Rousseau's perfectible man set free from the shackles of authority, Pound describes a rather different kind of enemy, the modern 'corporate' state: 'the work of the subtlest thinkers for the last thirty years has been a tentative exploration for means to prevent slavery to a "State" or a "democracy", or some such corporation, though this exploration has not been "organised", or "systematised", or coherent, or even very articulate in its utterance.' If Pound sees the resistance to the democratic state as disorganized, however, he is at least able in this essay to identify the tyrannical corporate state with Germany and to defend England as a place which has respect for individual freedom.[50] In future essays, he was to become more tentative about identifying both his ally and his enemy.

Between June and August 1919, the *New Age* serialized C. H. Douglas's book *Economic Democracy*. Its effects on Pound have been well documented. Hugh Kenner suggests that 'Having absorbed it, Pound immediately wrote *Mauberley* (his first work to mention usury) and then started the *Cantos* afresh.' As Nicholls argues, the crude oppositions of the early verse, between the materialistic bourgeoisie and aestheticism, become more subtle after Pound's reading of *Economic Democracy*. The book also encouraged Pound to extend his interest in the modern corporate state from Germany to Britain and the United States.

---

[50] Ezra Pound, 'Provincialism the Enemy', in *Selected Prose*, 164, 160.

In *Economic Democracy* Douglas argues that the Western nations have fought the First World War to 'make the world safe for democracy'. However, in doing so, Britain and the United States need to ensure that the state, as an externally imposed entity, does not become so powerful that it 'make[s] democracy ever more unsafe for the individual than it is at present'.[51] Douglas is worried about the position of the individual in the post-war democratic states, because he believes that modern democracies are grounded in the centralization of economic power in the hands of a few vast corporations and industries. Douglas claims that individual autonomy is threatened by this centralization of the modern corporate state. He constructs an economic account of individual identity, arguing that human autonomy in the modern world is consonant with economic autonomy.

He wants to recast the modern state so that power is devolved away from the centralized economic entities of the state or vast powerful industries, and given to the economic individual: 'we must build up from the individual, not down from the State', he insists. However, Douglas considers the state to be a vastly powerful entity which threatens to swamp the individual: 'It is the lifelong struggle between freedom and authority, between external compulsion and internal initiative,' he proclaims. However, he insists that these familiar struggles have a different significance in a modern context 'in which all the command of resources, information, religious dogma, educational system, political opportunity and even, apparently, economic necessity, is ranged on the side of authority; and ultimate authority is now exercised through finance'. He argues that one of two things will happen: '[E]ither a pyramidal organisation, having at its apex supreme power, and at its base complete subjection, will crystallise out of the centralising process which is evident in the realms of finance and industry, equally with that of politics, or else a more complete decentralisation of initiative than this civilisation has ever known will be substituted for external authority.'[52] Douglas was more convincing in his descriptions of the nature of post-war state power than on how power could be decentralized. Both of these questions, however, would haunt the critical essays and poems of writers in the post-war period.

---

[51] Pound, *Selected Prose*, 21.
[52] Major C. H. Douglas, *Economic Democracy* (London: Cecil Palmer, 1920), 7, 79, 80.

In *Hugh Selwyn Mauberley*, Pound, as Kenner suggests, immediately engaged with his new anxieties about the role of the artist in the modern state. The poem describes the redundancy of Pound's pre-war poetic achievements in terms of the legacy of the war. It also considers the nature of modern democracy. In the third section of *Mauberley*, Pound describes a series of epochal cultural shifts. The religious beliefs of Dionysus made way for Christianity, which, in turn, has been supplanted by the materialism of a contemporary culture of 'the marketplace'. The 'tea-gown', therefore, has replaced the fine muslin of Cos; the pianola, the ultimate symbol of the democratization of musical culture, has ousted Sappho's barbitos. Politically, the religious rituals of the wafer and circumcision have been replaced by the values of the press and the franchise. The latest manifestation of cultural power is post-war democracy. However, the democratic mechanisms of modern politics are not necessarily security against bad government:

> All men, in law, are equals.
> Free of Pisistratus,
> We choose a knave or an eunuch
> To rule over us.[53]

While we are 'free' of Pisistratus, the benevolent Athenian tyrant, the people are free to choose a bad or weak man to rule over them. Pound asks whether it is better to be ruled by a benevolent tyrant or by the tyranny of a misinformed democratic majority. The idea of freedom is thus put into question. Where does the freedom lie? In the freedom to choose a bad ruler?

Democracy, in *Hugh Selwyn Mauberley* as for Nietzsche, is merely the latest manifestation of a belief system stemming from the Dionysian rituals of ancient Greece through Christianity. This latest cultural epoch is famously 'botched' in the poem. Yet, if Christian values have been replaced by the mathematical and economic values which measure culture by means of quantity rather than quality, how does Pound envisage a different structure of value in the poem? How are we to get beyond the government of a bad man?

Pound's epigrammatic pictures of this botched civilization take us on a literary journey through mid- to late nineteenth-century verse and up to the present day. The contemporary moment is represented most potently by the twin figures of Mr Nixon, the man on the gilded yacht

---

[53] Ezra Pound, *Selected Poems*, 100.

who writes for money, and Lady Valentine, who oversees the exchange of cultural capital in her 'stuffed-satin' salon. As Michael Alexander puts it, the 'mock-tentative words—"precisely", "somewhat", "uncertain", "possible"' used to describe Lady Valentine's drawing-room are 'predictably Prufrockian'.[54] Does Pound, then, simply resurrect the feminized cultural sphere of Eliot's pre-war poem? There are differences between the two poems, and the differences are revealing. Lady Valentine fancies herself as a cultural hostess who uses poetry to blend 'lower and higher' classes, and her salon is a place which is threatened by revolution. Despite the fact that her cultural aspirations and political concerns are ironized, the idea that political questions cannot be kept safely at bay does invade the poem as a whole. The 'Mauberley' section of the poem presents us with the hopeless aesthete unable to respond to the political demands of the modern age: the 'glow of porcelain' fails to incite in Mauberley any 'reforming sense'; gazing on the woman he desires does not rouse him to consider the 'relation of the state / To the individual'; and he is simply mild 'amid the neo-Nietzschean chatter'. Pound ridicules the assumption that art has any intrinsic connection with a gentle politics of reform, just as he mocks the idea that a wayward hedonist would have any response to Nietzsche's philosophy. The retreat inwards which we have considered in the first part of this chapter is diagnosed as acutely as the wider cultural milieu. If Mauberley is bewildered, estranged, and isolated, all he is capable of creating out of this withdrawal is 'maudlin confession'. The drifting Mauberley bears some resemblance to Prufrock, and his aestheticism is consolidated through his withdrawal from snatches of pseudo-political and philosophical chatter. Both the withdrawal and the political chatter are inadequate responses to the violence of the war, as well as to the class destabilization and revolution which threaten to ravage Lady Valentine's salon.

H.D., who we will consider in the next chapter, makes a brief appearance in *Hugh Selwyn Mauberley* as a corollary to Mauberley's poetics of 'maudlin confession'. Pound had written a collection of poems about H.D. called 'Hilda's Book' during the first years of their relationship. In this book he often addressed her as 'Ysolt', or depicted her as a tree nymph. His early poem 'The Tree' was addressed to her, and bears all the hallmarks of Pound's early poetry; the archaisms, the aestheticism, the high seriousness. 'I stood still and was a tree amid the

[54] Michael Alexander, *The Poetic Achievement of Ezra Pound* (Edinburgh: Edinburgh University Press, 1998), 119.

wood, / Knowing the truth of things unseen before; / Of Daphne and the laurel bough.' In *Mauberley* Pound ridicules these lines:

> "Daphne with her thighs in bark
> Stretches toward me her leafy hands," —
> Subjectively. In the stuffed-satin drawing-room
> I await The Lady Valentine's commands.

H.D.'s subjective and leafy appeal is an example of the poetic introspection, the 'obscure reveries / Of the inward gaze', which are singularly unable to deal with the demands of the post-war moment. The judgement here cast on H.D.'s inwardness would be repeated in subsequent discussions of her work, and we will consider these in more detail in the next chapter. For the moment, it is important to note that Pound insists on the need to move beyond the poetic inwardness which had coloured the pre-war moment. He was not alone.

THE POST-WAR AVERAGE: THE NEW DEMOCRATIC STANDARD

The post-war literary imagination is haunted by the idea that an invisible force or a thing is in control of the individual. As Lewis put it in 1918, 'After this war, and the "democratisation" of all countries, no man will ever say what he means, yes, seldomer even than at present. *The thing that is not* will reign in the lands.'[55] For Lewis, the new democratic world order creates a form of self-imposed censorship which is more sinister than anything that has preceded it. Some writers wanted to concretize, and therefore make present, Lewis's imaginary 'thing'. Whereas Pound identified the 'thing' with usury, Lewis himself was often actually referring to the Jews when he described the invisible controllers of Western nations. Other writers kept the 'thing' which reigns deliberately vague. Kafka's characters are controlled by a law which may or may not actually exist. In Mina Loy's poem 'Apology of Genius', the 'thing that is not' is a secular, capricious, and powerful voyeur: the 'watchers of the civilized wastes' who 'reverse their signals on our track'. These watchers never come into focus in the poem.

In all of the essays we have looked at in this chapter, there has been an interest in the way in which democracy creates self-imposed forms of

---

[55] Wyndham Lewis, 'Imaginary Letters', *Little Review*, 4.12 (1918), 52.

censorship and control. In the post-war moment, the object of analysis shifts, and there is increased interest in how the political ideology of democracy veils the powerful economic interests which control society. In his post-war essay 'Democracy', written in 1919, Lawrence attacks democracy in these terms, but partly in order to defend what he calls a new democracy, a 'new order'.

This essay repeats Lawrence's pre-war criticisms of democratic equality, but is also interested in how democracy rests on what he calls the 'Law of the Average'.[56] Lawrence's 'Law of the Average' is a version of the 'mathematical logic' which he attacked in *The Rainbow* and *Women in Love*. It is grounded in Rousseauistic ideas of equality and social perfection: 'Rights of Man, Equality of Man, Social Perfectibility of Man: all these sweet abstractions'. The average, he states, is a particular kind of modern abstraction which takes its place alongside these older ideals. The average reduces humans to a 'mathematical unit', useful to 'measure by', 'to serve as a standard in the business of comparison', like 'the metre, or the gramme, or the English pound sterling'. Like the older ideals, we have erected the average into an ideal, a kind of 'fetish' or God which we bow down to and worship. By doing so, the modern idol of the average stands over and against the human. Lawrence brings this unit into sight, hauling it down from its pedestal, in order to 'examine it corporeally'. Once we have analysed this little 'monster' of the average man, we can see that he is simply the sum of his material needs. The average is thereby useful to 'make living together possible', but is unable to refer to spiritual and mystical needs. Lawrence erects a new kind of statue to symbolize the average man. Rather than being a kind of Rousseauistic idol, he is a shop mannequin of a man in pants and vests in a 'shop at the corner of Oxford Street'.[57]

Whereas before the war Lawrence focused on the illusions of equality which structure liberal democracy, in the essay 'Democracy' he produces a vivid depiction of a different kind of illusion: the clothes dummy on Oxford Street is a potent symbol of mass consumerism and mass culture. Lawrence describes the way in which modern men and women are marked psychologically by this new modern idol. He argues that power is transferred from institutional religion to the new idol of the human average. In doing this, humans have created a new system of secular beliefs to rule over them, a 'magnified unit of Consciousness, or Spirit'. By identifying with this universal consciousness, individuals

---

[56] Lawrence, *Phoenix*, i. 699, 701, 718, 699.   [57] Ibid. 699, 700, 701, 703.

believe that they have become little gods; that by embracing 'everything', they have become divine. Alas, the opposite happens, claims Lawrence. All that you really learn is that 'your *consciousness* is not *you*: that is the sad lesson you learn in your superhuman flight of infinite understanding'.[58] Lawrence argues, then, that this self-estrangement is a powerful new modern tyranny, which is all the more powerful for being self-imposed.

Lawrence sees these psychic splits as distinctly modern forms of conflict. They are the result of the materialism, new industrialism, economic expansion, and consumerism which produced the war. They are also, however, the legacy of the political and cultural discourse of humanism and democracy. Marsden had argued the same thing in the years before the war, seeing women as particularly subject to the psychic splits described by Lawrence. Should women, she asked, identify their interests with the progressive movements of modernization which would eradicate the differences between the sexes just as surely as modernization would eradicate the differences between nations? Or does the identification with a masculine average create a powerful self-estrangement in which sexual difference comes into play?

Lawrence, like Marsden, believed that women, in particular, were split apart by these modern contradictions. In 'Democracy' he argues that only a vigorous egoism can resist the self-estrangement which characterizes modern society. To make this argument, he separates out the ego from personality. Personality, suggests Lawrence, derives from the Latin *persona*, a player's mask or a character in a play. Personality, then, is a 'human being *as he appears to others*'.[59] The individual with personality is someone who is self-conscious about his or her appearance to others. An ideal self is set up over and against the actual individual, becoming like a personal god. The self-conscious Hermione in *Women in Love*, for example, is the product of an excess of personality as he defines it in 'Democracy'.

In the essay 'Democracy' Lawrence tries to produce a language for describing the strong ego. He is interested in the 'little identity; little, but real', in the man who is 'himself'. For Lawrence, this 'little identity' is beyond language, because it is singular: 'Every single living creature is a single creative unit, a unique, incommutable self. Primarily, in its own spontaneous reality, it knows no law. It is a law unto itself.' The core of individual identity can only be described negatively: 'We cannot analyse

---

[58] Ibid. 705, 706.   [59] Ibid. 710.

it. We only know it is there.'[60] Individual spontaneity is isolated as the key to a new democratic future: the 'spontaneous self' will walk 'naked and light', and will be the basis of 'the Democracy, the new order'. All that is possible between single selves is a 'strange recognition of *present otherness*'.[61] The transference from Rousseau's perfectible man, armed with ideals of equality and rights, to the robotic, mathematical idol of the mannequin average colours his understanding of the post-war moment.

The critique of the mass average also informs Ford's post-war writings. His 1923 volume *Women and Men* addresses the sex question. This is a rather chaotic text, which, like *The Soul of London*, mixes anecdote, personal impressions, and argument. Ford's theoretical starting-point is that 'there is no difference between men and women'; the text tests this theory by considering a number of highly personal experiences. Ford takes us back to 1906. He tells a story about an experience he had with a group of progressive 'Young Liberals' who were 'anxious to point out to me that they were the most advanced body of men that could be found in the world'.[62] Despite being at the cutting edge of progressive politics, however, these men were obsessed with a new book, Otto Weininger's *Sex and Character*. Weininger had exploded on to the British political scene because, to the relief of these Young Liberals, who for years had been burdened with the idea 'that women should have justice done to them', Weininger had proved to them 'that women were inferior animals'. Ford argues that this belief is accidentally populist. On this one issue 'Young Liberals' could feel themselves to be 'in agreement with the bagman, the music-hall singers and all those unthinking and jovial people who make up the man in the street'.[63] For Ford, then, the feminist demand for equality in 1906 pulls against two kinds of democratic power: both the democratic beliefs of progressive liberals and the populist, demographically democratic beliefs of the 'man on the street'.

For Ford, these two kinds of democratic power are, in general, separate. The former democracy, involving the discourse of rights and liberty, does not necessarily connect with the latter kind of democracy, which involves the beliefs of the 'unthinking' majority. As we have seen in Chapter 1, there was a general anxiety in the period about whether the democratic majority would constitute a progressive or reactionary

---

[60] Lawrence, *Phoenix*, i. 707, 708.   [61] Ibid. 718, 715.
[62] Ford Madox Ford, *Women and Men* (Paris: Contact Editions, 1923), 30.
[63] Ibid. 32.

political force. Ford argues in *Women and Men* that the sex question shows the limits of democratic forms of understanding, in either of their guises. Democracy is not attacked simply as a form of politics, however. Ford goes on to claim that democratic ideas impinge on our very categories of understanding. He is particularly interested in the way in which the idea of the majority is used as a powerful rhetorical tool by politicians, through the construction of something called the 'average' man or woman. 'What is the average?,' he asks. He claims that arguments for or against feminism tend to rely on constructions of this average man or woman. If we attempt to describe her, however, she disintegrates under the weight of particularities.

Like his consideration of the literary representation of women in 'The Woman of the Novelists', this book bases its claims on a defence of realism. However, Ford's ultimate argument in this text remains unclear. Is he attacking the 'democratic' language of the average as such, or is he suggesting that it is impossible to argue about the politics of sexual difference? At one point, for example, he claims that he is happier for the language of averages and approximations to be used in relation to ideas of nation: '[T]he differences between national characteristics will be much greater than the difference between the sexes.'[64]

Ford's attempt to downplay the differences between the sexes produces an idiosyncratically progressive position on women's social and political position. In his post-war novel *Parade's End*, this odd kind of feminism is developed in more detail. The character of Valentine Wannop, a feisty suffragette, falls in love with, and is loved by Tietjens, an intellectually brilliant Tory whom we are told repeatedly is 'pure eighteenth century'. Tietjens, in conversation with Valentine, argues that he agrees with the violent methods of the suffragettes, but that their aims are 'idiotic'. This is because, as he states, 'What good did the vote ever do anyone?' However, he agrees with suffragette violence, because it's the 'only straight method. It's the feudal system at work.' The real object of attack for Ford is not Valentine, the woman whom he sees as the key to the future, but a political and cultural milieu which lacks meaningful forms of political and ethical belief. Tietjens muses at one point, 'Perhaps the future of the world then was to women? Why not? He hadn't in years met a man that he hadn't to talk down to.'[65]

Like Marinetti and Lewis, Ford supports suffragette violence while denigrating suffragette aims. Rather than identifying freedom with a

[64] Ibid. 46.   [65] Ibid. 114, 115, 128.

formal political equality, these writers, like Orage and Marsden, locate liberty in individual action. As this chapter has suggested, this political scepticism informs a wide range of literary texts in the period. However, whereas before the war attacks on equality and rights often fuelled optimistic and exuberant visions of literary anarchy or egoism, after the war there is a shared anxiety about the powerlessness of the individual in the face of a state or market economy whose mechanisms of power are hidden from view.

These shifts inform the ideas of sexual difference which structure modernist texts in the period. Before the war women are often associated with the politics of romanticism and the egalitarian principles of the French Revolution. After the war women are often connected to the mass consumerism which Lawrence attacks in his image of the mannequin-god on Oxford street or with Ford's man average. Here the feminization of politics and culture is seen as being less a question of whether the citizen is understood as a bearer of rights and an individual with the capacity for moral action and more about whether the individual will be swamped by the tyrannical and anti-intellectual power of the feminized mass average. Whilst these two ideas of democracy often sit side by side, it is this latter idea, fuelled by the shifts towards mass democracy after the war, that lies behind many of the literary explorations of power and politics in the 1920s.

WOMEN EGOISTS

Critical accounts which have traced the impact of Stirner's and Nietzsche's philosophy on Anglo-American modernist writing have concentrated on the work of Hulme, Pound, Yeats, Lewis, Ford, Lawrence, and Eliot. Writers such as Gertrude Stein, Djuna Barnes, Dorothy Richardson, Virginia Woolf, Rebecca West, H.D., and Mina Loy have not figured in these accounts. The attempts to connect Stirnerian and Nietzschean ideas to feminist arguments in the *New* Age and the *Freewoman* have also not been analysed in detail. Levenson and Sherry simply ignore the connections between feminist thought and these philosophical ideas. Other critics, such as Benstock, stress the way in which an egoist philosophy facilitates the masculine posturing of Anglo-American male writers. By ignoring the fact that some feminist thinkers identified with Stirner's and Nietzsche's arguments, many critics have highlighted the 'masculine' nature of egoism, and have disregarded the fact that some feminists used these arguments to criticize what they saw as a debased parliamentary democracy.

I have been keeping male and female writers artificially separate in this chapter in order to consider the relationship between modernist writing, democracy, and sexual difference. In the book overall, however, I want to describe the connections between the responses to democracy by male and female writers. The ideas traced in Chapter 1 help us to understand a much wider range of modernist texts. Many women writers in the period focus on the psychic impact of the modern political contradictions discussed by Stirner and Nietzsche. Their writing often produces startling images of women as split apart by these contradictions. In particular, writers suggest that modern women embody wider political contradictions. The discourse of democratic rights and equality is often described as a powerful modern ideology which masks the recognition of sexual difference. Marsden had asked whether women should identify their interests with the emerging system of mass democracy, which would produce a levelling out of sexual differences? Many women writers also considered whether modernity involved collapsing female identity into masculine models of citizenship. Loy bluntly proclaims that women must 'Be BRAVE & deny at the outset—that pathetic clap-trap war cry, woman is the equal of man'. As we have seen, Loy's scepticism about the discourse of formal political equality was shared by a number of writers. Others create texts whose formal properties suggest a conflicted response to modern democracy.

Let us take the early work of Gertrude Stein, for example. On the face of it, Stein presents us with a radically new aesthetic which seems to embrace the new democracy of the twentieth-century United States. In her early text *The Making of Americans*, she writes a kind of inclusive modernist prose: 'Some time then there will be every kind of a history of every one who ever can or is or was or will be living.'[66] As a corollary to this belief in the value of everyone's history, Stein levels out language so that there is seemingly no organizing principle of hierarchy. *Three Lives* (1909), with its focus on the lives of three ordinary, working-class women, had begun this project of literary inclusion. Wyndham Lewis, in discussing Stein's work in *Time and Western Man* (1926), saw her work in precisely such terms. He argued that the writing style of *Three*

---

[66] Gertrude Stein, *The Making of Americans, Being a History of Family's Progress* (Paris: Contact Editions, Three Mountains Press, 1925), 124.

Lives is 'undoubtedly intended as an epic contribution to the present mass-democracy'.[67] It is hard, then, to imagine a literary project whose politics is more at odds with the work of Ford, Hulme, Lewis, Pound, and Lawrence.

Yet, let us pause before we accept this characterization of Stein's work. What exactly is Stein trying to achieve in her early text *Three Lives*, and in what way is the writing 'democratic'? In her early texts, Stein writes what she called a 'continuous present' which deliberately tries to do without nouns and adjectives, and instead focuses on 'prepositions and conjunctions and articles and verbs and adverbs'. This is because, as Peter Nicholls puts it, 'In Stein's view, nouns tie us to the world of thought, providing counters which are endlessly familiar and denying us the excitement of immediate perception.'[68] This antipathy to the deadness of familiar language is close to Hulme's attack on words being used as 'counters' in his essay 'Romanticism and Classicism'. Hulme, Pound, and Eliot argue that the counter-language of romanticism should be replaced by a noun-based poetic language which foregrounds the object. In *Three Lives* Stein comes to the opposite conclusion. Her interest in the composition of language shifts attention from the object to the structure of the writing. It is in the minute differences produced through linguistic repetition that she reveals the nature of the language which structures identity.

For Lewis, Stein's experiment with a 'continuous present' in *Three Lives* fails because it produces a prose which is abstract, 'dead', and 'mechanical'. He regarded the modern mass democratic state in similar terms. Democracy, he argued, produced dead and mechanical individuals incapable of independent thought. For Lewis, then, rather than giving us the history of everybody's individual life, Stein's writing actually effaces the individual. When he attacks her writing as dead and mechanical, he accuses her of replicating the dynamic of political effacement which controls the modern democratic state. As we read Lewis's attack on Stein, however, something odd happens. Rather than suggesting that Stein's writing is a celebration of democracy, he seems to argue that her writing is one of the most potent expressions of the failures of democracy. Her 'history of everyone' creates a language based on a sinister uniformity, in which each individual seems to be the same

---

[67] Wyndham Lewis, *Time and Western Man*, ed. Paul Edwards (Santa Rosa, Calif.: Black Sparrow Press, 1993), 60.
[68] Nicholls, *Modernisms*, 203.

individual. It is Stein, rather than Lewis, who produces a prose in which the singularity of the individual is truly shattered.

This is interesting, not least because Lewis attempted to capture the repetitions of psychic mimeticism in his own prose. In *Tarr*, for example, characters struggle to shake off the social masks which control them. Even at the most intimate of moments, characters perform little stage plays for imaginary audiences: Kreisler, we are told, 'conformed for the sake of the Invisible Audience haunting life'. A little later in the novel, he is seen 'struggling and perspiring in the grasp of a shadow'.[69] Certain exceptional and wilful individuals, such as Tarr and Anastasya, resist these self-imposed audiences. It is through the differences between independent and mimetic personality types that Lewis attacks the structures of modern democracy.

Lewis chiefly objected to Stein's writing because, in his view, she presents us with no vantage-point outside the characters she describes: Stein adopts 'the simplicity, the illiterateness, of the mass-average of the Melancthas and Annas'. By mimicking the language of the 'mass-average', her writing is incapable of giving order or meaning to the mechanical lives she describes. Her aesthetic, then, gives proof of 'all the false "revolutionary," propagandist *plainmanism* of her time'.[70] This 'plainmanism' is false because it masquerades as an accessible form of literary realism, but is actually language at its most artificial, organized by means of an externally imposed rhythm of an 'obsessing time'. It is notable that Lewis diagnoses and reveals the masks of modern men and women, the 'invisible audiences' haunting life. Stein's writing, in contrast, suggestively captures the difficulty of individuation in the context of a standardized language.

There is a conflict between the aesthetic parameters of *Three Lives* and *Tarr* which suggestively captures two different strands of the modernist critique of democracy. Lewis's main objection to Stein's writing is that she fails to give meaning to the mechanical lives she describes. The differences are focused on the issue of order, and this will be central to my more detailed discussion of the poems of H.D., Eliot, and Loy in the following three chapters.

It is perhaps not surprising that women writers might have a troubled relationship to the adoption of literary authority. However, I want to suggest that these writers do not identify intellectually with the political and cultural move towards democracy in a way which enforces Huyssen's

---

[69] Lewis, *Tarr*, 151, 159.   [70] Lewis, *Time and Western Man*, 60.

dichotomy between male and female modernist writing. Instead, they are often critical, along with their male contemporaries, of liberal democratic principles of equality, rights, morality, and sentimentalism. The following chapters explore how these ideas fuel the poetry of H.D., T. S. Eliot, and Mina Loy.

3

H.D.: Egoist Modernism

Of the three poets discussed in the following three chapters, H.D. is the least obviously politically engaged. She rarely occupied herself with wider political events, although anti-Semitic Vienna and the violence of the Blitz are significant backdrops in *Tribute to Freud* and *Trilogy*. Yet, running through her writing is a consistent interest in the nature of power and subjection. In fact, mastery, whether as patriarchal regulation, as scientific rigour, as psychoanalytic reason, or as legal rule, dominates H.D.'s writing. She seems to erect a series of counter-values to these regulatory discourses: poetic mysticism, female prophecy, and poetic introspection. In terms of Hulme's, Babbitt's, and Eliot's romanticism–classicism opposition, it would seem that H.D. is best placed on the side of romanticism, despite the fact that her poems are famously like 'the Greek'. Along with Pound in *Hugh Selwyn Mauberley*, then, it is common to see her as an introspective, late romantic poet whose classicism is nostalgic, expressive of personality, democratic, and feminine, rather than modern, impersonal, authoritarian, and masculine. Recent books on H.D. by Cassandra Laity and Eileen Gregory have re-evaluated these central modernist terms, but reinforced the claim that H.D. has poetic affiliations with romantic and *fin-de-siècle* decadent poets.[1]

In the previous two chapters I have uncovered a range of material from the early twentieth century, some familiar, some less familiar, that has questioned the validity of this interpretative framework. For a number of writers, the modernist construction of romanticism and classicism is dependent on other oppositions: introspection versus impersonality, democratic versus authoritarian, and feminine versus masculine. These oppositions are haunted by a third term, egoism. Egoism is a theory of human agency in which individualism is separated out from ideas

---

[1] Eileen Gregory, *H.D. and Hellenism: Classic Lines* (Cambridge: Cambridge University Press, 1997); Cassandra Laity, *H.D. and the Victorian fin de siècle: Gender, Modernism, Decadence* (Cambridge: Cambridge University Press, 1996).

of personality and introspection. In a literary sense, poetic techniques of irony, detachment, and imagistic concretion hold the ego at a firm distance from the object of contemplation, the opposite of the self-absorption seen to characterize decadent poetry. Politically, egoism focuses on the rampantly wilful, self-oriented nature of human identity in the context of the breakdown of the cohesive ideological norms of religion and modern politics. Modern democracy and liberal individualism are seen as secular ideologies that have replaced institutionalized religion, but which in effect represent a continuation of religious structures and values. Some male modernists attempted to construct egoism as essentially masculine. The male artist is threatened by the sentimentality, introspection, and democratic mimesis of modern life, factors all classed as 'feminine' and held at bay by the wilful assertion of male autonomy.

A number of modernist writers, then, attempt to use egoism to marry ideas of literary value, politics, and sexual difference. A theory of style is Hulme's starting-point in 'Romanticism and Classicism'. His end-point is the authoritarian politics and culture of the new classicism. Egoism, like the new classicism, then, specifically peels away the romantic, moralistic, and civic ideals of citizenship which accompany liberal conceptions of individuality. It stops short, however, of any identification with an authoritarian modern state. Modernist writers shuttled back and forth between egoist and authoritarian positions in the 1910s, but both were responses to the altruistic, sentimental, and romantic notions of subjectivity of the previous generation.

The relationship between egoism and theories of sexual difference, however, was a fraught one. Hulme, Lewis, Pound, and Eliot align romanticism with sentimental femininity in order to produce a sexualized theory of modern poetry, in which feminine introspection is countered by masculine impersonality. A number of feminist intellectuals, however, challenged the connection of femininity with sentimentalism and self-absorption, arguing that egoism is a theory of human agency which destabilizes the dichotomy of masculinity and femininity.

In this chapter I will reconsider H.D.'s poetry in the light of these historical debates. Gregory, in her excellent book on H.D., argues that in terms 'of the structural map of modern classicism, H.D. is undoubtedly situated with the romantic'. She goes on, however, to make some suggestive comments about this romanticism: 'H.D.'s affiliation with [romanticism] goes far beyond her connection with romantic or Victorian writers: it represents a deliberate choice for an alternative perspective and tradition that she senses can address the realities of disillusion and loss yet evade the kind of authoritarian order given in modern classicism.' Gregory substantiates the claim that H.D. adopts a 'deliberate' position within the modernist debate about romanticism and classicism, in which personal nostalgia counters modernist authority, by situating H.D.'s classicism in the context of early twentieth-century traditions.[2] Walter Pater, in *Greek Studies* (1897), discusses the 'two distinct' classical traditions of the Ionian and the Dorian. As Gregory puts it, the Ionian is 'manifest in Athenian democratic institutions', while the Dorian identifies with order and Spartan militarism. Gregory argues that Hulme and Eliot are 'severely reasserting the Dorian over the Ionian, the rational masculine over the "myriad-minded," effeminate traditions'. However, there is a fertile history of Ionian Hellenism running through nineteenth- and early twentieth-century literature which focuses on the 'discrete, the fragmentary, and the rationally obscure', emphasizing the 'erotic and the visionary', and 'affiliated politically with democracy and freedom'.[3] It is this latter tradition with which H.D. identifies.

In this chapter I want to suggest that it is less easy to place H.D.'s work in relation to the modernist oppositions outlined by Gregory. In order to understand H.D.'s work, we need to register the obvious differences between her identification with classicism and the construction of classical models by contemporaries such as Pound, Eliot, and Hulme. They use classicism and romanticism to explain the co-ordinates of an impersonal rather than a mimetic modernism, but their subject-matter is resolutely contemporary by comparison with H.D.'s 'Greek', non-modern poems. Her absolute refusal to include any reference to modern commodities or landscapes in her poems is her most consistent statement of aesthetic value. In this chapter I attempt to understand the nature of this hostility to modernity, and how this can be married to the 'democratic' project identified by Gregory. By reading H.D.'s work in the light of Chapters 1 and 2, I want to suggest that modernity and feminism are in conflict in H.D.'s writing. As a result, both the individualism and the feminism which control her work are ambivalent towards modern democracy.

This chapter, then, will bring into focus the idea of individualism, which regulates many of the other ideas in her poems. Does she function with a category of the liberal individual, defined by ideas of rights and duties? Or does she presuppose an idea of the new democratized subject of mass politics, defined by economic or sociological categories of understanding? Or does her work focus on an egoist, anti-liberal, wilful individual, defined precisely through his or her difference from the democratized masses?

Through a close analysis of H.D.'s poems, it becomes clear that the images of power and subjection in her poems are inflected with natural, wilful, and individual, as opposed to social, registers: it is individual male will, rather than patriarchal systems of power, which energize the male figures in her poems; it is individual strength, rather than economic power, which regulates the relationship between individuals; poetic and linguistic value resides in a spiritual gift-inheritance, rather than in structures of social mediation or education; the poems contrast singular objects or gifts with economic or standardized value; and the poetic legislators who feature in her work are defined against the crowd.

H.D., THE *NEW FREEWOMAN*, AND EGOISM

H.D. arrived in London at the end of 1911. In 1912, Pound famously stabbed at her poems with a pencil and, according to him, created both Imagism and H.D.'s poetic persona. As she remembered it years later, Ezra 'chizzled' at 'Hermes of the Ways' so that it 'emerged like a stalactite'.[4] Her new poem, along with 'Priapus' and 'Epigram', was quickly dispatched to Chicago for publication in *Poetry* magazine in January 1913. In Britain, it was in the *New Freewoman* that H.D. first found her way into print. Her poem 'Sitalkis' appeared alongside other Imagist poems by Richard Aldington, Amy Lowell, Skipworth Cannell, F. S. Flint, and William Carlos Williams in September 1913. In addition to publishing her poems, the *New Freewoman* and the *Egoist* were also forums for her translations and poetry reviews, and for criticism of her work. F. S. Flint reviewed her poetry for the 1 May edition of 1915; her translation of 'Choruses from Iphigeneia in Aulis' was published on 1 November 1915; and she also published her own poetry reviews.[5] Richard Aldington, whom H.D. had married in 1913, took over the post of assistant editor of the *Egoist* on 1 January 1914, and she helped

---

[4] H.D., 'Letter to Peter Russell', 24 Jan. 1950, in H.D. Correspondence, Beinecke Library, Yale University, New Haven, Conn., folder 604.

[5] By 1916 the *Egoist* had reduced its publication to one edition a month.

him considerably with his editorial duties.[6] Aldington joined the British Army in May 1916, when military conscription became inevitable with the passing of the Military Service Act of March 1916. Whilst he was at the front, H.D. took over as assistant editor of the *Egoist* in June 1916. During this period, one of her poems appeared in every issue of the *Egoist*, and she also published further poetry reviews.[7] Due to the breakdown of her marriage, H.D. stopped editing the journal in June 1917, and T. S. Eliot became assistant editor in her place.

The fact that editorially H.D. had such close links with the *New Freewoman* and the *Egoist*, and published poems alongside Marsden's editorials until 1917, does not mean that there is a necessary connection between Marsden's egoist philosophy and H.D.'s writing. However, there is some evidence that she was interested in Marsden and in debates within British feminism from her unpublished short story called 'The Suffragette'.[8] The story is undated, but was probably written when H.D. first arrived in London in 1911–12. It describes a young American woman who meets a woman called 'Miss Marston' at a London party. On the title-sheet to the story there is written in pencil, probably by Norman Holmes Pearson: 'sounds like Dora Marsden, but am not sure when Hilda met her'. In the story the young American woman with a 'determined chin' begins by criticizing the suffragettes for being law-breakers: ' "I don't care who is arrested,——serve them all right!" ' A burly Englishman agrees with her: ' "Quite right, miss, I agree with you! A set of law breakers and rioters——outrageous performance." ' The American girl asks Miss Marston to defend her cause, and Marston suggests that there would be no point in the present company. This prompts the American girl to self-reflection: ' "Surely it was better to take active interest in the affairs about one, if only for the whetting of one's intellect, than to drift on and on, following ever the conventional, the platitudinous.——to this!' The desire to meet intellectual challenges

---

[6] H.D.'s letters of autumn 1914–16 reveal her contributions to the editorial duties of the *Egoist* to be extensive. She writes: 'I am so tired typing for Egoist': Letter to F. S. Flint, 12 July 1916, in 'Selected Letters from H.D. to F. S. Flint: A Commentary on the Imagist Period', ed. Cyrena N. Pondrom, *Contemporary Literature*, 10.4 (1969), 575.

[7] H.D., ' "Goblins and Pagodas" by John Gould Fletcher', *Egoist*, 3.12 (1916), 183–4.

[8] H.D. 'The Suffragette' (n.d.), H.D. Papers, Beinecke Library, Yale University, New Haven, Conn., folder 952. The story is signed by 'J. Beran', 'Upper Darby, Pa'. The story is undated. Confusingly, it is signed at H.D.'s parental home in Pennsylvania, yet having left there in 1911, she did not return until her visit to the USA in 1921. It is highly likely that it was written during H.D.'s initial trip to London in 1912.

prompts the American to accompany Miss Marston through the streets of London. While they walk, the American girl questions Miss Marston's beliefs: ' "You have a wonderful city," she said, "so peaceful and well ordered I wonder that you try and better it." ' Marston answers her by pointing to a young woman: ' "You haven't seen it all," she said, "now that——" the girl pointed down a narrow little court, ... "have you ever seen *that*, for instance?" ' The emphasized pronoun refers to a young woman who has just been sacked from her job. The American experiences a strong reaction: 'Something stirred within her, deep down it had its origin, among the primal causes of unjust allotements [sic].' They turn to a discussion of the labour market. Marston tells her that women are sacked because, while they do the same work, 'they're women, that's all, because there is an alarming majority of women in this country, and women are cheap, because if this new bill goes through, all men will have the vote, no women, because such women as Maggie and Jennie and a thousand others have no social power, nor any hope of power in the future'.[9] The story concludes with the American woman translating detached laughter into action: 'She wanted to laugh, but something caught in her throat.' Instead of laughing, she accompanies Miss Marston to the suffragette meeting.

We don't know whether the real Dora Marsden had as much persuasive power over H.D. as the fictional Miss Marston has over the young American poet. However, this story suggests that H.D. had an interest in feminist questions of suffrage and women's employment rights in the early 1910s. Marston is made to represent the suffragette feminism which the real Dora Marsden repudiates in the *Freewoman*, the *New Freewoman*, and the *Egoist*, making it hard to know whether H.D. was aware of Marsden's evolving feminism in the period when H.D. first lived in London.

This minor short story is interesting, however, because it introduces us to a number of ideas which are important in H.D.'s later writing. The defining feature of the young American woman is her intellectual autonomy, which separates her from the aggressive feminism of Miss Marston. But this intellectual autonomy also means that, rather than dismissing the questions raised by Marston, she is intrigued by them.

---

[9] H.D., 'The Suffragette', 4, 6. The 'bill' that Miss Marston refers to is probably the 1912 Franchise and Registration Bill, which aimed to grant full manhood suffrage, but which excluded the issue of women's suffrage, which had been central to the Conciliation Bills of 1910 and 1911.

The American believes that her autonomy is secured by the democratic law and order which she spiritedly defends. Yet when Marston shows her the poverty of working women in London, she reveals the way in which the supposedly 'democratic' law actually discriminates against women. The American finds herself confronting the political link between economic inequality and gender difference, and questioning her own 'autonomous' position. She is defined both by the intellectual detachment to which she aspires and the fact that she is a woman. In the conclusion to the story, the American woman replaces detached intellectual curiosity and laughter with a kind of feminist commitment.

The language of the story is interesting too. While the law is described as a form of 'social power', the American's identification with the working woman is described as 'primal'; perhaps a primal empathy with individual injustice; or a primal feminism, which identifies with the specific injustice towards women. Within the logic of the story, primal empathy is a human recognition which counteracts the seemingly neutral justice of the state. There are, then, two kinds of justice at work in the story: one is civic, legal, and abstract; the other is grounded in a form of individual recognition based on experience. In the story H.D. suggests that if we could strip away the false legalism which grounds the categories of justice and power, we would find a natural justice grounded in empathy.

As we saw in Chapter 1, the critique of legalistic forms of justice through the lens of natural justice was central to discussions about democracy and modern subjectivity in the pre-war period. H.D., however, does not simply dwell in the primal empathy which forms one side of this opposition. Both social power and empathy are collective demands which threaten to dissolve the egoism necessary for the creation of poetry. H.D.'s prose is often at its most powerful when it describes the conflicts involved in being a modern female artist. She represents the historical pressures which enforce a specific model of modernity onto modern women. Essentially, she sees the artist as the individual who is able to withdraw from these external pressures. On the one hand, she presents us with women who are defined by history, modernity, and civic conceptions of cultural inclusion. On the other hand, her female characters want to withdraw from these collective demands and promote a wilful artistic nature.

If 'The Suffragette' is an early attempt to stage these conflicts, she was to continue to explore them throughout her life, but in more sophisticated ways. Her late prose work *Bid Me To Live* was written and revised over a number of decades, before being published in 1960. In it she describes being a modern woman as a 'tightrope act', suggesting that it entails a precarious performance which is irreconcilable with being a female poet. The novel is set during the First World War, and being modern is described as an oppressive burden that threatens to destroy the protagonist, Julia. Contemporary history is an external force which is weighted with images of bombs, the army, and masculine power: it is 'cosmic, comic and crucifying'. One of the key forms of pressure in this novel is to *be* a successful modern woman. Yet her writing deliberately obscures, rather than reveals, the nature of this injunction. It could be that this pressure comes from Julia's husband, Rafe Ashton, or from the 'rowdy actual lost generation' who gabble of 'Oedipus across tea-cups or Soho café tables'.[10] Or, it could be that this demand comes from somewhere within Julia herself.

H.D. presents us with characters who respond to the pressure of modern history by withdrawing into the self. As in Lawrence's writing, this retreat fuels certain stylistic experiments. The images that H.D. uses to consolidate the idea of external force are complicated. In *Bid Me To Live*, an object falls from the sky, but H.D. shifts into a metaphorical register which serves to obscure, rather than illuminate, its nature: 'Leviathan, a whale swam in the city dusk.'[11] The change of register here is partly motivated by the fact that the object has 'drifted from sight'. The Leviathan image is sufficiently ambiguous that it could refer to the smoke left drifting in the sky after a bomb blast or to the after-image left on Julia's mind after the object has disappeared from view. The ambiguity reveals much about H.D.'s aesthetic interests. She focuses on the borderline between interior and exterior worlds. There is a causal logic to this interest. In the face of the weight of history, Julia, and the writing, retreat into a realm of poeticized language which is produced through experiential and localized reactions. Poetry is defined as a private language grounded in the psychically charged relation to objects. 'We walk among stones, paving-stones, but any stone might have been our tomb-stone, a slice of a wall falling, this ceiling over our heads.'[12] Here, the external world is indeterminate, since it seems as though the protagonist is in the street at the same time as she is in a room. The reality of this external world seems less important than the fact that the stones prompt our protagonist to consider death. Even

---

[10] H.D., *Bid Me To Live* (London: Virago Press, 1984), 7, 8.
[11] Ibid. 11.   [12] Ibid. 16.

more disorientating, it seems as though it is as much the word 'stones' as the object itself which has encouraged the thought process.

Many years earlier Ford had defended a literary impressionism in the face of a modern world too large to be 'seen whole'. In H.D.'s writing, this retreat inwards has become the informing principle of the work. Yet, her model of the writer's role is different from that envisaged by Ford. At times, the external pressures of life threaten to invade and destroy the writer. At other moments, however, the writer seems omnipotent in her ability to aestheticize and transform her world. The quotation above, 'We walk among stones', for example, is not simply a description of human activity in a bombed-out London. Instead, considerations of time and space are disregarded, and the writing appears to be a series of overlapping memories based as much on word associations as on geographical reality. The 'real' dimensions of the phenomenal world shrink as the artist plays with linguistic associations. This is a rather different kind of 'tightrope' act, one in which H.D.'s writing performs a precarious balancing act in which images seem to refer to both psychological states and external objects. The result is to break apart any stable definition of art's legislative role. At times, the psychological focus of her work means that it feels as though her writing is spiralling into a frightening solipsism or an aesthetic decadence. But at other times, H.D. seems to be exploring the limits of the individual's withdrawal from the phenomenal world. As she put it in *The Walls Do Not Fall*, 'I sense my own limit, / my shell-jaws snap shut.' This is more a meditation on the fate of the self in the context of a hostile modernity and the impossibility of transforming the world through art. The question of what constitutes both the individual's and art's 'limits' was one which preoccupied H.D. throughout her writing career.

ROMANTIC OR CLASSIC?: H.D.'S EARLY POEMS

H.D.'s poems, like her prose pieces, explore the borderline between psychological states and the world of objects. The language, however, is more abstract and pared down; and she sets her poems in an ahistorical, pseudo-classical landscape. Her early poems seem to exemplify Pound's Imagist and Hulme's classical principles of composition by presenting objects in a direct and specifically non-sentimental manner. The first poem of *Sea Garden*, 'Sea Rose', for instance, is seemingly a simple poem about a rose, in which she departs from sentimental registers by evoking the raw energy of the natural world. The poem presents us with a static picture of a rose, only immediately to undercut this image through references to disfigurement, evoked in the joyless words 'marred', 'stint', 'meagre', and 'sparse'. The third and final stanzas continue to describe an impaired object which is controlled by external forces:

> Stunted, with a small leaf,
> you are flung on the sand,
> you are lifted
> in the crisp sand
> that drives in the wind.[13]

The third stanza shifts the register by introducing references to energy and force: the diminutive rose is a passive object which is tossed about by the wind. The poem's effects are dependent on the evocation of an arbitrary natural force which acts on a single, fragile object. The suggestion that, despite its spoiled appearance, this rose is 'more precious' than a wet rose ascribes value, seemingly arbitrarily, to the qualities of fragility and helplessness.

Whereas in 'Sea Rose' the wind arbitrarily flings the disfigured rose on to the sand, in 'Mid-Day', defeat and damage are created by the indistinct external force of the light. It is the 'I', rather than the rose, which is metaphorically flung around by the elements:

> The light beats upon me.
> I am startled—
> a split leaf crackles on the paved floor—
> I am anguished—defeated.[14]

Here, the poetic 'I' is startled and defeated because of the external light. Yet, the later line 'My thoughts tear me' suggests a self-destructive laceration which disrupts the causal relationship between outward light and inner response. The idea that there is an identifiable difference between thoughts and selfhood is unsettling. However, the poem further splits apart its poetic 'I' by shifting perspective again: 'My thoughts tear me, / I dread their fever.' Not only is the poetic 'I' separate from her thoughts; we here witness a self considering her fear of her own thoughts. The self is split at least three ways.

---

[13] H.D., 'Sea Rose', in *Collected Poems: 1912–1944*, ed. Louis Martz (New York: New Directions, 1983).
[14] H.D., 'Mid-Day', in *Collected Poems*, 10.

There is a layering effect in the poem, in the sense that it moves steadily inwards until the self is 'scattered', before moving outwards again to pin words on objects in the natural world. The seeds in the following simile, for example, represent, in a physical way, the internal state of the poet: 'I am scattered like / the hot shrivelled seeds.' The effect of this shuttling back and forth between psychic processes and natural objects is to trouble our sense of where to locate agency: it seems to reside both in the external light with which the poem began; and in the self whose scattered nature is mirrored in external objects.

The volume *Sea Garden* is remarkably consistent in its language and ideas. The poems all focus on similar kinds of power dynamics. The external agency is an elemental force or a capricious Greek god. In 'The Shrine', for example, H.D. addresses a 'you' who is 'great, fierce, evil', and it is men who have 'perished' on the cliffs. The poem is a rewrite of 'The Shrine by the Sea' by Anyte of Tegea, which refers to sailors who gaze on the Cyprian's 'bright image'. In H.D.'s poem, the contemplative distance between the 'we' and the 'you' is disrupted:

> and you strike us with terror
> O bright shaft.
>
> Flame passes under us
> and sparks that unknot the flesh,
> sorrow, splitting bone from bone,
> splendour athwart our eyes
> and rifts in the splendour,
> sparks and scattered light.[15]

It is ambiguous whether the light is 'scattered' because the bright shaft has disrupted the sailors' quality of vision, or because the source of the light itself has splintered apart. The description of geographical destabilization coincides with, rather than precedes, human dismemberment.

The scattered, fractured selves of *Sea Garden* merge with the rhythms of the landscape, and seem to disrupt the poetic detachment praised by Pound and Eliot. H.D. uses Imagist techniques to represent individuals who, rather than controlling the phenomenal world, find themselves at its mercy. By doing so, she depicts asocial and ahistorical selves who are defined by 'natural', naked, and brutal power dynamics. The diminutive objects or characters are helpless in the face of the capricious power of an elemental, divine, or human force. The poems do not present

---

[15] H.D., 'The Shrine', in *Collected Poems*, 9.

us with a moral perspective from which to criticize the exertion of force; it is simply a fact of nature. This lack of moral perspective is obviously explained partly by the fact that these poems are so 'Greek' in language and subject-matter. Greek gods do not have moral scruples when it comes to dishing out punishments and rewards. But explaining the constellation of values in H.D.'s poems is not as simple as that. If there are elements in these poems which are like the Greek, as a whole the poems are thoroughly 'modern' in the elements they synthesize.

As we have seen in Chapters 1 and 2, the interest in selves stripped bare of civic or moral categories is a shared one in philosophical and literary writing in this period. H.D.'s poems participate in this focus. They present us with naked selves in a landscape prior to Christian moral democratic culture. Hers is an idiosyncratic take on the wider modernist attack on progressive, 'Rousseauistic' models of human emancipation. In her poems, the forces which generate psychic disintegration are natural, irrational, and impenetrable. Her poems imply that the brutal exertion of power and psychic fragmentation are facts of nature, as impossible to escape as the heat of the sun.

'SOME OUTER HORROR': THE LANGUAGE OF POETRY

H.D.'s early poems represent a pre-Christian landscape severed from moral or civic conceptions of subjectivity. Her understanding of individualism, then, partakes of this amoral focus. Stirner argues that the artist is, by necessity, an egoist in the sense that artistic greatness is always a result of someone being 'more than other men (the "masses")'.[16] Artists are able to give expression to the unique thing which makes us who we are. H.D., like Lawrence, also sees art as what originates in and represents singularity. Individualism in the sense of singularity controls her understanding of aesthetic value. In 'Cities', the concluding poem of *Sea Garden*, beauty is described as 'rare, measureless'. The word 'rare' is central to H.D.'s vocabulary, because it incorporates both the physical quality of an object, that it is thin and sparse, and a value-judgement, that beauty is refined and that which is not common. The idea that

---

[16] Max Stirner, *The Ego and its Own*, ed. D. Leopold, trans. S. T. Byington (Cambridge: Cambridge University Press, 1995), 120.

beauty is 'measureless' also specifically opposes beauty to standardized objects. Unlike the other poems in *Sea Garden*, the 'hideous' city of 'Cities' is depicted as a place in which nature, truth, and beauty are absent: 'he had crowded the city so full / that men could not grasp beauty'.[17] The crowded city is monotonous and standardized: 'street after street / each patterned alike'. These repetitive streets are metaphorically linked to the 'souls' who inhabit them: 'And in these dark cells, / packed street after street, / souls live, hideous yet—/ O disfigured, defaced.' The streets and souls which are 'patterned alike' are 'hideous', because they lack the beauty of singularity. The poet's task, as it is presented in the poem, is to discover beauty by transcending this geographical and human monotony.

The search for beauty in the context of a monotonous cityscape is a common topic in modernist poetry. H.D. repeats the terms of this opposition, describing the city crowd as 'seething life' akin to 'larvae'. In so doing, she comes close to the register of Eliot's line in the first draft of *The Waste Land*, in which he compares the crowd in the city to swarming, breeding insects. The line involves standing over the city and creating order from above.

H.D.'s lines also involve a voyeuristic perspective on modern life which stands over a city only to condemn its insect-like inhabitants. As in *The Waste Land*, H.D. asks how poetic beauty can be created in the context of these repetitive and mechanized lives. Her answer in this first volume is to suggest that the 'old splendour' and the beauty of the future constitute imaginary landscapes which blot out the 'hideous' waste of modernity. The poem seems to suggest that both the past and the future are embodied in the 'timeless', 'rare', singular nature of poetic language itself.

It is not just that power and subjection are individualized, natural dynamics in H.D.'s poems, then. It is also the case that aesthetic value is specifically associated with singularity. The concept of individuality which controls these various aspects of H.D.'s writing is defined in opposition to the standardized emotions of the crowd. We find the crucial 'us' intruding importantly in 'Cities', the collective pronoun which, like many of the features of *Sea Garden*, was repeated throughout H.D.'s writing. This collective pronoun, described in *Trilogy* as the 'select little band', describes the poet, and poetic language, as outside and above the crowd. The fact that H.D. concludes *Sea Garden* with

---

[17] H.D., 'Cities', repr. in *Collected Poems*, 40.

'Cities' implies that she wants to make a wider claim about the nature of poetry in this first volume, to create her own description of the 'outer horror' which stamps beauty.

H.D. sets up a series of counter-values to standardization, commodification, and the crowd, the most important of which is that of the gift. The gift is central to H.D.'s poetry and prose, because it embodies a number of qualities: a gift is an object in the real world; a gift is also a human quality. The gift, then, is a perfect literary tool for H.D., because it can be that which is both external and internal to the self. In addition, the gift embodies ideas of aesthetic value: a gift is a form of value which is not commodified; and the value of a gift is dependent on personalized recognition. We will consider the nature of H.D.'s literary 'gifts' to Lawrence and Pound later in this chapter. For the moment, I simply want to discuss how these combined ideas of value are central to H.D.'s understanding of literary value in her early poetry. The poem called 'The Gift' begins:

> Instead of pearls—a wrought clasp—
> a bracelet—will you accept this?
> You know the script—
> you will start, wonder:
> what is left, what phrase
> after last night? This:[18]

The poem begins by specifying a number of valuable objects, 'pearls', 'a wrought clasp', and 'a bracelet'. The addressee of the poem is asked if she will accept in the place of these tokens of value, 'this'. The pronoun seems to refer to the poem itself: instead of these ornaments, will you accept this, the poem itself, as a gift?

The poem opens, then, with the question of value. The familiar 'script' is placed alongside other circulating objects in the poem. The poem is identified as one possible object or gift among others. As opposed to the pearls, the value of which is social and economic, the value of the poem is singular, dependent on a moment of recognition on the part of the addressee. 'The Gift' presents a dialogical notion of value in which recognition is central.

The desire to create an aesthetic language which stands outside of materialistic forms of value is a common one within modernist writing. As Peter Nicholls notes in relation to Pound, 'Cantos XXXI–LI seek

---

[18] H.D., 'The Gift', repr. in *Collected Poems*, 15. (First published as 'The Last Gift', in *Egoist*, 3 (1916), 35.)

to generate values through the evocation of objects and activities which resist transmutation into commodities.'[19] Yet, H.D.'s avoidance of objects which might suggest the 'congealed labour-time' of price or commodified value is more complete than that of any other modernist poet.[20] She simply excises all modern commodities from her poems.

If 'The Gift' begins by presenting an opposition between individual and social value, however, it proceeds by unsettling this opposition. It is in her poems which explore these oppositions that H.D. is at her most powerful. The poetic 'I' seems to be overpowered by her desire for the addressee: 'I who have snatched at you'. Yet, the 'you' is as scattered as the 'I' of 'Mid-Day'. The addressee of the poem is only ever described through the things she owns: a comb, a gold tassel, a scarf. She is *in* the many things she has touched. Her belongings, we are told, possess traces of their owner. Yet, H.D. complicates this idea of possession. These objects are in the process of being discarded: 'a comb / that may have slipped', 'a gold tassel, unravelled'. Is the comb, then, still part of the addressee, or has it slipped away from its owner? Where do we locate the boundary which separates self from world? In this stanza H.D. introduces a simile to clarify the image. But, as in *Bid Me To Live*, the simile serves to complicate the idea of possession: 'You are like the children / who haunt your own steps / for chance bits—a comb / that may have slipped.' The line likens the addressee to the children who haunt her, thereby suggesting that she is haunted by herself. This idea of self-haunting could refer to the fact that her childhood ghosts haunt her adult personality. Yet, in the context of the poem's wider meditation on the nature of writing, the image of self-haunting also seems to refer to the poem's relationship to a literary past.

Writing is always a rewriting of sorts, but H.D.'s poems, novels, and stories are distinctive for their obsessive interest in the process of rewriting. Not only does she rewrite mythical stories and retranslate Greek poems, she also rewrote her own story, particularly her experiences of the First World War, again and again. She also rewrites the self, often within a single poem or paragraph. Take this opening passage from her novel *Her*: 'Her Gart went round in circles. "I am Her," she said to herself; she repeated, "Her, Her, Her." Her Gart tried to hold on to

[19] Peter Nicholls, *Ezra Pound: Politics, Economics and Writing: A Study of the Cantos* (London: Macmillan, 1984), 59.

[20] Karl Marx, *Capital: A Critique of Political Economy*, i, trans. Ben Fowkes (Harmondsworth: Penguin Books, 1976), 130.

something.'[21] The word 'her' is as scattered as the addressee in 'The Gift' and the poetic 'I' in 'Mid-Day'. The narrator tries to 'hold on to' the self through pronominal repetition, but the effect is to destabilize, rather than unify, the self.

Returning to 'The Gift', we can see how in the poem this destabilization is a condition of writing. If the comb and the tassel are on the borderline between owner and world, then the poem itself also occupies this fragile borderline state. Is the poem, then, owned by the writer or by the person to whom it is addressed? And, more generally, is a poem a bit like one of the 'chance bits' which the street children want to snatch? In other words, once writing is in the world, it is 'scattered' among the different people who read it. It belongs to everyone, and no one. Writing which seems to be concerned with the self, as in the opening passage from *Her*, flips over into its opposite.

H.D.'s interest in how writing haunts and scatters the self informs her relationship to Greek myth. Rather than using myth to order the present, as Eliot does, mythical stories appear as scattered scraps which haunt the present. In many ways, she also creates myths about her own life by telling and retelling the story of her 'lost generation'. There is no definitive narrative version of this story. Each rewriting seems to be an attempt to make present the event being described, just as by repeating the word 'Her' discussed above Hermione tries to realize herself. This fraught relationship between self and language troubles our sense of H.D. as an 'introspective poet', as Pound characterized her. In 'The Gift' she implies that writing always externalizes the self.

This aspect of H.D.'s writing is important, as it complicates our understanding of her position in relation to the modernist oppositions outlined at the beginning of this chapter. In a number of respects her writing participates in the wider modernist hostility to commodification, standardization, and the crowd. Yet, rather than embracing forms of literary authority and tradition to take control of the chaotic and threatening facts of modern life, her work connects aesthetic value to the isolated objects and selves which shrink from an impenetrable modern world. She takes to an extreme the literary preoccupation with the self's circumscribed role in modern culture. Yet, she does not simply dwell in a poetic solipsism disconnected from the phenomenal world. She is preoccupied with the way in which writing constructs and defines the self. For H.D., words are weighted with the semantic and mythic

---

[21] H.D., *Her /HERmione/* (New York: New Directions, 1981), 3.

histories which cling to them. In her texts, there are minute differences in the ways in which individuals relate to these collective histories. At times, these ghost-like histories threaten to haunt and control the self. At other times, artistic individuality resides in the ability to re-visualize the stories which make us who we are. A theory of the interpretation of myth and history lies at the heart of H.D.'s aesthetic project. As I will go on to argue, it is also at the centre of her feminism.

The gift is the basis for a whole theory of aesthetic value in H.D.'s work. The idea that poems are akin to gifts, rather than commodities, intrudes on *Sea Garden* and H.D.'s *œuvre* in a wider sense. Gifts, gift giving, and gifted artists appear repeatedly in H.D.'s work: her poems are often constructed as a kind of gift or tribute to an unidentifiable 'you', a Greek or Egyptian god, or one of the many male writers with whom H.D. was intimate in her life, such as Ezra Pound, Richard Aldington, D. H. Lawrence, Sigmund Freud, Lionel Durand, or St John Perse. The reason for this focus on the gift is partly because 'The Gift' and the collection *Sea Garden*, as well as H.D.'s other volumes of poetry, partake of a literary tradition of gift-books. For instance, Catullus, who was one of H.D.'s favourite poets, begins his poetry books by announcing that they are gifts to a patron, and a language of the gift features centrally in his poems.

H.D. adopts the terms of this tradition by creating poems which are dedicated to, and dependent on, a patron. H.D. was dependent on gifts of money, primarily from her lover Bryher, all her life. Bryher's earliest letters to H.D. offer her praise and money: she writes to her on 22 December 1918: '[I]f another few pounds would be useful to you in a month or so, you will not hesitate to ask for it.'[22] As Barbara Guest states, H.D. 'had the mentality of one to whom things are given, but are not earned, not even rightfully inherited'.[23] Brigit Patmore, in a rather harsher description of H.D.'s relationship to Bryher, suggests that Bryher's 'gifts' actually functioned as a means of tyrannical control:

The child [Bryher] had generous ideas, but when it came to action she was cramped and ugly, and had a strange bargaining sense—for some much money or its equivalent she expected so much in return, principally in submission, for

---

[22] Bryher, letter to H.D., 22 Dec. 1918, H.D. Correspondence, Beinecke Library, Yale University, New Haven Conn., folder 80.

[23] Barbara Guest, *Herself Defined: The Poet H.D. and her World* (New York: Doubleday, 1984), 265.

she loved power .... She [Bryher] pressed Helga's [H.D.'s] freedom away with little importunities and wistfulness and protection and gifts.

Notwithstanding the fact that Patmore's description is partly fuelled by her personal dislike of Bryher, the idea that a gift can actually function as a means of control filters importantly into H.D.'s writing.

In Patmore's description, the gift, which we might think of as that which is offered freely, turns into its opposite, becoming instead a powerful form of personalized control. The power of the gift resides not in that which is socially explicit, such as the financial transactions of the market, but in subtle demands for psychic submission. H.D. was consistently interested in how the latter kind of power worked. We have already seen how in her poems objects function as concentrated forms of power, because they are infected with the personality of the giver. H.D. uses the gift to imagine an object language which can bind individuals into structures of personalized control.

H.D. also has a tendency to conflate the human and object status of the gift, and it is therefore also an important way of pin-pointing the nature of identity in her writing. In *Her*, for example, characters are identified both with the things they give and with the special skills with which they are gifted. Her's brother, Bertrand, has an 'incredible gift for mathematics'. She reaches out for 'Celestial Mechanics', but, we are told, it 'proved a barrier'. The implication is that it is a barrier, both to mathematics, and to Bertrand. He, in turn, has bought her *Jane Eyre*, so that she can 'be one with Bertrand'. Here, fictional characters are identified with the isolated characteristics or 'gifts' which define them. Rather than presenting complex, multi-faceted personalities, characters are stripped down to their wilful, anti-social, singular drives.

Returning to 'The Gift', the poem destabilizes any stable idea of individuality by suggesting that if we are in the things we give and receive, then the self is scattered and dispersed. This logic is magnified when H.D. goes on to write gifts and tributes to particular individuals, such as Lawrence, Freud, and Pound. Here, the personalities of both giver and receiver infect the gift-text, and the self is scattered in relation to a particular addressee. Patmore's description of the will-to-power at the heart of Bryher's gift giving will be kept in mind as we read these tributes. These dynamics are central to her depictions of male mastery and female subjection, which I will discuss in the next section.

---

[24] Brigit Patmore, *No Tomorrow* (London: Century Co., 1929), 56.
[25] H.D., *Her*, 18.

'UNACKNOWLEDGED LEGISLATORS': MODERNIST POETS

If H.D.'s poems violate Pound's rules about poetic objectivity and impersonality, she concurs with his belief that the artistic self is defined through its ability to assert its difference from modernity. H.D.'s early poems, then, foreground the value of singularity, the gift, and the 'select little band', entities which are defined through their opposition to standardized value, the commodity, and the democratic crowd. These values are reinforced by the overriding idea that art is produced through the individual withdrawal from these facts of modern life. In letters and critical essays, H.D. was often explicit about the terms of this withdrawal. In a letter of 1937 to Norman Holmes Pearson, for example, she describes a sharp disjunction between 'outer horror' and the poet's imagination: 'the inner world of imagination, the ivory tower, where poets presumably do live, in memory, does stand stark with the sun-lit isles around it, while battle and din of battle and the whole dreary, tragic spectacle of our times, seems blurred and sodden and not to be recalled, save in moments of repudiation, historical necessity.'[26] Here, H.D. unashamedly associates beauty with a nostalgic and romantic inner world of memory severed from the violence of war and more general ideas of modernity. In this letter, however, H.D. also tacitly admits that at times of intense historical pressure, it is impossible to maintain the strict boundary separating poetry from the 'tragic spectacle of our times'. The relationship between poetry and modernity, then, is more complicated than she sometimes admitted in her letters and essays. She also suggests that the phrase 'the inner world' is not confined to one person: it is a tower where poets, in the plural, live.

In a review of Yeats's 'Responsibilities', which H.D. probably wrote in 1916, she makes some revealing comments about her artistic contemporaries and the nature of modern artistic boundaries. She argues that the artist always has an enemy in the 'so-called middle-classes and general heaviness of the world'. Yet, for her generation, there is a more potent enemy: the 'great overwhelming mechanical daemon, the devil of machinery, of which we can hardly repeat too often, the war is the

---

[26] H.D., 'Letter to Norman Holmes Pearson', in Donna Krolik Hollenberg, ed., *Between History and Poetry, The Letters of H.D. and Norman Holmes Pearson* (Iowa City: University of Iowa Press, 1997), 8.

hideous offspring'.[27] H.D. believes that this secular devil is powerful because her artistic generation has internalized its values. She targets Futurist, Cubist, and Vorticist aesthetic values: 'inasmuch as its cubes and angles seem a sort of incantation, a symbol for the forces that brought on this world calamity'. The machine, she suggests, is now worshipped as a god by sections of the avant-garde, but this is a 'devil over whom neither they nor we have any more control'.[28]

Here, by embracing the modernity of the machine, the avant-garde has internalized the very forces which will destroy it. As we saw in Chapter 2, it is common in this period to argue that writers have internalized the beliefs of a secular modernity just as surely as the previous generation prostrated themselves before a fictional religious deity. For H.D. the avant-garde has taken a wrong turn. Rather than incorporate and transform a mechanical and standardized modernity, she argues that artists should withdraw into a poetic language in which the present is re-connected to the past. In *Notes on Thought and Vision*, which she wrote during 1919, H.D. argues that the 'new schools of destructive art theorists are on the wrong track'. Instead of creating the new through destruction, artists should re-enter the world of Leonardo and his kind. To encounter this world involves a particular kind of attentive perception. This comes out most clearly in her discussion of the poet Lo-Fu. She tells us that he looked at a branch of a tree. When he looked, however, he 'really did see it'. He then went inside to his room and 'closed his eyes'. When inside his room, he 'saw that branch more clearly, more vividly than ever. That branch was his mistress now, his love.' Through this process of perception, internalization, and love, 'she was his forever'.[29] The value placed on Lo-Fu's internalization of an external natural object specifically sees introspection as the basis of art.

Returning to the 1937 note, we can see that in her critical essays and letters H.D. sustained the idea that poetry is the language of a collective 'inner world' separate from the 'tragic spectacle of our times'. This reasoning helps explain H.D.'s refusal to allow her poems to be contaminated by references to modern commodities, industrial landscapes, or details of contemporary life. Art's enemy is clearly defined here: the middle classes, and their 'heavy' democratic values, a

---

[27] H.D., 'Responsibilities', in *Agenda: H.D. Special Issue*, guest edited by Diana Collecott, 25. 3–4 (Autumn/Winter 1987/8), 52.

[28] Ibid. 53.

[29] H.D., *Notes on Thought and Vision & The Wise Sappho* (San Francisco: City Lights, 1982), 23, 44.

mechanized modernity, and modern warfare. The 'inner world' actually seems to be consonant with poetic language in her writing; it is a shared imaginary place sealed off from the modern world, and composed of the select little band of poetic legislators.

Yet, the values which inform her poems are not as straightforward as this. The aesthetic principles which control her work are based on the idea of withdrawal. As we have seen in 'Cities', 'The Gift', and *Bid Me To Live*, her poems and novels often present images of an inner world under threat. Rather than successfully sealing art against the outside world, her writing is at its most subtle when it stages a dynamic between introspection and external pressure, and between self and world. After 1916, she would associate this question with the representation of sexual difference.

MEN AND WOMEN: H.D. ON LAWRENCE

The year of *Sea Garden*'s publication, 1916, represented a wider turning-point in H.D.'s life. It was around this time that her marriage fell apart, and she began to communicate with Lawrence. As she narrates it in *Bid Me To Live*, during this time the two writers had a number of fraught exchanges on the subject of writing. She admitted to John Cournos that she feared Lawrence's impact on her, declaring rather melodramatically in 1916 that 'There is power in this person to kill me', and 'if he comes too near, I am afraid for myself'.[30]

In *Sea Garden* the dynamics in H.D.'s poems revolve around the words 'great', 'mighty', 'strength', 'splendour', and 'terror', and they focus on the mystical power of gods and nature. In 'The God', 'Adonis', 'Pygmalion', and 'Eurydice', all published in 1917, the words 'power', 'mastery', 'arrogance', 'ruthlessness', 'unconscious', and 'nothingness' enter H.D.'s poetic vocabulary. The introduction of these words forms part of a new kind of interest in whether art can be seen as secular in origin. The key categories in H.D.'s vocabulary are now the will, understood as the aggressive, active, self-legislative core of the self, and the unconscious, associated with an irrational life force. The will is seen as consonant with artistic form; it is able to take control of the unconscious, associated with modernity, matter, and femininity, and mould it into shape.

---

[30] H.D., 'Letter to John Cournos', H.D. Correspondence. Beinecke Library, Yale University, New Haven, Conn.

As we have seen in Chapter 2, the idea that art can order the unconscious matter of modernity was central to modernist writing in the 1910s and 1920s. In H.D.'s poems these issues appear as questions. In 'Pygmalion', a poem published in the *Egoist* in 1917, for instance, H.D. asks whether it is simply arrogant to assume that artistic creativity originates in the individual will. This idea assumes the truth of a secular account of historical progression in which art is detached from the gods and handed over to the artist. The poem, then, asks whether Pygmalion's artistic fire comes from himself or from an external deity:

> have I made this fire from myself?
> or is this arrogance?
> is this fire a god
> that seeks me in the dark?[31]

Here, creativity is mysterious, originating either in a god who selects Pygmalion and sets him apart from his peers or in a self-generated artistic impulse which seizes control of the material world and moulds it into shape: 'am I the master of this fire, / is this fire my own strength?' However, there is a fatal cost to Pygmalion's hubris, as the poem concludes with the idea that power has reverted to the gods whom Pygmalion attempted to make 'less than men' through his art. The poem ends by questioning whether art secularizes creation and brings imaginative power down to earth: 'am I the god? / or does this fire carve me / for its use?' Here, instead of the artist moulding matter, the gods shape the self.

In this poem she maintains the ambiguity as to whether art originates in the individual will or in the injunction of an external god. H.D. stages this key question about the sources of artistic creativity, and in so doing develops a particular theory of historical interpretation. She seems to understand history as a subtle combination of two things. The gods and their stories are both the most important form of collective historical knowledge and a panoply of images heavily invested with personal significance. The external and the personal meet: Pygmalion in H.D.'s poem, for example, is both a fragment of collective history, and a figure with highly charged personal meaning.

In her personal descriptions of artistic inspiration, she also flirts with the idea that creativity is something that comes from outside. In a letter of 1916 to John Cournos, H.D. declares that the artistic 'flame is my

---

[31] H.D., 'Pygmalion', in *Collected Poems*, 49.

very Daemon driving me to write'. A day later this half-way spirit has become more distant, as she admits that the poems she is writing 'seem absolutely dictated from without'. She uses a couple of analogies to flesh out this statement: 'I am burning all the time like an early Christian, like a mad fanatic in the desert, well, like a poet.'[32] In these descriptions artistic authority is surrendered to an external entity, and the disturbing image of the gods carving Pygmalion for their use is seen as consonant with a kind of madness, or loss of self-control.

In both 'Pygmalion' and these letters to Cournos, H.D. specifically seems to counter the idea that modernist art confronts a chaotic modernity and moulds it into a meaningful shape. Instead, something external to the self, and beyond human understanding, threatens to send the artist spiralling into insanity. It is almost as though H.D. inhabits the passive, abject, decadent position assigned to femininity by Pound, Eliot, and Lewis.

I want to suggest, however, that rather than submitting to this gendered construction of 'feminine' art, H.D. actually tries to disrupt it. In a number of new poems, a series of male 'masters' take the place of the external god in 'Pygmalion', creating an aesthetic in which sexual difference splits apart the creative process. For example, in 'Eurydice', which was published in the *Egoist* in 1917, H.D. again explores artistic egoism, but here she connects it with masculinity. 'Eurydice' replays the dynamics of earlier poems, but the structures of power and subjection are now heavily marked by ideas of sexual difference. Helen Sword helpfully notes that H.D. 'rejects the familiar myth of Orpheus as the faithful lover whose glance back at his wife signals at once his aspiration and his human imperfection. Orpheus' backward glance, this Eurydice suggests, is more a gesture of greed.'[33] H.D. retells the story of Orpheus and Eurydice, but presents us with Eurydice's point of view as she addresses Orpheus:

> you who have your own light,
> who are to yourself a presence,
> who need no presence[34]

Unlike both Eurydice and the scattered selves of *Sea Garden*, Orpheus appears to be a self-possessed, self-present, heroic subject. Eurydice is

---

[32] H.D., 'Letter to John Cournos', 5 Sept. 1916 and 6 Sept. (?) 1916, H.D. Correspondence, Beinecke Library, Yale University, New Haven, Conn., folder 581.

[33] Helen Sword, 'Orpheus and Eurydice in the Twentieth Century: Lawrence, H.D., and the Poetics of the Turn', *Twentieth Century Literature*, 35.4 (1989), 414.

[34] H.D., 'Eurydice', in *Collected Poems*, 51.

characterized as the precise opposite of this: 'So for your arrogance / I am broken at last.' The poem proceeds to describe the psychic dislocation which she experiences because of the actions of Orpheus: 'everything is lost', 'I have lost the earth'.

This poem both replays themes discussed in relation to *Sea Garden* and engages with a different set of issues. While 'Eurydice' retells a familiar mythical tale, H.D. adapts the naturalistic language of *Sea Garden* to make the story fit her own concerns. The structural relationship between helpless objects and external forces of light, wind, and sea recurs in this poem, but H.D. uses this dynamic to represent the relationship between two characters. Eurydice is a diminutive thing: the penultimate stanza describes her spirit as 'small against the black / small against the formless rocks'. As with the natural objects of *Sea Garden*, Eurydice is tossed about by the actions of Orpheus: she is 'swept back' to reside amongst lichen and moss; she is 'broken', and she is 'swept into nothingness'. While Eurydice shrinks into nature, becoming a 'reflex of the earth', Orpheus is a wilful, empowered subject who is 'above the earth', whose freedom is expressed in his arrogant sense certainty. Like the 'I' of 'Mid-Day', who was torn apart by her thoughts, Eurydice is also torn apart, but here it is her physical being which is separated from her imagination. Orpheus, heroic and all-seeing, stands above the feminine matter beneath him, and controls its destiny. This appears to be the ultimate expression of modernist egoism, in which the self seizes control of the material world.

As with 'The Gift', however, H.D. disrupts any simple reading of the Orpheus–Eurydice story by introducing a central ambiguity: 'so for your arrogance, / I am broken at last, / I who had lived unconscious, / who was almost forgot'. The two subjects in these lines slip into each other. There is the 'I' who lives unconscious and the person or people who have forgotten Eurydice. The unconscious could be Eurydice's or somebody else's. By connecting these ideas together, H.D. puts a question mark over the identity of the 'I' and the unconscious of the poem. Is this a poem about the dramatic story of two characters, Orpheus and Eurydice, or is it about Orpheus and his memory of Eurydice? In other words, is the 'I' of the poem Eurydice, a separate character, or is the pronoun a memory in Orpheus's mind? The poem can be read both ways.

We have seen H.D. manipulate the ambiguity over what is internal or external to the self in a number of other texts, and she uses it to great effect in this poem. If Eurydice is taken to be a separate character, the poem focuses on a gendered dynamic in which female subjection is a consequence of male arrogance. But if the poem's 'I' is actually Eurydice as a memory, we are presented with a psycho-drama focused on Orpheus's failed attempt to assert himself as a unified subject. Lines such as 'you have swept me back' and 'myself thus / swept into nothingness' are visually vibrant descriptions of psychic repression. This picture of Orpheus's failed attempt to forget Eurydice is in tune with H.D.'s more general exploration of the 'scattered', fractured selves of *Sea Garden*, but here she seems as interested in the costs of his self-delusion as anything else. Male egoism is dependent on sweeping away the female element, whether this is a particular person or a part of the psyche. Orpheus, however, is haunted by the very thing he arrogantly tries to control.

In this, the poem chimes with H.D.'s more general interest in writing as a form of self-haunting. Both 'Pygmalion' and 'Eurydice' suggest that artistic freedom resides in a wilful seizure of matter, but 'Eurydice' points us forward towards H.D.'s future poetic interests. The poem engages directly with the central modernist preoccupation with form and matter, male and female. In this she confronts Lawrence, one of her main artistic adversaries, suggesting that masculinity is not only dependent on the repression of femininity but that this leads to a kind of artistic blindness.

Lawrence saw egoism as a less troubling force, indispensable to the modern artist, allowing the individual to break from religious, familial, and social ties. Before the war, Lawrence attacked democracy and defended the will in ways which reflected his reading of Nietzsche. His *Study of Thomas Hardy*, which he began in 1912, but which was not published until the 1930s, shows the influence of Nietzsche most extensively. It is dominated by ideas of cultural and religious crisis. His attack on the democratic state is the foundation of his defence of egoism: 'Which is greater', he asks, 'the State or myself? Myself, unquestionably, since the State is only an arrangement made for my convenience.'[35] Arguing that the individual, however, must battle against the demands of society, Lawrence insists, as Nietzsche had done before him, that there is a contradiction between genuine individuality and the individualism promoted by liberal democracy: 'The glory of mankind is not in a host of secure, comfortable, law abiding citizens, but in the few or more fine, clear lives, beings, individuals, distinct, detached, single as may be

---

[35] *The Cambridge Edition of the Works of D. H. Lawrence: Study of Thomas Hardy and Other Essays*, ed. Bruce Steele (Cambridge: Cambridge University Press, 1985), 38.

from the public.' Lawrence's theory of art is grounded in this critique of law-abiding citizens. He goes on to describe the relationship between art and the average in a way that echoes with Nietzsche's theory of *ressentiment*, arguing that 'the community' is 'determined to destroy all that is [not] the average'. For Lawrence, art can be produced only by those individuals who stand outside the average: 'By individualist is meant, not a selfish or greedy person anxious to satisfy appetites, but a man of distinct being, who must act in his own particular way to fulfil his own individual nature. He is a man who, being beyond the average, chooses to rule his own life to his own completion, and as such is an aristocrat.' This is a clear description of the modernist connections between individualism, the average, and ideas of a natural, rather than hereditary, aristocracy. 'The artist always has a predilection for him',[36] Lawrence declares.

At one time Lawrence was going to give the *Study* the Nietzschean title 'Le Gai Savoir'. However, he was critical of aspects of Nietzsche's work. In particular, he attacked Nietzsche's 'Wille zur Macht', as he called it, because it underestimated the importance of sexuality. As we saw in Chapter 1, other British Nietzscheans wanted to inject Nietzsche's ideas with theories of sexual difference. In *The Birth of Tragedy* Nietzsche distorts, in order to accentuate, the Apollonian and the Dionysian artistic impulses to substantiate his theory that Greek tragedy is the product of polarized metaphysical principles. In doing so, he excises the role of women in the Dionysian cults, for which there was much archaeological evidence. Orage, in his book *Nietzsche in Outline and Aphorism* (1907) reinjects the Dionysian and the Apollonian with ideas of sexual difference, although he equates the Dionysian impulse with masculinity, and the Apollonian impulse with femininity, which he elsewhere connects to 'conservatism'.[37] There were references to women's association with convention in Nietzsche's work, although not in relation to Dionysus and Apollo. In *Human, All Too Human*, Nietzsche aligns women with convention, citizenship, the law, and 'the recognised authorities and concepts of society'. In contrast, men are connected to individuality and will.[38]

[36] *Cambridge Edition*, 47, 49.

[37] A. R. Orage, *Friedrich Nietzsche: The Dionysian Spirit of the Age* (London: T. N. Foulis, 1906), 27.

[38] Friedrich Nietzsche, *Human, All Too Human: A Book for Free Spirits*, trans. R. J. Hollingdale (Cambridge: Cambridge University Press, 1986), 159.

In the *Study of Thomas Hardy*, Lawrence repeats the ideas that women are on the side of convention and men are on the side of individuality, but extends them into a much more developed theory of sexual difference. For Lawrence, male and female embody opposed forms of will-to-power which are normally in states of tension and struggle, but are capable of momentary reconciliation or balance. In the second chapter of the *Study*, for example, he attacks the women suffragists for their legalistic fantasies of power: 'The women ... want the vote in order to make more laws.'[39] Women are agents of political conservatism, at the forefront of the liberal politics which would place more and more power in the hands of the lawyers. As we saw in Chapter 1, there was a shared discourse in this period that the law was a means by which the weak exerted power over the strong, and that this constituted a 'feminine', or passive, political impulse. For Lawrence, women are the key signifiers, agents, and ultimate victims of democratic modernization. By embracing modern democracy, women loosen their connection to their sensual nature. In the *Study* as a whole, women are aligned with convention and law, and men with individuality, love, and flux. Lawrence connects women to the conservatism which wants to destroy the artistic individual. Later on in the *Study*, Lawrence discusses women's connection to the law in a more metaphysical sense, by opposing love to law: 'Now the principle of Law is found strongest in Woman, and the principle of Love in Man.' This is no longer the modern law which is under such attack in the *Egoist* and the *New Age*. Instead, it is a philosophical notion of law, or form. He explains this dichotomy by aligning love with creativity, and law with stasis: 'In every creature, the mobility, the law of change is found exemplified in the male, the stability, the conservatism is found in the female.' Stability and mobility are the organic images which ground Lawrence's political claims: 'The woman grows downwards, like a root, towards the centre and the darkness and the origin. The man grows upwards, like the stalk, towards discovery and light and utterance.' This reiterates claims made earlier in the essay, where Lawrence argues that the female is 'utter stability and permanence in Time', and the male is mobility. He goes on to define these two principles as the centripetal, which is female, and the centrifugal, which is male.[40] Lawrence here mimics Pater's use of these terms in *Greek Studies*, in which centripetal means Dorian, and centrifugal means Ionian. By doing so, he counters our expectations, as

---

[39] *Cambridge Edihon*, 15.   [40] Ibid. 127, 73, 75.

the female is associated with militaristic order, and the male with occult and pagan classicism.

What would such statements mean in terms of everyday life? In Lawrentian fashion, he used such images and metaphysical concepts to make sense of his own relationships. H.D., then, is fed through this rather crude dichotomous framework. In a letter to Cecil Gray of November 1917, he discusses the way in which his relationship to H.D. is based on a fraught power dynamic: '[M]y "women", Esther Andrews and Hilda Aldington etc, represent, in an impure and unproud, subservient, cringing, bad fashion, I admit,—but represent none the less the threshold of a new world, or underworld, of knowledge and being.'[41] H.D.'s status as one of the representatives of the female 'underworld' is obviously at the heart of her response to Lawrence in 'Eurydice' and *Bid Me To Live*. She implies in 'Eurydice', however, that by gazing too hard into her 'underworld' Lawrence has paralysed her.

The associations of women with subterranean darkness and of men with transcendent light were by no means Lawrence's invention. There was a range of myths based on precisely such ideas, and these were familiar to readers of the *New Age*. This was partly because both Lawrence and the writers of the *New Age* used Nietzsche's ideas to imagine human nature stripped of civic ideas of citizenship and morality. By peeling off the ideological layers, writers could toy with organic descriptions of sexual difference. Hastings, for example, under the pseudonym 'Tesserae', argued in 1914 that 'Men have to do with morals—woman with conventions ... her law is the physical law of terrestrial Nature.'[42] Hastings goes on, however, to claim that if women were stripped of their conventions, the 'amoral law' which lies at the 'bottom of female consciousness' would stand revealed in its 'awful nakedness'. Lawrence also refers to two different kinds of 'Law' in his *Study*. One is a political or juridical law, with which the suffragettes associate their interests. The other is an organic or natural law, which lies behind these layers of legal and social conventions. It is the latter which constitutes the truth of female and male identity.

Lawrence tries to associate women with two seemingly contradictory impulses in the *Study*; they are connected both to legalistic abstraction

[41] D. H. Lawrence, 'Letter to Cecil Gray', 7 Nov. 1917, in *The Letters of D. H. Lawrence*, iii, ed. James T. Boulton and Andrew Robertson (Cambridge: Cambridge University Press, 1984), 179–80.

[42] Tesserae, *New Age*, 14.11 (1914), 340.

and to a static and unreflective matter. In the previous chapter I discussed how a number of modernist writers also flirted with the idea that women are the agents and signs of modernity, because they embody these two contradictory impulses. In Chapter 4 I will consider in detail how Eliot attempts to make similar connections.

Lawrence's *The Rainbow* and *Women in Love*, which he had begun as a single work in March and April 1913, are remarkable for the way in which single characters embody universal human drives and epochal shifts in forms of cultural organization. Human conflicts are embodiments of shifts from pagan ritual to Christianity to scientific, industrial civilization. These epochal changes fuel stylistic considerations. For Lawrence, urban, industrial civilization, represented in *Women in Love* by London and the coal mines, is depicted in hard, geometrical, abstract images. Hermione and Gudrun, in their self-conscious, intellectual disconnection from organic nature, are seen as embodiments of this abstract imagery. He describes Ursula Brangwen in *The Rainbow* in the following way: 'Her nature had gone hard and smiling in its own arrogance, in its own antagonistic indifference to the rest of them.'[43] Ursula's 'arrogance' here arises at the moment she asserts herself against her mother and father and insists on going out to work as a schoolteacher. The feminist impulse towards economic independence necessarily involves a break with her family, and is the result of a wilful assertion of independence in which she disregards the demands of others. For Lawrence, then, egoistic arrogance is a necessary response to modernity.

The idea that particular images are connected to particular kinds of social or cultural organization also controls his poems. Lawrence was influenced by the Imagists, of whom he regarded H.D. as the most interesting, in the period 1914–16, when he turned away from conventional poetic forms and developed his own kind of free verse.[44] He was also interested in Italian Futurist theories of free verse. He was living in Levici in the early summer of 1914, during which time he read *I Poetici Futuristi*, which had been published in Milan in 1912. He here came into contact with Marinetti's, Paolo Buzzi's, and Soffici's theories of Futurism and free verse. In a letter to Arthur McLeod in June 1914, he states that he is particularly interested in the Futurist 'purging of the

---

[43] D. H. Lawrence, *The Rainbow* (London: Penguin Books, 1981), 415.
[44] Lawrence wrote: 'H.D. is good: none of the others worth anything': 'Letter to Arthur McLeod', 21 Dec. 1916, in *Letters of D. H. Lawrence*, iii. 51.

old forms and sentimentalities', but that he finds Futurism too 'male', 'intellectual', and 'scientific'.[45]

In his article 'The Poetry of the Present', which was published as an introduction to the American edition of *New Poems* in 1918, but which, he states, should have been a preface to *Look! We Have Come Through!*, Lawrence defends free verse on the grounds that it is the only form which truly captures the sexual 'conjunction' he describes in 'Manifesto'. He argues that the poems of the Greeks, and of Keats and Shelley, are perfect because their form mirrors their subject-matter: the eternal truths of 'the far future, exquisite and ethereal', or the 'voice of the past, rich, magnificent'. Both kinds of truth are flawless, because they are 'far off' from the human lives of the present: 'Eternity is only an abstraction from the actual present.' In contrast, Lawrence's poems represent 'The quivering nimble hour of the present, this is the quick of Time. This is the immanence. The quick of the universe is the *pulsating, carnal self*, mysterious and palpable.' Free verse captures this 'carnal self', because it expresses the moment: 'free verse is, or should be, direct utterance from the instant, whole man. It is the soul and the mind and body surging at once, nothing left out.'[46] Lawrence defends free verse, because it constitutes a poetic concretion which moves beyond the 'abstract' formal perfection of his predecessors. Only 'whole' men, in whom soul, body, and mind are one, can create poetry.

These comments on free verse help us to understand his volume of poems entitled *Look! We Have Come Through!*, which was published in 1917, and which contained poems written between 1912 and 1917. It was originally going to have the title, 'Man and Woman', then 'Poems of a Married Man', before he finally settled on *Look! We Have Come Through!* It is a kind of poetical record of Lawrence's early married life. In his preface to the volume, Lawrence describes the sequence: '[t]he conflict of love and hate goes on ... till it reaches some sort of conclusion, they transcend into some condition of blessedness.'[47] The poem sequence, then, is partly an account of the polarized male and female wills in tension and struggle described in the *Study*.

The female is consistently connected with the 'underworld' and with night or dark, and the male with that which is above ground and with

[45] D. H. Lawrence, 'Letter to Arthur McLeod', 2 June 1914, in *The Collected Letters of D. H. Lawrence*, i, ed. Harry T. Moore (London: Heinemann, 1962), 279–80.

[46] D. H. Lawrence, 'The Poetry of the Present', Preface to *New Poems* (London: Martin Secker, 1918), 183, 184.

[47] D. H. *Lawrence, The Complete Poems* (Harmondsworth: Penguin Books, 1993), 191.

illumination. 'Hymn to Priapus' begins: 'My love lies underground / With her face upturned to mine.' 'Bei Hennef' addresses a woman: 'You are the night, and I the day.' This sequence of images continues in the next two poems, 'First Morning' and 'And Oh—That the man I am might cease to be—', in which the poet embraces his love by asking her, and the darkness, to engulf him: 'I wish it would be completely dark everywhere, / inside me, and out, heavily dark / utterly.'

When the two begin to 'transcend into some condition of blessed-ness', the dark/light imagery is used to signal this togetherness: in 'Frohbleichnam', the man and the woman stand together on a balcony looking down on the street: 'Out of the sunshine into the shadow, / Passing across the shadow into the sunlight, / Out of sunlight to shadow.' The poem concludes with the image of the two together: 'Two white ones, sharp, vindicated, / Shining and touching, / Is heaven of our own, sheer with repudiation.' This love, fuelled by its sharp 'repudi-ation' of others, destabilizes the poet's isolated self: 'What should I be, I myself, / "I"? / What would it mean, this / I?,' he asks in 'Humiliation'. The love between the two creates a new kind of wholeness. In 'Bei Hennef' the condition of blessedness merges night and day, female and male: 'And at last I know my love for you is here; / I can see it all, it is whole like the twilight, / It is large, so large, I could not see it before.'

The poems connect individual relationships to epochal ideological shifts. In 'Paradise Re-entered', the sensual relationship between the man and the woman takes them 'back beyond' Christian imagery: 'back beyond good and evil / Return we. Eve dishevel / Your hair for the bliss-drenched revel / On our primal loam.' As the poem sequence continues, the meaning of having 'come through', as the title of the volume has it, resonates with this sense of having 'returned' 'back beyond' a Christian notion of good and evil. In 'Spring Morning', the following lines encompass both the isolated relationship between a man and a woman and a sense of cultural and spiritual regeneration: 'We are not our old selves any more. / I feel new and eager / To start again.' This new 'start' is connected to the 'primal loam' of 'Paradise Re-entered', an embrace of the elements and human sensuality. 'Spring Morning' continues: 'It is gorgeous to live and forget. / And to feel quite new.' 'One Woman to All Women' is written from the point of view of a woman, and this return is 'a motion human inhuman, two and one / Encompassed, and many reduced to none, / You other women'. In 'New Heaven and Earth', the new world is one of a feminized underworld:

'The unknown, strong current of life supreme / drowns me and sweeps me away and holds me down/to the sources of mystery, in the depths.'[48]

The condition of 'transcendent' 'blessedness', then, is one in which the male and the female combine, whilst maintaining their singleness. In 'Manifesto', singleness is the condition of freedom: 'It is in pure, unutterable resolvedness, / distinction of being, that one is free, / not in mixing, merging, not in similarity.' He goes on, 'one clear, burnished, isolated being, unique / and she also, pure, isolated, complete, / two of us, unutterably distinguished, and in unutterable conjunction'. For Lawrence this 'conjunction' is visually imagined in the figure of the angel, an image which captures the idea of a spiritual body, as well as that which is neither simply male nor female.

RECOGNITION IN H.D.'S MATURE POETRY

In her early poems, H.D. shares with Lawrence an interest in an aristocratic band of poetic legislators who stand above the crowd. In a number of poems, including 'Eurydice', she also repeats Lawrence's associations of women with the subterranean and men with that which is above the earth. However, she uses such imagery to challenge his claim that women are aligned with law, convention, abstraction, and *ressentiment*. H.D. is acutely aware that the modernist understanding of sexual difference is grounded in the interpretation of history and myth. She thereby puts interpretation, and the process of interpretation, at the heart of her aesthetic interests. For instance, in associating men with transcendence and women with the subterranean, both Lawrence and H.D. had a rich mythical and literary tradition on which to draw. H.D. was consistently interested in discovering and writing about pre-Christian myths. She was helped by Bryher. In August 1924, for instance, Bryher got hold of a book on Babylonia, and wrote excitedly to H.D. about it. She sent a series of notes to H.D. detailing the cult of Tammuz, meaning 'the faithful son', which was of Sumerian origin. She describes how Tammuz was worshipped in Babylonia: 'Like the Egyptians they [the Babylonians] believed that the union of heaven, the male principle with earth the female principle, gave rise to a series of forms of material things which ultimately resulted in an ordered

---

[48] *Lawrence, The Complete Poems*, 261.

world.'[49] The story of Tammuz encourages us to consider the mythical sources of male and female principles, and how matter can be fused with form to create order. As we saw in Chapter 2, both questions were major preoccupations among modernist writers, and were often considered as inseparable.

H.D.'s and Bryher's interest in the male and female principles, however, was different from that of Hulme, Babbitt, Eliot, and Lawrence, and these differences fuelled distinct understandings of history and myth. Bryher also notes other factors of Babylonian life: 'Babylonian women', she writes, 'enjoyed more privileges and security than they do now except in one or two countries of Europe.'[50] Seven days later she is still sunk 'completely and deep in Babylonia which seems to have had a better civilization and more humane laws in many respects than the civilizations of today'. In particular, this humanity is signalled by the fact that 'Women had a splendid position in Babylon.' She goes on: '[A]s a rule they lived perfectly free lives by themselves.'[51]

Bryher's letters are full of such excited interest in women's enlightened role in ancient civilization, an interest that was clearly matched by H.D. Even Freud, it seems, commented on this during his analysis of H.D. Bryher writes in 1933: 'I am a bit inclined to agree with Papa, you ARE more interested in antiquity than anything else.'[52] It is important that H.D. found in antiquity evidence of women's high social status, as she uses this as a weapon with which to battle with her male contemporaries over the construction of history.

In the 1920s and 1930s H.D.'s poems began to focus on how masculinity and femininity are controlled by a murderous battle of wills. Her poem 'Toward the Piraeus', for example, is structured in a similar way to 'Eurydice'. However, it replaces the diminutive 'earthy' Eurydice with a combative female poetic voice which challenges the addressee's attempts to 'break' her apart: 'You would have broken my wings', 'You would have snared me.' But despite this brutal fight, the wilful and aggressive male is also the source of her artistic confidence: 'but the fact that you knew / I

[49] Bryher, 'Letter to H.D.', 18–22 Aug. 1924, H.D. Correspondence, Beinecke Library, Yale University, New Haven, Conn., folder 82.
[50] Bryher, 'Letter to H.D.', 19 Aug. 1924, H.D. Correspondence, Beinecke Library, Yale University, New Haven, Conn., folder 82.
[51] Bryher, 'Letter to H.D.', 26 Aug. 1924, H.D. Correspondence, Beinecke Library, Yale University, New Haven, Conn., folder 82.
[52] Bryher, 'Letter to H.D.', 3 Mar. 1933, H.D. Correspondence, Beinecke Library, Yale University, New Haven, Conn., folder 99.

had wings, set some seal / on my bitter heart', and 'the very fact that you saw, sheltered me, claimed me, / set me apart from the rest'.[53] The 'you', by recognizing the 'I', confirms her status, which is enforced because she is female: 'If I had been a boy, / I would have worshipped your grace.' Her gender both distinguishes her and focuses the battle for mastery described in the poem. The female first person describes her 'weapon' as being 'tempered in different heat'. The poem yields victory to the male, while coyly endorsing the 'fine' and 'fiery' nature of her difference. Despite her weapon being 'lesser,' it is 'still somewhat fine-wrought / fiery-tempered, delicate, over-passionate steel'. Here, female artistic power is specifically connected to an unsentimental dynamism and will, qualities which create the recognition afforded by the hostile male.

The idea that recognition rests on a wilful assertion which takes control of the material world, is important to H.D.'s work, because it fuels her 'tributes' and gifts to Lawrence, Freud, Pound, and others. If male and female are locked into mutually dependent power dynamics in 'Eurydice' and 'Toward the Piraeus', H.D.'s poems of the 1920s and 1930s repeatedly depict women who are defined by the fact that they are chosen ones, selected by a divinity, a powerful male master, or a male poet. In these scenes, the value of women's words is secured by absorbing the power of male authority. Men adopt the position of power which in previous poems had been occupied by more abstract ideas of the elements or of a divinity. In some senses, then, these later poems are secular versions of the early focus on mythic subjects.

H.D. wrote a number of literary tributes, the prose works *Tribute to Freud* and *End to Torment*, as well as the poems which she envisaged as a sequence: 'Priest', 'The Master', 'The Dancer,' and 'The Poet'. 'Priest', part of the series of poems composed in the early 1930s about male 'masters' in H.D.'s life and a tribute to Peter Rodeck, stages a battle of wills between a female 'I' and a male 'you': 'your will, set to my will'. The 'I' demands that the 'you' recognize her 'equal' status with him, bemoaning the fact that he prefers 'a woman under the earth'. Here, she splits apart the feminine by erecting an opposition between a subterranean female principle and a transcendent female artist figure.

This split female principle is also central to her other tributes. In 'The Poet' she takes up Lawrence's thoughts on matter and transcendence,

<hr>

[53] H.D., 'Toward the Piraeus', in *Collected Poems*, 176. (First published in *Heliodora* (1924), 61–6.)

female and male, and responds. The poem is a touching memorial to Lawrence, who had died in 1930. Lawrence is addressed as a brother, who shares her untimely presence in the world: 'we, who were not of the years'. If they are both dislocated from their modern context, this distance at least allows them to see it as a stage in the epochal cycles of human history. She implies that in life Lawrence hid behind irony, and in death hides behind the shrine that has been erected in his name. While she admits that she fails to understand him, she claims to be able to touch the mysterious core of him. 'I put out a hand, touch a cold door.' Here, matter, in the form of the door, can be envisaged as both an entrance and a barrier. Two lines later, the sensuous encounter with matter has transmuted into something altogether more spiritual: 'I touch something imperishable.' In touching the mysterious thing which cannot decay, the door is here imagined as an entrance to Lawrence. A few lines later Lawrence's presence is seen in the opposite sense, as a barrier: 'why should he guard a shrine so alone'. H.D.'s ambivalent relationship to Lawrence in life, it seems, extends to her experience of him in death. For this reason, the poem implies, he still manages to intimidate her, and this keeps her waiting at his threshold. The poem has the repeated refrain 'I am almost afraid', written in relation to sitting near and looking at the windows of his shrine and speaking to him. The poem concludes with the lines 'I am almost afraid to think to myself, / *why,* / *he is there.*' The dialogical structure of the poem, in which the poet addresses 'you', ends when she finds that she must 'think to herself'. She might do this thinking in his presence in this poem, but the implication is that Lawrence's death has in some sense set her free.

If Lawrence's poems sought an imagistic union of male and female, H.D.'s fractured selves are resolved in the final lines of 'The Poet', where she is finally able to 'think to herself'. Each of her tributes seems to have had the freedom afforded by such unity partly in mind. In *End to Torment* (1958), memories of her engagement with Pound are interspersed with meditations on his incarceration. The book concludes with H.D.'s visit to the Pounds immediately after his release from St Elizabeth's. She styles this book as her gift to Pound, in return for his generosity to her in life: 'He gave, he took. He gave extravagantly. Most of the tributes to his genius, his daemon or demon, have come, so far, from men. But at least three women, whether involved in the emotional content or not, stand apart; he wanted to make them, he did not want to break them; in a sense, he identified himself with them and their art.'[54] Here, H.D. acknowledges the power dynamics which had always featured in her literary explorations of gifts and mastery: that Pound's extravagant generosity to the chosen women in his life also involved a hectoring attempt to control them and their work. At the same time, however, his recognition of her artistic status as one who 'stands apart' is central to her writing.

EGOCENTRIC HISTORY: *TRILOGY*

> I sense my own limit,
> my shark-jaws snap shut
>
> at invasion of the limitless,
> ocean-weight; infinite water
>
> can not crack me, egg in egg-shell;
> closed in, complete, immortal

I have discussed how H.D. explores the self's limits in her writing, and these ideas come to fruition in her most important poem, *Trilogy*. The 'ocean-weight' of the Second World War threatens to wipe out the 'I' of this poem, as well as the poetry she values so highly. The poem is punctuated with references to the barriers which the self erects as self-protection, but, as in these lines, they are often woefully inadequate. An egg-shell hardly seems the most powerful defence against a limitless ocean. As in previous poems, H.D.'s ocean and shell imagery translates contemporary historical realities into mythical registers. She also repeats the references to a diminutive first person pronoun, 'be firm in your own small, static, limited / orbit', positioned against an overwhelming external force, 'the shark-jaws / of outer circumstance'. As in 'Eurydice', she values the way in which small but powerful poems can resist the 'shark-jaws' of history, employing the language of the gift to emphasize this resistance: 'be indigestible, hard, ungiving'.

Yet, there are important differences in this poem. The scale is larger. The historical pressure of 'incidents' and the removal of rails for armaments are much more historically concrete. The sense of potential psychological breakdown in the face of this violence is also, therefore, more historically specific. The opening image of a room 'open to the

---

[54] H.D., *End to Torment: A Memoir of Ezra Pound by H.D.* (Manchester: Carcanet New Press, 1982), 49.

air', for instance, incorporates a disturbing idea of a revealed brain which is raw and sensitive to the impact of inescapable incendiary.

The main argument of the poem is that poets do have a significant cultural role in the context of the war. H.D. identifies the following qualities: poets have linguistic expertise, are able to understand the mythical cycles of history, have a mystical insight specifically at odds with the utilitarian values of practical life, and are 'the keepers of the secret' which 'binds all humanity'.[55] 'Tribute to the Angels' and 'The Flowering of the Rod' reveal the secret spiritual ideas of rebirth which, amid the 'rain of incendiary', will lead us forward imaginatively.

Critics have disagreed about the nature of H.D.'s redemptive vision of rebirth in *Trilogy*, although they have concurred in interpreting this vision as central to her understanding of sexual difference. Rachel Blau DuPlessis argues that the poem challenges 'authoritarian' and 'absolutist' forms of male 'revelation' by exploring epiphanies which have 'both a spiritual and a feminist dimension'.[56] Friedman argues that H.D. considers the way in which 'a world at war has lost touch with the female forms of divinity'.[57] Susan Edmunds, more recently, has argued that in fact the poem is more personal, exploring 'the conflict between [H.D.'s] pacifism and her own destructive and self-destructive tendencies'. Edmunds discusses *Trilogy* in relation to H.D.'s interest in Kleinian theories of female aggression, tracing the images of 'poisoned food, maternal violence, infantile sadism, and fears of persecution' in the poem.[58]

These readings imply that the poem is written in the interstices of the war, sexual difference, and selfhood. Edmunds's book is helpful for showing how aggression is at the core of H.D.'s understanding of female subjectivity. Yet, for Edmunds, 'the war' impacts on H.D.'s poem in terms of opposed cultural representations of motherhood during wartime: she argues that the maternal is a destructive, rather than regenerative, force in H.D.'s poem, and connects this to H.D.'s ambivalent and troubled pacifism.

In this chapter I want to suggest that *Trilogy* mounts a defence of the poet's and women's will-to-power in the context of an understanding

[55] H.D., *Trilogy* (Cheadle, Cheshire: Carcanet, 1973), 24.
[56] Rachel Blau DuPlessis, *H.D.: The Career of that Struggle* (Bloomington, Ind.: Indiana University Press, 1986), 93, 94.
[57] Susan Stanford Friedman, ' "I Go Where I Love": An Intertextual Study of H.D. and Adrienne Rich', *Signs*, 9.2 (1983), 231–2.
[58] Susan Edmunds, *Out of Line: History, Psychoanalysis, and Montage in H.D.'s Long Poems* (Cambridge: Cambridge University Press, 1994), 23, 32.

of the mythic cycles of human history. It is a modern epic in which subjectivity is tied to epochal shifts from pagan to Christian to modern beliefs. The poem insists that the 'now' is connected to a past when Christian morality did not control the way we understand women and their history. To see what remains when we strip away the Christian morality of Western culture *is* the redemptive vision that the poem celebrates. Poetry battles with science in the interpretation and construction of history. The vision of pre-Christian female resurrection with which the poem ends is a comment on this history making.

As in previous poems, there is a question mark over agency in *Trilogy*. While the bombed out houses are a feature of the cityscape in the poem, there is never any focused description of where the bombs have come from. The large-scale natural images of 'infinite oceans', 'storm-winds', etc. serve to mythologize, rather than particularize, their historical referents. Instead, the real enemy in the poem is internal, rather than external, to the state. This enemy is the ideology which insists on utilitarian values such as 'the practical issues of art' and 'new-world reconstruction', and those who claim that poets are 'useless'.[59] This utilitarian ideology is at its most sinister when it infiltrates the very language of the poem, appearing in a pseudo-scientific vocabulary.

As in previous poems, the poet's spiritual gifts are specifically set up in opposition to economics, science, and use value. H.D. enforces this dichotomy through the use of Latinate, rather than Greek-based, vocabulary. Latin phrases such as 'corrosive sublimate' are often connected to the sinister, ideologically laden 'you' of the poem. In contrast, Greek and Egyptian gods and Greek-based words stand as imagistic, concrete nouns, wedded to their referents: 'Thoth, Hermes, the stylus'. H.D. specifically defends the poet's linguistic expertise: 'if you do not understand what words say, / how can you expect to pass judgement / on what words conceal?', the poem asks.[60] The Latinate, pseudo-scientific words in this poem are severed from their referents, and this linguistic abstraction is contrasted to the solidity of Greek nouns. Words thereby say more than they mean; they also tell us about the different relationship between word and world at the very origins of civilization.

Despite the differences between science and poetry, they both comprehend the amoral, pre-Christian forces which drive human history. The poet's various skills coalesce in the ability to understand and manipulate this amoral power. The poets, like the Greek words valued so highly

---

[59] H.D., *Trilogy*, 11, 22.   [60] Ibid. 16.

in this poem, are 'indifferent to your good and evil'. Their insight into etymology and semantics importantly involves an understanding of the mythical origins of power: 'idols and their secret is stored / in man's very speech'. Poets, then, see further than others. In doing so, they are able to wield the power represented by the rod of Hermes, the god of literature and interpretation: 'Let us, however, recover the Sceptre, / the rod of power.'[61]

In this understanding of history, the utilitarian ideology which wishes to banish 'useless' poets from the new world order is merely the latest manifestation of a will to destroy poetic seers. The conflict between poetry and science is as old as the Greeks. According to Nietzsche, Greek tragedy records the struggle between art and Socratic scientism. The Euripidean drama enshrines the domination of Socratic reason over Dionysian ecstasy, a development from which world civilization has never recovered. Despite their different views of Euripides and of the role of women in the Dionysian cults, H.D. shares Nietzsche's sense that the battle between ecstasy and reason stands at the heart of Greek culture and art; and that Western culture is still playing out the consequences of this conflict. Like Nietzsche, she also believes that these intellectual impulses are grounded in opposed understandings of reason and subjectivity.

Trilogy describes the tension between brittle structures of selfhood based on reason and the loss of identity through the embrace of nature. Consider section 30 of 'The Walls Do Not Fall': 'if you surrender / sterile logic, trivial reason; / so mind dispersed, dared occult lore'. This opposition between logic and psychic dispersal continues with images of the self merging with the elements: 'lost in sea-depth, / sub-conscious ocean'. The poem creates another image of the self's absorption in a collective and elemental subconscious: 'when identity in the depth, / would merge with the best'. This section of the poem ends with the celebration of a Dionysian loss of identity: 'oneness lost, madness'.[62]

The rebirth celebrated in *Trilogy* is seen to come from a female kind of pre-Christian ecstasy, based particularly on Dionysian rituals and the spirit of Hermes. For instance, the poem opens with a reference to the 'Pythian' who 'pronounces'. The Pythian refers to the Delphic oracle belonging to Apollo. The latter was thought to have been preceded by an earth goddess whose serpent, Python, he slew before ousting the goddess. The site of the oracle used to be called 'holy Pytho', and also assisted in propagating the worship of Dionysus. The Pythian priestess

[61] H.D., *Trilogy*, 20.   [62] Ibid. 40–1.

is catapulted into a present-day London blasted by the Blitz, but the pronouncement is left blank. It is possible that H.D. envisaged her poem as itself a kind of Pythian pronouncement, spoken in the spirit of Dionysus and Hermes.

'Tribute to the Angels' and 'The Flowering of the Rod' explore in more detail this female mysticism. Both poems concentrate on the origins and meaning of the name Mary: H.D. begins with the words 'marah' and 'mar', and then considers the way in which these words 'change and alter, / mer, mere, mère, mater, Maia, Mary, // Star of the Sea, / Mother'. *Mer*, the word for sea, transmutes into *mater*, the word for 'mother', Maia, the mother of Hermes, Mary, the mother of Jesus, to the post-Christ naming of the Madonna as 'Stella Maris', or 'Star of the Sea'. These semantic shifts encompass the development of the Christian veneration of the virgin Mary out of Greek and Egyptian rituals.

This female lineage is important to H.D., because it is a mythical source of 'the counter-coin-side / of primitive terror'. Primitive terror means mainly war to H.D., a terror that continues to dominate world history. At the same time, however, the Christian version of femininity is rejected: 'she is no symbolic figure / of peace, charity, chastity, goodness, / faith, hope, reward'. *Trilogy* implies that the modern reader is well situated to see with new eyes the Venus—Aphrodite—pre-Christ vestal virgin—Mary genealogy. Her generation, she implies, is escaping the rigid Christian ideology which controls our understanding of the mythical past. The interpretation of history will, therefore, be 'different yet the same as before'.[63] Despite the semantic and intellectual shifts recorded in *Trilogy*, H.D. insists that there are some elements of what it means to be human that do not change, what she calls 'the eternal urge'.[64] She equates this urge with the will: 'the will to enjoy, the will to live', 'the will to flight, the will to achievement, / the will to rest after long flight'. While the will to life stays the same, the representation of history changes from generation to generation. H.D. reconstructs the past by writing in the character of Mary Magdalene, who pronounces: 'through my will and my power, / Mary shall be myrrh'. This takes us back to the pagan legend of Adonis, whose mother, Myrhhä, was turned into a myrrh tree as punishment by the gods. The name Myrhhä is a variation on Mary.

One of the source books for *Trilogy* was Arthur Weigall's *The Paganism in Our Christianity* (1928). The main argument of the book

---

[63] H.D., *Trilogy*, 104–5.   [64] Ibid. 119.

is that if Christianity is to survive, we must strip away the pagan legends of miraculous happenings which surround the figure of Christ. Weigall argues that we find these aspects of Christianity increasingly difficult to take, encouraging us to question Christianity as a whole. He wants to 'get back to the real and credible Jesus', because the value of Christ is 'the man Jesus, the teacher of divine truths, the supreme example of the perfect life'. We should see 'the Master's life as an example to be followed'.[65] H.D. seems to have been interested in Weigall's humanist interpretation of Christ's life stripped bare of the trappings of institutionalized Christian teachings. Her own interpretation of Mary Magdalene's life similarly embellishes the fragments of her story handed down to future generations.

Above all, then, this poem promotes a particular concept of interpretation, both of history and of reality. Like Nietzsche, H.D. questions the idea that science looks at 'reality' more accurately than poetry. In an unpublished prose work called 'The Ghost', of 1941, H.D. interrogates the self-satisfied scientific realists who claim to have a handle on 'reality': 'Were bombs reality? If so, were the realists, who theorized about the new Britain, the new England, the new World, in the thick of it?' She continues: 'Was what went on here, these ghosts in this house, tangible presences [sic], real? If so, she was one of the realities. Did they know, the realists, the reality of the ghost-world?' The ghosts referred to here are the spirits of writers. 'Shelley was real. Proust whom they now anathematized was real. The late Mrs. Woolf who walked into a river, but a few weeks ago, was real.'[66] As in 'The Gift', writing is figured as a form of self-haunting in the sense that books are ghosts which haunt and inform the representation of the present. The utilitarian knowledge denounced by H.D. cannot account for the layers of language and stories which construct our relationship to the phenomenal world. In addition, however, she queries the idea that there is a firm distinction between reality, ideas, and self. Here, the ideas that we imbibe from books are as real as the bombs which fall from the sky. She foregrounds the self in her writing because she wants to account for the highly personal significance of these ghosts. In 'The Walls Do Not Fall' H.D. describes the small but significant differences between people:

[65] Arthur Weigall, *The Paganism in our Christianity* (London: Hutchinson, 1928), 28, 86.
[66] H.D., 'The Ghost' (1941), H.D. Writings, Beinecke Library, Yale University, New Haven, Conn., folder 1004, 9 and 10.

> my mind (yours)
> has its peculiar ego-centric
> personal approach
> to the eternal realities
> and differs from every other
> in minute particulars

H.D. foregrounds the 'ego-centric' differences in the way people interpret reality. In 'The Ghost', for example, she will write with the recent death of Woolf haunting her alongside a panoply of other literary ghosts. In *Trilogy*, poetry is figured as a form of egocentric interpretation which admits the presence of these past and present ghosts.

Hugh Dowding, in a cautionary letter to H.D. in 1945, insists on the importance of a historical interpretation which foregrounds an intense engagement with the dead, but in the context of an extinction of personality: 'The importance of the past lives is that we may ration the extreme <u>unimportance</u> of the present personality which seems to us to occupy such an important place in the scheme of things. The personality is nothing: it is the individuality which inhabited all these masks of flesh which is important and eternal.' He grounds his understanding of the self in this theory of historical interpretation: 'It helps the great Ego, or true self, to separate itself from the personality.'[67]

Throughout her writing career, H.D. wrote about selfhood in a similar way. We have seen how H.D.'s writing, like that of other modernists such as Pound, Lawrence, and Eliot, is based in a critique of modernity and modernization: poetic value is situated against the crowd, the commodity, standardization, sentimentalism, moralism, and modern science. In *Trilogy* she pin-points a distinctively modern form of *ressentiment*: the utilitarian values dominant during the war attempt to stamp out poetry through the powerful and insidious gesture of contempt. Poetic value, in contrast, is connected to values seen as in conflict with the modern: the 'select little' band of poetic legislators, the gift, singularity, 'hard-edged' poetic language, the natural will, and artistic egoism. H.D. develops a feminist model of interpretation out of these opposed values, in which women from the past are blasted into the present. Eurydice, Mary Magdalene, Helen of Troy, and others are stripped of the moral-historical interpretations which have muffled our

---

[67] Hugh Dowding, Letters to H.D., 15 and 8 Nov. 1943, H.D. Correspondence, Beinecke Library, Yale University, New Haven, Conn., folder 315.

responses to them, and are reimagined for the present. Art, for H.D., is intrinsically connected to this re-energized feminist vision of mythical history. Art's radical force, however, lies in the fact that it stands outside the modern. Rather than embracing the democratic forces which seem inherently connected to modern feminism, H.D. sees her art as in conflict with them.

4

T. S. Eliot, Women, and Democracy

In this chapter I explore two points of literary departure. First there are women, whose voices echo vacuously through domestic interiors and whose bodies straddle men and give promise 'of pneumatic bliss'—women who consolidate ideas of male subjectivity in modernist writing.[1] Second, there is the idea of a politicized romanticism which 'made the revolution', the 'idea of liberty', of humanism, progress, democracy, and liberalism—ideas against which the new classicism in the arts and a new reactionary politics of authority and discipline are defined.[2]

Both departures are crucial for Anglo-American modernist writing and for Eliot's work, yet these two moments have only rarely been brought into dialogue with each other. There are connections, however, between Eliot's depiction of women and his political understanding. There have been a number of important discussions of Eliot's poetic representation of women, including Albert Gelpi's detailed analysis of the way in which 'fear of women as the stimulants of an enslaving, defiling sexual passion is obsessive' in Eliot's early poems, Carol Christ's discussion of gender and voice in his early poems, and Lyndall Gordon's biographical analyses of Eliot's poems in relation to the women in his life.[3] Michael Levenson, Michael North, and Kenneth Asher have meticulously analysed the importance of ideas of romanticism,

---

[1] T.S. Eliot, 'Whispers of Immortality', in *T. S. Eliot: The Complete Poems and Plays* (London: Faber & Faber, 1969), 52.

[2] T. E. Hulme, 'Romanticism and Classicism' (1911), in *Speculations: Essays on Humanism and the Philosophy of Art*, ed. Herbert Read (London: Routledge & Kegan Paul, 1960), 179.

[3] Albert Gelpi, 'T.S. Eliot: The Lady between the Yew Trees', in *A Coherent Splendor: The American Poetic Renaissance, 1910–50* (Cambridge: Cambridge University Press, 1987), 93; Carol Christ, 'Gender, Voice and Figuration in Eliot's Early Poetry', in R. Bush, ed., *T. S. Eliot: The Modernist in History* (Cambridge: Cambridge University Press, 1991), 23–40; Lyndall Gordon, *T.S. Eliot: An Imperfect Life* (London: Vintage, 1998).

classicism, liberalism, and democracy for modern aesthetics.[4] Yet these accounts have ignored one of the key aspects of the shift toward mass democracy and legal equality: the political and cultural position of women in British and American society.

Michael Tratner, in *Modernism and Mass Politics: Joyce, Woolf, Eliot, Yeats*, importantly discusses the relationship between Eliot's politics and his representation of women, focusing particularly on the way in which the crowd is figured as 'feminine' in *The Waste Land*. His discussion of Eliot's work is part of a wider analysis of the way in which modernist writing responds to the 'transformations of English, European, and American politics that occurred in the early twentieth century', which he characterizes as 'the shift from individualism (or liberalism) to collectivism'. He looks at Eliot's poetry in relation to what he calls the 'modern' premiss 'that individuals cannot control their own lives'. Instead, he argues, 'vast collective entities such as classes, genders, and nationalities shape the individual mind'. In this chapter I use Tratner's work as an important starting-point for understanding Eliot's poetry. However, there are also differences in our approaches. Tratner is interested primarily in the way in which the crowd is feminized in Eliot's work, how 'women are involved in mysterious ways in the emergence of anarchic mobs'.[5] This chapter considers the way in which Eliot also connects women to the principles of individualism and liberalism which were displaced by collectivism in the period. In other words, Eliot constructs women as agents and representatives of two different forms of the modern. This chapter explores the connections between these two ideas of contemporary history, and how Eliot sexualizes them. The liberal individualist target sustained its importance for Eliot. In 1932, ten years after he had declared that liberalism had 'died', we find him attacking its domination of British culture.

Eliot was always an astute, if selective, commentator on political affairs. This chapter will look at four key moments in his career when he engaged with wider political events or arguments to defend a particular understanding of literature. First, in 1916, Eliot delivered a series of

---

[4] Michael Levenson, *A Genealogy of Modernism: A Study of English Literary Doctrine 1908–1922* (Cambridge: Cambridge University Press, 1984); Michael North, *The Political Aesthetic of Yeats, Eliot and Pound* (Cambridge: Cambridge University Press, 1991); Kenneth Asher, *T. S. Eliot and Ideology* (Cambridge: Cambridge University Press, 1995).

[5] Michael Tratner, *Modernism and Mass Politics: Joyce, Woolf, Eliot, Yeats* (Stanford, Calif.: Stanford University Press, 1995), 172, 3, 171.

lectures on modern French literature in Oxford, in which he discussed the politicized categories of romanticism and classicism. The focus of interest suggested by the notes to these lectures will be used as a starting-point for considering his poems written from 1909 to 1915. Second, in the early 1920s, Eliot made a number of statements about the displacement of liberalism by new forms of authority. I will analyse these claims in relation to *Ara Voc Prec* and *The Waste Land*. Third, in 1928, Eliot's 'Commentaries' for the *Criterion* become insistently interested in the question of the 'dilution' of individual agency in modern democracy. He became worried by the spectre of a feminized tyranny of the majority. I will consider the wider effects of these claims on his writing. Fourth, I will conclude by discussing Eliot's famous attack on liberalism in *After Strange Gods* (1933), in which the triumphalism of his post-war declarations gives way to a pessimistic account of the dominance of liberal thinking. Why does Eliot claim that society is 'worm-eaten' by liberalism when, in the 1930s, as John Gray argues, 'there were few leaders of opinion who did not consider themselves critics or opponents of liberalism'?[6]

This chapter will claim that his representations of women, so central to many of his early poems, are informed by his political understanding. It will therefore look at his poems alongside his comments on liberalism and mass democracy, paying attention to the shifting meaning of these key political categories in the period.

ROMANTICISM AND CLASSICISM

In 1916, Eliot gave a series of lectures on modern French literature. No full transcript of these lectures survives, but we do have a record of Eliot's syllabus notes summarizing the content of the lectures. In these notes, he uses the terms 'romanticism' and 'classicism' to discuss French literature, mainly because this opposition had been an established feature of French literary debates since the establishment of the Third Republic with parliamentary democracy in the 1880s and the Dreyfus affair. In such debates, the 'romantic' progressive ideals of the French Revolution were pitted against a reinvigorated classicism, connected to monarchism and authority. Rousseau was seen as the most important 'romantic' philosopher, the proponent of the ideals of the French Revolution.

---

[6] John Gray, *Liberalism* (Milton Keynes: Open University Press, 1986), 36.

These ideals were challenged by a group of rather disparate contemporary intellectuals which included Charles Maurras, who organized the group called L'Action Française, as well as Auguste Barrès and George Sorel.

Eliot's lecture notes on French literature and culture repeat the terms of this French debate. He connects political democracy to ideas of cultural democratization, and adopts the broad categories of romanticism and classicism to summarize complex political and cultural debates: 'Rousseauistic' political and literary values are described as the 'purely personal expression of emotion' in literature, and are opposed to a new classicism based on a defence of '*form* and *restraint* in art, *discipline* and *authority* in religion, *centralization* in government (either as socialism or monarchy)'.[7] Eliot connects socialism and monarchism here, because within France the syndicalist, Sorel, and the monarchist, Charles Maurras, had a common enemy in the liberal politics of the Third Republic and the system of democracy: 'Both currents express revolt against the same state of affairs, and consequently tend to meet.'[8]

Despite the fact that the liberal tradition was rather different in France than in England and the United States, these lectures also, I want to suggest, map out the co-ordinates of an Anglo-American literary agenda, in which the aesthetic is accorded a crucial role in resolving the contradictions and dislocations of modern politics. Romanticism, Eliot claims, involves three things: the 'purely personal expression' in literature, excessive emotion, and excessive realism, which he describes as 'devotion to brute fact'. Modern classicism departs from all three of these things through a 'growing devotion to form'. Eliot's claims about the literary consequences of romanticism and classicism were the basis for subsequent important critical essays. In 'Tradition and the Individual Talent', for example, he discussed in more detail the need for the 'extinction' of personality and emotion in literature.

Eliot was not the only Anglo-American writer to define what he was doing by means of the French intellectual context, and to use the broad categories of romanticism and classicism to criticize democratization and to politicize the modern preoccupation with form. We have seen how T. E. Hulme set out a similar programme for modern art in his essays 'A Tory Philosophy' and 'Romanticism and Classicism'. In 'Romanticism and Classicism' he insists that politics cannot be divorced

---

[7] The lecture notes are reproduced in A. D. Moody, *Thomas Stearns Eliot, Poet* (Cambridge: Cambridge University Press, 1979), 41–9, at 44.

[8] Ibid. 45.

from arguments about aesthetics: 'I make no apology for dragging in politics here; romanticism both in England and France is associated with certain political views.'[9]

The reading list for Eliot's lecture series also includes *The Masters of Modern French Criticism*, by his Harvard tutor, Irving Babbitt. In this book Babbitt traces a similar genealogy of ideas. He connects 'Rousseauist democracy' to the democratization of culture, and advocates a return to order and impersonal standards of political, moral, and literary value.[10] Babbitt's later 1919 volume *Rousseau and Romanticism*, extends this discussion. He again characterizes Rousseau as 'the great modern romancer', and argues, like Hulme, that romanticism involves an excess of imagination without restraint. Like Hulme, Babbitt defines romanticism and classicism by contrasting different understandings of what it means to be human: he claims that 'a general nature, a core of normal experience, is affirmed by all classicists'.[11]

Hulme, Babbitt, and Eliot, then, share a sense that in the Anglo-American context, romanticism is an expression of the liberal individualism which controls nineteenth-century politics, in which the individual is seen as 'an infinite reservoir of possibilities', and progress involves setting the individual free from church and state. How, then, do women fit into such a picture? Changes in women's political position in the nineteenth century were intrinsically connected to two kinds of liberal argument: first, to a liberal egalitarianism which argued that all persons should be accorded the same moral status, and which denied the relevance to the legal and political order of differences among human beings; second, the argument that liberty involves an entitlement to take part in the collective decision making of government. The latter argument, that individual liberty involves civic participation, was foundational to John Stuart Mill's defence of women's emancipation in *The Subjection of Women* (1869), in which he argued that equal political, educational, and financial rights were central to women realizing themselves as full human beings.

The new political and literary programme of anti-liberal reaction in France and Anglo-America questioned both egalitarian and libertarian arguments for individual freedom. The focus on what Hulme sees as

---

[9] Hulme, 'Romanticism and Classicism', 115, 116.

[10] Irving Babbitt, *The Masters of Modern French Criticism* (London: Constable, 1913).

[11] Irving Babbitt, *Rousseau and Romanticism* (Boston: Houghton Mifflin, 1919), 31, 30.

a 'static' human nature refutes the idea that political participation will create enlightened subjects. The anti-liberalism of this diverse group of intellectuals also involved a critique of the legalism, or formalism, of liberal accounts of human agency and emancipation. It is this common foundation that binds together the diverse beliefs of syndicalists and monarchists. Eliot's anti-liberalism is also expressed most forcefully in his attack on legalism, formalism, or what he called 'verbalism' in 'The Perfect Critic'. Where they differed was in the kinds of authority with which they wanted to reorder the world.

When these writers attacked romanticism, democracy, and legalism, they were also partly attacking women's recent attainment of political, social, and cultural freedoms. Their attitudes to this question differed. Hulme, for example, barely mentions women in his work. Babbitt associates women with romanticism and introspection in *Rousseau and Romanticism*.[12] Eliot does not mention women in his notes to his Oxford lectures. Yet his classicism is specifically situated against a feminized decadence, in which a literary solipsism overrides his demand for the separation of word and thing. In his poems, then, he consistently connects legalism, formalism, 'verbalism', and introspection with women. In his early poems, written from 1909 to 1915, he presents us with a series of gendered dramas in which men assert control over a feminized environment. This feminized environment is 'romantic' in the sense sketched in the syllabus to the lectures: the subjectivism or egoism that Eliot associates with romanticism is connected with women; and women are agents of excess, both in terms of emotion and in terms of an unreflective physicality. Above all, women are key signs of the modern moment in Eliot's poems and essays, a modern moment severed from a meaningful history or tradition.

BOURGEOIS WOMEN IN ELIOT'S EARLY POEMS

Individual alienation from the political, legal, or social sphere is often a starting-point for European and Anglo-American modernist writing, and it is central to Eliot's first poetic achievements. What is notable is that Eliot sexualizes both the estrangement and fragmentation which is central to his poetry and the idea of cultural power. In 'The Love Song

---

[12] Ibid. 22.

of J. Alfred Prufrock', which was originally called 'Prufrock Among the Women', the opening simile, 'When the evening is spread out against the sky / Like a patient etherised upon a table', is powerful because the image of a helpless and unconscious individual whose fate lies in the hands of a scientist, or surgeon, is one which is central to the poem as a whole. Prufrock, like the patient, is controlled by, and estranged from, the exact, scientific judgements of others, and struggles to free himself from an etherized or drugged existence. Prufrock's awakening or beginning will happen by spitting out the formulated phrases of his cultural milieu, by awakening from the sleepy, sensual afternoons, by risking his overwhelming question.

By implication, he is also struggling to awaken and to differentiate himself from a vacuous bourgeois society. This is a paranoid vision of estrangement, of what Pound called being 'out of key' with his time, which is common in modernist writing. Yet, where Joyce and Kafka depict forms of civic alienation related to law, work, commodification, religion, or family, Eliot sees alienation as a gendered issue: it is women who fix Prufrock in formulated phrases, whose sensual perfume makes him digress, whose smooth fingers induce a soporific inaction, who insist that he has misunderstood their meaning. By focusing on the relationship between the sexes, Eliot seems to want to explain estrangement in this poem, to identify the cause of alienation, with the cultural and sexual power of bourgeois women.

A similar dynamic of female cultural power and male estrangement controls 'Portrait of a Lady', in which the poet shrinks away from the lady's claim upon his friendship, recoiling from her suggestion that their relationship should involve a meaningful form of recognition. This withdrawal is connected to the idea that her demands, like her words and her gestures, are insincere, as they parrot received opinions about friendship, rather than recognizing the poet's individuality. Eliot is here being ironic about the disjunction between the lady's social ideas of friendship, 'all our friends, / They all were sure our feelings would relate', and the false note of the poet's solipsistic reality. For their relationship to work, the poet would have to perform a rather absurd social personality. Notwithstanding the 'hammering' invocation of their 'friendship', a word repeated ten times in the poem, the poet and the hostess remain in the dark when it comes to understanding each other. The poet's withdrawal into a tentative, incomplete self-possession and the lady's insistence on their friendship produce each other: her words force him to shrink into himself; and the more he recoils, the more she invokes the idea of friendship which they have failed to attain.

In both poems, bourgeois women are depicted as being outside a cultural language that they use and abuse. In 'Tradition and the Individual Talent', Eliot distinguishes between the poet, who has 'absorbed' the texts and beliefs of a tradition, and the individual, who sees knowledge as a 'useful' tool for examinations and the drawing-room. The drawing-rooms of Eliot's early poems are, of course, largely populated by bourgeois women who do precisely that, 'who come and go/talking of Michelangelo'. The hostess in 'Portrait of a Lady' also talks 'of', rather than through, friendship. Both are poetic images of humans who use words as symbols of cultivation or intimacy, rather than as meaningful forms of communication or recognition. Their words thereby remain external to their ostensible referent, a painting by Michelangelo or the particular friend of the poem, and rebound back onto the speaker, creating a linguistic and emotional egotism. This modern egotism, for Eliot, constitutes a particularly dangerous kind of fragmentation, in which the stability of language itself is threatened.

Eliot saw this individualistic use of language as a key feature of contemporary history. In 'The Perfect Critic' (1917), he claims that 'words have changed their meanings. What they have lost is definite, and what they have gained is indefinite.'[13] He describes indefinite language, in which words have become severed from their objects, as a 'verbalism', or 'abstraction'. The category of abstraction is central both to Eliot's critical vocabulary and to his understanding of history and tradition. The 'abstraction' and 'verbalism' he attacks in 'The Perfect Critic' are dangerous features of a contemporary 'feminine' culture. In a letter to Pound of 1915, he bemoans the 'monopolisation of literature by women', although he suggests that it is 'imprudent' to admit it.[14] In his essays he is less direct, but the impulse to characterize contemporary culture as feminine is similar. In 'Reflections on *Vers Libre*' (1917), for example, he paints a picture of contemporary cultural exchange. The essay begins with a lady's pronouncements on modern poetry: she claims that she can no 'longer read any verse but *vers libre*'. This declaration is a sign of the modern moment:

---

[13] T. S. Eliot, 'The Perfect Critic', in Frank Kermode, ed., *Selected Prose of T. S. Eliot* (London: Faber & Faber, 1975), 55.

[14] T. S. Eliot, Letter to Ezra Pound, 15 Apr. 1915, in Valerie Eliot, ed., *The Letters of T. S. Eliot, i: 1898–1922* (San Diego: Harcourt Brace Jovanich, 1988), 96.

vers libre is *the* modern verse form; and the lady is modern because
of her susceptibility to fashion. Her interest in *vers libre* is 'abstract'
because she is fascinated by its novelty and fashionableness, not by
the thing itself. To understand the thing itself, the essay argues,
she would need to know about the history of poetry. Without this
knowledge, the woman is interested in novelty for the sake of novelty,
and freedom for the sake of freedom. Just as the romantics believe
in the illusion of free will, liberals believe in the illusory freedoms of
the individual, so the freedom of *vers libre* is deceptive. When Eliot
insists that 'there is no freedom in art', it is partly because he believes
more generally that freedom is a social, rather than an individual,
category.[15]

If Eliot is sceptical about a feminine abstraction, however, he is
equally critical of the unreflective realism, or 'devotion to brute fact',
of romanticism, as he describes it in his 'Extension Lectures'. His early
texts often focus on the relationship between physical formlessness and
literary form, and he turns repeatedly to a depiction of the relationship
between men and women to dramatize this relationship. Eliot's focus
on women's sexual invasiveness is perhaps most startlingly illustrated in
his 1915 prose piece 'Hysteria', in which an overwhelmingly physical
femaleness vies with the writer's desire for autonomy: 'I was drawn in by
short gasps, inhaled at each momentary recovery, lost finally in the dark
caverns of her throat, bruised by the ripple of unseen muscles.' The text
ends: 'I decided that if the shaking of her breasts could be stopped, some
of the fragments of the afternoon might be collected, and I concentrated
my attention with careful subtlety to this end.'[16] This is close to bawdy
farce, a tone central to the poems later published in *Ara Vos Prec*, rather
than to the more tasteful ironies dominant in the rest of *Prufrock and
Other Observations*. The writing bluntly dramatizes the movement of
dissociation, the shift from a moment of female engulfment to the
writer's fastidious withdrawal. The suggestive familiarity of the terms
of this dissociation are revealing. Here, rather than the textual and
political fragments of *The Waste Land*, it is the afternoon, or perhaps
the man's mind, which is in fragments, and which is 'collected' through
'concentration', 'attention', and 'careful subtlety'.

Eliot has transposed a language of fragmentation and formal organization, implicit in the shift from erratic to regular prosody in 'The

15   T. S. Eliot, 'Reflections on *Vers Libre*', in Kermode, ed., *Selected Prose*, 31, 32.
16   T. S. Eliot, 'Hysteria', in *Complete Poems and Plays*, 32.

Love Song of J. Alfred Prufrock' and present in the ideas of discord and musical arrangement in 'Portrait of a Lady', on to a moment of physical exchange between a man and a woman. In all three texts, the man, whether Prufrock, the poet, or the writer, withdraws in the face of the woman's physical or intellectual demands. In all three texts this withdrawal allows space for poetic reflexivity, particularly on the nature of poetic form.

DEMOCRATIZED VOICES: *ARA VOS PREC* AND *THE WASTE LAND*

The individualized dramas of Eliot's early poems are displaced by the more collective concerns of *The Waste Land*, with its images of the crowd on London Bridge and the revolutionary hordes over distant mountains. This shift from a concern with a romantic solipsism classed as feminine to an interest in wider historical forces is mirrored in his essays. In the early 1920s, he triumphantly announced, on a number of occasions, that liberal individualism was dying. Instead, he became increasingly concerned with the status of art in the context of the new era of mass democracy.

Many commentators have discussed the fact that Eliot both represents the feminized working classes in *The Waste Land* and is disdainful of them. As Peter Nicholls puts it, '[T]he practice of textual imitation always uses the cultural echo to reveal a vacancy within the modern event to which it is ironically applied.' The poem, then, both engages with the democratic forces unleashed after the First World War, and relies on static models of cultural and political authority to keep those forces in place. As Nicholls goes on to argue, the poem relies on a 'timeless' moral perspective to order or ironize the modern scenes: Eliot's 'version of the "mythic method" thus tends to produce a high degree of local specificity at the level of tone and idiom, while securing a parallel abstractness in its referents'. In Nicholls's logic, then, the separation of cultural echo and localized modern event produces precisely the kind of abstraction that Eliot attacks in 'The Perfect Critic' and 'Reflections on *Vers Libre*'. The poem is 'ambivalent', because the literary and mythical allusions remain external to the contemporary moments with which they are supposed to connect. Instead, as Nicholls puts it, 'Nothing can redeem the blight of sexuality which afflicts the poem, and the equation of modernity with figures of an unregenerate femininity chokes any kind of narrative or dialectical movement.'[17] In essay after essay, Eliot asks how pattern, form, structure, and order can be generated out of the 'chaotic, irregular, fragmentary' experience of the ordinary man, a 'mass' of perceptions and 'the chaos of contemporary history'.[18] Nicholls suggests here that Eliot imposes literary and mythical allusions on the chaos of contemporary history in *The Waste Land*, rather than connecting the past and the present.

In this section I want to explore this ambivalence in more detail. Eliot's response to post-war mass democracy was contradictory. On the one hand, during the war he embraced the historical forces which were destabilizing a complacent liberal culture. On the other hand, he was troubled by the cultural and political consequences of these democratic forces.

In the first of his 'Reflections on Contemporary Poetry', published in the *Egoist* in 1917, Eliot provides a suggestive insight into the new poems he was writing in 1917, which were published in *Ara Vos Prec* in 1919. He describes how modern poetry departs from a liberal humanist literary sensibility: 'One of the ways in which contemporary verse has tried to escape the rhetorical, the abstract, the moralizing, to recover (for that is its purpose) the accents of direct speech, is to concentrate its attention upon the trivial or accidental or commonplace objects.'[19] Eliot argues that contemporary verse escapes abstraction and moralism by attending to the particularity of the contemporary object, in all its accidental, commonplace dimensions. He also states that contemporary verse escapes abstraction by capturing the accents of direct speech. The corollary of attending to the particularity of the object is a recognition of the particularity of people, a particularity he locates in voice. He seems to be saying that direct speech, then, will involve both an object-centred language and the cadences of contemporary, class, and gender-specific voices.

Eliot's early poems are dependent on the farcical distance between linguistic registers. In 'The Love Song of J. Alfred Prufrock', the prosaic, conversational register of women's voices is contrasted to the literary register of Prufrock's imagination. Eliot continued to focus on the significance of voices throughout the 1910s, but their meaning was to

---

[17] Peter Nicholls, *Modernisms: A Literary Guide* (Basingstoke: Macmillan, 1995), 257, 258.

[18] T. S. Eliot, 'The Metaphysical Poets', 'The Perfect Critic', 'Ulysses, Order and Myth', in Kermode, ed., *Selected Prose*, 64, 58, 177.

[19] T. S. Eliot, 'Reflections on Contemporary Poetry', *Egoist* (1917).

change. In the early poems, 'The Love Song of J. Alfred Prufrock', 'Portrait of a Lady', 'Mr Apollinax', and 'Cousin Nancy', the cadences and sentiments of pretentious Boston drawing-rooms are mocked by means of a clash of linguistic registers. As Eliot's work developed, however, he became interested in incorporating a much wider range of human voices into his poems, in removing the quotation marks which frame these voices, and in thereby making these voices integral to the language of the poem.

This difference corresponds to a radical change of register, form, and direction of satire in Eliot's new poems of 1917. His poetic characters, Burbank, Sweeney, and Pipit, are vehicles for basic rhymes and scatological detail, and the satire shifts from the vacuity of polite Boston chit-chat to the 'broadbottomed', 'straddled' bodies of sensual individuals, from the drawing-room to the boarding-house, from the literary dressing up of empty emotions to the attempt to capture working-class idioms. In 'Sweeney Erect', for instance, Eliot includes the idiomatic, 'Mrs Turner intimates/It does the house no sort of good', and in 'A Cooking Egg', he rhymes 'Sir Philip Sidney' with 'heroes of that kidney'.

There is a tastelessness to this sequence of poems which flouts the diction that Eliot had ironized in earlier poems. He connects taste to the vacuous feminine culture which he seeks to transcend. In 'Sweeney Erect', for instance, Eliot flouts refinement by depicting a vulgar female body, and by ridiculing a female sense of propriety. It is a female body which is caught in convulsive seizures, which could be the result of either epilepsy or the sexual act. And it is women who are ridiculed for characterizing this violent confusion of images as a question of taste:

> The ladies of the corridor
> Find themselves involved, disgraced,
> Call witness to their principles
> And deprecate the lack of taste.

The female body is the site of a repulsive violence, and women lack a meaningful moral register by which to understand this violence. Their reversion to principles which are farcically inadequate signals both their inability to deal with the particularity of the situation and the redundancy of their moral principles. In addition, however, Eliot smuggles in a reflexive reference to his poem's 'lack of taste', signalling that the shocked audience for his poem will be similar to the disgraced witnesses of Sweeney's erection.

Eliot described himself as 'intensely serious' about these poems, claiming that 'Sweeney Among the Nightingales' and 'Burbank' were 'among the best' that he had ever done.[20] Writing to his brother in 1920, he was worried, however, that his mother would be shocked by 'Sweeney Erect'. Yet at some level the poem's vulgarity is obviously designed to shock a refined, feminine, moral literary sensibility. Other modernist and avant-garde writers also violated good taste by means of sexually explicit detail and non-poetic registers. When Laforgue compares the sun to a 'gobbet of pub-spit' in his late poem 'L'hiver qui vient', for instance, he uses the simile ironically to undermine a particular idea of poetic language.[21] Avant-garde writers such as Apollinaire and Marinetti took such shock tactics to new levels, and specifically saw their tastelessness as a challenge to the dominant bourgeois, sentimental culture. Eliot's tastelessness participates in this departure from the sentimental artistic past.

Eliot's turn to 'direct speech' also involves an idiomatic shift. The attempt to capture the linguistic dimensions of class, racial, and gender-inflected idioms is important for other modernist writers such as Gertrude Stein and James Joyce. Eliot's own concern with voice in the poems of this period and *The Waste Land* forms part of this wider interest. This helps explain the language and structure of both the poems in *Ara Vos Prec* and *The Waste Land*, particularly the first draft of the latter, which collects together fragmented voices in a way which gestures towards the component parts of a wider, encompassing historical totality. Eliot adopts a rather surprising intellectual position here. He seems to be saying that the poetic revolt against bourgeois culture will produce a democratization of voice in modernist poetry, a kind of linguistic inclusiveness.

In an essay on Marie Lloyd, in 1923, Eliot, in discussing her achievements as a music-hall actress, suggests how we might read the meanings he attaches to voices in *The Waste Land*. He uses the same logic and terms of his argument about contemporary poetry to discuss class and cultural distinctions in England. Marie Lloyd was able to embody and express the moral virtues of the working class through exactly the same mechanisms as he had identified in his description of the new poetic language: through her 'tone of voice' and by using

---

[20] T. S. Eliot, Letter to Henry Eliot, 15 Feb. 1920, in V. Eliot, ed., *Letters of T. S. Eliot*, 363.

[21] Jules Laforgue, 'L'hiver qui vient', in *Selected Poems*, trans. Graham Dunstan Martin (Harmondsworth: Penguin Books, 1998), 218.

particular objects as signifiers of class, age, and gender. Her success was due to the fact that she understood and sympathized with the working class, and was recognized by them. For Eliot, this mutual recognition amounts to a form of embodied, cultural morality. In contrast, Eliot attacks the middle class, whom he regards as the political force of democratization in England, and who are gradually inheriting cultural and political authority, because they lack both a distinct morality and a particular form of cultural expression.

Marie Lloyd is an important symbol of Englishness and a crucial component of the English nation in this review. Any attempt to represent the totality of the English nation would need to incorporate her voice, as *The Waste Land* might be seen to do. Yet, this idea of embodiment is dependent on the maintenance of a steady sense of class distinctions. Class mobility, in the form of Bradford millionaires and young house office clerks, creates a confusion and dislocation in which an embodied, aestheticized morality is impossible.

There are two contradictory impulses controlling *The Waste Land*, one which wants to incorporate the modern voices which constitute contemporary history, and another which wants to maintain rigid class and gender hierarchies. This is because there are two objects of attack in this poem: the tasteful poetic language of a liberal feminized culture and the mass politics of the crowd unleashed after the war. The contemporary voices, however, are peculiarly hollowed out and morally bankrupt, and the sources of aesthetic value are located firmly in the past. Is the language of the poem, then, controlled by the very voices that Eliot believes to be morally and culturally vacuous? And if so, have the democratic masses destroyed the art object which sought to contain them? This was the question with which Eliot began to engage after the publication of *The Waste Land* in 1922.

'AUTHORITY NOT DEMOCRACY': ELIOT'S ESSAYS OF THE 1920S

In Eliot's commentaries for the *Criterion* through the early 1920s, he often addresses the consequences of modern democracy. Eliot knowingly created a poetic combination of historical specificity and hierarchical notions of value. For example, he declared in a number of articles that the liberal or humanitarian values which inform the work of a writer such as George Bernard Shaw are dying. Instead, a new set of values, 'of authority not democracy, of dogmatism not tolerance, of the extremity and never the mean', are taking their place.[22]

In 1924 Eliot reviewed T. E. Hulme's posthumously published book, *Speculations*. He used the occasion to declare that Hulme's philosophy is the harbinger of a new set of values. In this review, Eliot polemically reiterates the dichotomies of the debate he had discussed in his lectures on modern French literature, and states that 'Hulme is Classical, reactionary, and revolutionary; he is the antipodes of the eclectic, tolerant, and democratic mind of the last century.' Notwithstanding the fact that Hulme had died in the war in 1917, and that Eliot is reviewing his work retrospectively, it is significant that he wants to define Hulme's modern classicism in relation to a historical moment which has already been politically displaced, the 'democratic mind of the last century'. This is particularly relevant because Eliot uses this retrospective idea of democracy as a foundation for a definition of modern art and culture. He goes on to define the democratic 'mind' in terms of its dislocation from authority and belief: 'We say democracy advisedly: that meanness of spirit, that egotism of motive, that incapacity for surrender or allegiance to something outside oneself, which is a frequent symptom of the soul of man under democracy.' This loose definition allows Eliot to move quickly from a discussion of political democracy to a statement about cultural and artistic democratization, arguing that the absence of authority means that art is rejected in favour of a debased culture: '[The] aversion for the work of art, [the] preference for the derivative, the marginal, is an aspect of the modern democracy of culture.'[23]

Eliot moves quickly from the democratic mind of the last century, to a general description of this democratic mind, to a comment about the modern democracy of culture. The phrase 'modern democracy of culture' could refer to the cultural ideas of the last century or to those of the post-war period, but it is important that, while politically these two historical moments are different, Eliot fuses them together. Eliot's rhetorical slip from the past to the present allows him to construct a particular definition of modern art. Art is defined through its connection to authority, and a democratized culture is identified with notions of the self in which the individual ego is consolidated at the expense of authority. His criticism of 'the incapacity for surrender or allegiance to something outside oneself' seems to attack classically liberal notions

[22] T. S. Eliot, 'A Commentary', *Criterion*, 3.9 (1924), 4.
[23] T. S. Eliot, 'A Commentary', *Criterion*, 2.7 (1924), 231, 235.

of the self, as a grounded entity which exists prior to articulated and historically specific ends. It is this kind of liberal, democratic, individual subject who focuses Eliot's attacks on democracy in this period.

Eliot's attacks on democracy were to become increasingly insistent through the 1920s, but his focus on the individual was to shift dramatically as he succeeded in bringing into focus the mass democracy he studiously side-steps in his review of Hulme. It is not 'the incapacity for surrender or allegiance to something outside oneself' which is the problem in the context of mass democracy. Instead, he begins to be worried by two rather different things: first, that individuals surrender themselves to things outside themselves far too easily, and to the wrong forms of authority; and second, that, obeying a sinister kind of dialectical logic for Eliot, the masses will actually start to occupy the position of external authority which controls the individual. Not only will Marie Lloyd's embodied, aestheticized morality be destabilized by this arbitrary allegiance, but Eliot's own cultural position will start to look rather tenuous. The terms of his critique of democracy, then, become complicated, as Eliot wants to continue to criticize liberal definitions of the subject, whilst also attacking mass democracy.

His 1928 essay 'The Humanism of Irving Babbitt', which was a review of Babbitt's 1924 book *Democracy and Leadership*, is an important moment in Eliot's attempt to bring together these two different impulses. He criticizes Babbitt for reverting to a liberal idea of the individual subject, in order to criticize mass democracy. Eliot agrees with Babbitt that the political shift towards democracy involves the weakening of the outer restraints of political and class authority.[24] Babbitt is critical of mass democracy on the grounds that it creates a tyranny of the majority. As he puts it: 'For the conscience that is felt as a still small voice and that is the basis of real justice, we have substituted a social conscience that operates rather through a megaphone.'[25] Babbitt's humanistic philosophy is based on the idea of a secular ethical will which he identifies with a vigorously individualist conception of justice, right action, and the work ethic.

Eliot agrees with Babbitt's criticisms of the tyrannical aspects of mass democracy, but disagrees with Babbitt's humanism, which Eliot argues is an abstraction which dislocates subjects from 'their contexts of race,

---

[24] T. S. Eliot, 'The Humanism of Irving Babbitt', in Kermode, ed., *Selected Prose*, 280.
[25] Irving Babbitt, *Democracy and Leadership* (Boston: Houghton Mifflin, 1924), 200.

place, and time'. Instead, Eliot argues that the ethical will cannot be grounded in the self, and that only religion can provide the authority and structure for ethical belief. He criticizes Babbitt's attempt to separate humanism from religion, arguing that humanism flourishes only in a religious context. Without it, Babbitt's ethical will is itself formalistic, without content. Only religion and the church can create the restraint that leads to social harmony. Eliot claims that Babbitt misunderstands religious belief by seeing it as something which is external to the individual, as that which has to be enforced as though 'by policemen'.[26] He argues that this sharp distinction between inner and outer belief is untenable: religious belief, if it is experienced profoundly, has already become a form of 'inner control'. For Eliot the religious individual is so saturated in the beliefs of the church that the boundary between individual belief and religious authority dissolves.

Eliot's critique of his old tutor, Babbitt, is important, because it captures his ongoing sense of the limitations of a self-grounded moral consciousness, but within the new context of an engagement with the mass democracy of the megaphone. Yet it was hard not to revert to liberal categories of the self in the context of the realities of mass politics in the 1920s and 1930s, and at times we find Eliot doing precisely this. In his 'Commentary' for April 1931, for instance, he criticizes democracy for the way in which it allows for the invasion of privacy: 'The extreme of democracy—which we have almost reached—promises greater and greater interference with private liberty.... In complete democracy, everyone in theory governs everyone else, as a kind of compensation for not being allowed to govern himself.'[27]

This fragile balance between a defence of private liberty in the context of the invasions of mass democracy and an attack on liberal categories of the individual subject is also integral to his comments about women in this period. In his review of 'The Literature of Fascism', published in December 1928, the same year in which Eliot announced that he was a 'classicist in literature, royalist in politics, and anglo-catholic in religion', he insists that British democracy has been destroyed by mass enfranchisement, has been 'watered down to nothing', as he puts it: 'With every vote added, the value of every vote diminishes.'[28] Eliot responds to specific political events here. A large number of votes had

---

[26] Eliot, 'Humanism of Irving Babbitt', 281.
[27] T. S. Eliot, 'A Commentary', *Criterion*, 8.32 (1931), 379.
[28] T. S. Eliot, 'The Literature of Fascism', *Criterion*, 8.31 (1928), 281.

recently been added to the British electorate through the Representation of the People Act of 1928. The Act dramatically shifted the gender balance of the electorate by extending the franchise from women over 30 to women over 21, and removed the remaining property qualifications of the 1918 Act. For the first time, women became the majority of the electorate, comprising '52.7 percent of the potential voters'.[29]

In this review, Eliot, in his defence of the 'idea of Democracy', as he puts it, against a 'watered-down democracy', is partly attacking women's entrance into the political process: 'A real democracy is always a restricted democracy, and can only flourish with some limitation on hereditary rights and responsibilities.'[30] He criticizes the language of individual rights, which was central to liberal understandings of the individual's relationship to the state and to both liberal and conservative feminist arguments for equality in the 1920s: '[F]rom the moment when suffrage is conceived as a *right* instead of as a privilege and a duty and a responsibility, we are on the way merely to government by an invisible oligarchy instead of government by a visible one.'[31] For Eliot, liberalism prioritizes individual rights over the collective good, the law over ethical life, the framework of democracy over the intellectual content of the democratic citizen. As he goes on to argue, 'The modern question as popularly put is: "democracy is dead; what is to replace it?" whereas it should be: "the frame of democracy has been destroyed: how can we, out of the materials at hand, build a new structure in which democracy can live?" '[32]

Three years later, Eliot returned to this question, and explicitly injected it with the gender categories which lie just beneath the surface in 1928. In his *Criterion* commentary of January 1931 he returns to the question he had posed in December 1928 by mocking the insistence that women's full participation in the democratic process is essential to a modern democracy. *The Times* has put forward 'the irresistible contention that the framework of democracy would not be complete

---

[29] Harold L. Smith, *The British Women's Suffrage Campaign, 1866–1928* (London: Longman, 1998), 81.

[30] Eliot, 'Literature of Fascism', 287.

[31] The feminist groups agitating for equal franchise extended across the political spectrum in the 1920s. It included the Conservative Party's women's organization and Labour Party women, as well as the 'National Union of Societies for Equal Citizenship' run by Eleanor Rathbone, Lady Rhondda's 'Six Point Group' and Lady Astor's 'Consultative Committee for Women's Organisations': Eliot, 'Literature of Fascism', 287.

[32] Eliot, 'Literature of Fascism', 287.

without—without what?—without the young women of twenty-one'. He goes on to ask, 'what, now that this tasteful piece of joinery, the "framework of democracy", is complete, is the character of the canvas to be found within it?'[33] Eliot's language is revealing here. Not only is it the case that democracy has been destroyed because of women's inclusion in its framework, but he also links together ideas of democracy, women, and taste. We seem here to have returned to the logic animating 'Sweeney Erect', in which democratization, women, and a tasteful, empty bourgeois culture produce each other. As in his poems, then, women represent both a particularly potent symbol of democratization in these discussions, as well as being the embodiments of an enfranchised, but disconnected citizenry.

Eliot's rhetorical slips, in which cause and effect become confused, have dangerous intellectual and political consequences. There is a continuity between his poetic depictions of estrangement and his later critique of ideas of modern citizenship. Eliot suggests that the focus on the formal mechanisms of democracy and legal equality is achieved at the expense of real political debate, and leaves a dangerous political vacuum in which Fascist and Communist forms of authority have a misplaced appeal. He also argues, however, that the belief in the individual as a bearer of rights and in the political process as a kind of lawcourt has created a legalization of politics. Legalism corresponds to a kind of verbalism in these discussions: both create a discursive freedom which masks or distorts the way in which individuals are estranged from politics and culture. Eliot's argument that there has been a dangerous shift of emphasis in understandings of democracy, from seeing the vote as a duty to seeing the vote as a right, also mimics the logic of his earlier critiques of the democratization of culture. The 'egotism of motive' of the soul of man under democracy is structurally similar to that of the individual who sees his or her relation to the political process as one of rights rather than duties. But, if, returning to the questions I posed at the start of this chapter, and, as I hope I have shown, the categories of democracy and gender difference do serve to define each other in Eliot's work, then this conceptual interdependence functions to empty out the content of both categories. Both the 'feminine' and the democratic represent a linguistic, cultural, and political formalism. Eliot uses concrete images and instances of the former to visualize these political factors.

[33] T. S. Eliot, 'A Commentary', *Criterion*, 10.39 (1931), 307.

AGAINST LIBERALISM: AFTER STRANGE GODS

Eliot's notorious critique of a society 'worm-eaten by liberalism', in his 1932 lectures, published as *After Strange Gods* in 1933, attempts to find stability in an idea of tradition connected to the land. These lectures describe a number of threats to this vision of stability: economic determinism, 'free-thinking Jews', 'extreme individualism in views', Irving Babbitt's cultural cosmopolitanism, a writer's separation from tradition, the replacement of religious morality with personality, and the religious and literary 'liberalism' which has undermined religious and literary authority. Eliot envisages the land as a fusion of time and space, and opposes the historical forces which have dislocated the individual from his or her racial community, and the intellectual liberalism which has dislocated the individual from religious and literary authority. His declaration that society needs to 're-establish a vital connexion between the individual and the race', then, offers a racialized solution to what he sees as the liberal individualism of modern society.[34]

Eliot's claim that the struggle of his time is 'against liberalism' repeats the terms of much political polemic in Britain in the early 1930s. After the 1929 Wall Street Crash, the global effects of which were quickly apparent, thinkers from both the socialist and the emerging fascist wings of British politics argued, in different ways, that a liberal political agenda was unable to deal with the severe political problems facing the country: parliamentary democracy was seen as a slow, cumbersome, and conservative political mechanism; and the liberal, *laissez-faire* economic strategy of Ramsay MacDonald's government was seen as inadequate in the face of the world-wide economic slump.

The category of democracy is often pulled in two directions in political theory in this period: as both a political system in crisis and the term whereby to call this system to account. Eliot's toxic mixture of perceived threats in *After Strange Gods* is energized by this deeply oppositional and increasingly violent political debate. In these lectures, he is primarily interested in the consequences of religious and literary, rather than political and economic, liberalism. However, he incorporates politically charged objects of attack into his argument: that mass democracy is a system which lacks a cohesive authoritative centre and thereby creates

[34] T. S. Eliot, *After Strange Gods: A Primer of Modern Heresy* (New York: Harcourt, Brace and Co., 1959), 12, 18, 34, 57, 22, 53.

radically dislocated and atomized individuals; that free-thinking Jews are the cause of religious disunity; and that cultural cosmopolitanism is a threat to community. He specifically dislodges these things from what he calls the 'god' of economic determinism, and attempts thereby to identify these modern realities as causes of 'heresy'.

As we have seen, Eliot's 1932 lectures were the culmination of a sustained engagement with the consequences of liberalism and mass democracy. As in previous essays and poems, he concretizes his wider political claims about 'liberalism, progress and modern civilisation' by means of sexualized images. In the second lecture, Eliot analyses three short stories: *Bliss* by Katherine Mansfield, *The Shadow in the Rose Garden* by D. H. Lawrence, and *The Dead* by James Joyce, all of which deal with the issue of 'disillusionment'. He uses these stories to illustrate his wider argument about the relationship between tradition and individualism, terms which he injects with a moral and religious register by renaming them as orthodoxy and heresy. Whilst Lawrence is 'an almost perfect example of the heretic' and Joyce is 'ethically orthodox', Mansfield, in contrast to both writers, is described as 'feminine'.[35] This third term is oddly out of place in Eliot's argument, as nothing has prepared us for its inclusion. Mansfield's story drops out of the discussion as it proceeds, and Eliot ties up his argument where he began, with a contrast of Lawrence's heresy and Joyce's orthodoxy.

So what is Mansfield's 'feminine' writing doing in his lecture in the first place? What purpose does her writing serve? Eliot claims that it is interesting to think about these three texts together because of the 'differences in moral implication'. In *Bliss*, according to Eliot, the 'moral implication is negligible', because the story restricts its focus to the 'wife's feeling'. In contrast to this 'limited' aesthetic, a word Eliot uses twice in his discussion of Mansfield's story, Lawrence's and Joyce's stories have moral significance, because they function on both an emotional and an intellectual level. Despite the fact that Eliot criticizes Lawrence's story as an example of literary heresy, then, it nevertheless offers us a 'great deal more than' Mansfield's story.

The feminine is mentioned very briefly in this text, yet it functions as a crucial conceptual foundation for moral and, by implication, literary value. Eight pages later, Eliot explicitly makes this connection: without moral 'struggle', he argues, art will be 'inoffensive', and characters will be 'vaporous'. In the third lecture, in the context of another discussion

---

[35] Eliot, *After Strange Gods*, 41.

of Lawrence's writing, Eliot states that the 'insensibility to ordinary social morality' is so alien to his mind that he is 'completely baffled by it as a monstrosity'. It is Mansfield's text, not Lawrence's, which ultimately lacks a social morality, and which is an expression of the 'liberalism, progress and modern civilisation' that both Lawrence and Eliot criticize.[36]

The ideas of liberalism, progress, and modern civilization come into focus in the concrete particularity of Mansfield's 'feminine' writing. Yet Eliot wants to claim that her writing both embodies these wider political and historical forces and is also confined to a limited focus on feeling. If her writing does represent these wider forces, then within the terms of his own logic it can do so only negatively, in the sense that it lacks an intellectual register, rather than in the sense that it positively incorporates a liberal or progressive agenda. If we look at the argument more carefully, we can see that this is exactly what Eliot means. Her writing is an example of liberalism and progress, because her limited writing is disconnected from and unconscious of the historical and political forces which nevertheless control its terms of reference and its aesthetic ambition.

This chapter has considered Eliot's depiction of women in relation to his shifting attitude to liberalism and mass democracy from 1909 to 1932. As we have seen, he announced that liberalism was dying, and that new kinds of aesthetic authority would take its place in 1916 and 1924. Yet, he resurrected the spectre of a culture dominated by liberal values in 1932, just when liberalism seemed to be at its most vulnerable. While from 1909 to 1916 he connects women with a romantic introspection in which the individual is privileged over cultural and political authority, in 1928 he sees their participation in political affairs as a 'dilution' of democracy. Throughout his writing, he believes in the need for the cultural authority of the poetic legislator, to control a debased modernity controlled by democratic mimesis and romantic introspection.

[36] Ibid. 38, 46.

5

Mina Loy: Psycho-Democracy

When Mina Loy's first four 'Love Songs' appeared in the first volume of the New York magazine *Others* in 1915, their sexually explicit subject-matter, Futurist content, explosive wit, and use of free verse were a fitting beginning to a new magazine devoted to 'the new verse'. In the November 1915 issue, the magazine's editor, Alfred Kreymborg, in a foreword, quotes from J. B. Kerfoot, who claims that the new poetry entails a new political sensibility: 'By the way, the new poetry *is* revolutionary. It is the expression of a democracy of feeling rebelling against an aristocracy of form.'[1] In 1914 Pound had described the new poetry in precisely the opposite sense, defending what he called the new 'aristocracy of the arts' against artists who dabble in democracy. Whereas Pound and Eliot defend poetic authority against an expressive individualism, here those values are reversed, as expression is privileged over form.

Where should Loy's 'Love Songs' be positioned in relation to these opposed ways of understanding the relationship between poetry and authority? We might expect Loy, who explicitly identifies herself as an international 'psycho-democrat' in 1921, and whose poems had a prominent position in *Others* over a number of years, to align herself with Kerfoot's 'democracy of feeling'.[2] Yet Loy's poems do not sit happily with the expression 'democracy of feeling', as they are perhaps most distinctive for their extinction of personality, foregrounding of aesthetic artifice, and, according to Pound, lack of 'emotion'.

It was not just Pound and Eliot who were sceptical about the idea that poets should abandon formal considerations in favour of self-expression. Alice Corbin Henderson, the co-editor of *Poetry* magazine,

---

[1] Alfred Kreymborg, 'Foreword', *Others,* 1.4 (1915). J. B. Kerfoot was a critic associated with the *Others* group. See, e.g., J. B. Kerfoot, *How to Read* (Boston and New York: Houghton Mifflin, 1916).

[2] In 1917, e.g., the journal planned to publish a special pamphlet of her poems. See *Others,* 3.5 (Jan. 1917).

for one, ridiculed the fact that this cultural inclusiveness seemed to amount to little more than a repetitive use of the first person pronoun, a prioritization of the self which could be read either as 'revolutionary' or as boringly self-absorbed: 'Replacing the outworn conventions of the I-am-bic school, we have now the I-am-it school of poetry.'[3] Henderson was right to view the journal's 'revolutionary' aesthetic as involving a radical foregrounding of the self. In 1918, the editorial foreword to *Others* clarifies the connection between expressive individualism and literary value:

Anyone is free to come in or stay out of the magazine, subject of course to the none-too-infallible judgement of the editors. The curriculum is taboo; the only question asked is: 'Does a man express himself, and if so, how well?' ... [the editors] do not sit on judicial or pedantic pedestals; primarily, they ask that they be permitted to evolve their own individualism, if they possess any, and to permit other folk to evolve theirs.[4]

There was subtext to this programme for literary freedom: Kreymborg's experience of literary censorship in 1916. Kreymborg's short story *Edna: The Girl of the Street*, which he had written in 1904 when he was 23, had been published by Guido Bruno in 1914. The story seems rather innocuous now. It is about a young male sociologist who has an encounter, which is not sexual, with a prostitute. In December 1916, Bruno was arrested for selling a copy to an agent for the Society for the Prevention of Vice. He was charged with selling 'indecent literature', but, it seems, was then exonerated. No legal record of the case has been located, but Bruno republished the story in 1919 with a letter by George Bernard Shaw defending Kreymborg's story against the censor and a new foreword by Bruno insisting on his right to publish it. Bruno discusses the right and the qualifications of John Sumner, the new Secretary of the Society for the Prevention of Vice, to decide precisely what is and what is not 'obscene literature', and then to sit on a 'judicial pedestal'. As Bruno puts it ironically, 'Verily an extraordinary mind is needed to pass judgement on ordinary minds.'[5]

Literary freedom of expression was an important principle for modernist or avant-garde writers in these years in New York, because of the censorship activities of the Society for the Prevention of Vice. Most

---

[3] Alice Corbin Henderson, 'Our Contemporaries: A New School of Poetry', *Poetry*, 3.2 (1916), 103.

[4] 'Foreword', *Others*, 5.1 (1918).

[5] Alfred Kreymborg, *Edna: The Girl of the Street* (New York: Guido Bruno, 1919), 4.

famously, in 1921 the *Little Review* was taken to court for publishing *Ulysses*, which was deemed to be obscene. However, the conflict between the courts and modern writing had been going on for many years. A new era in this relationship began when Theodor Dreiser's naturalistic novel *The 'Genius'* was threatened with prosecution for obscenity in 1915. It was at this moment that authors began to organize collectively to support each other's right to freedom of expression. Bruno's defence of Kreymborg's story and the *Others* foreword are a continuation of this debate, in which 'individualism' and freedom are linked, and opposed to the 'authority' of the courts.

Yet the definition of 'freedom of expression', and its relationship to a literary or cultural democratization, is more complicated than these opposed positions suggest. Anthony Comstock, the infamous Secretary for the Prevention of Vice, and John Sumner, the man who succeeded him on his death in 1915, were not sophisticated intellectual opponents in this battle. In fact, their rigid, puritanical Christian values, which involved seeing novels as slightly suspect to begin with, presented an easily identifiable common enemy for modern writers.

The more complicated question for writers was whether there should be limits on the principle of freedom of expression. It was one thing to defend the rights to literary freedom against the oppressive authority of Comstock's and Sumner's Vice Society. It was another to sponsor a more vigorous political anarchism or socialism which positioned the artist as an opponent of the state, or to defend the actions of an avant-garde which wanted to smash apart the bourgeois cultural class. Further, the principles of freedom of expression were often contested by avant-garde artists who saw ideas of literary inclusiveness as problematic. It was not simply, then, that avant-garde groups such as the Italian Futurists or Pound's Vorticist group defended the cultural authority of the artist against a democratization of cultural expression. It was also the case that the idea of self-expression was importantly questioned in writing of this period.

Others, in trying to provide a non-judgemental space for new writing, embodied some of these tensions. This was nowhere more true than in its cultural feminism. The September 1916 issue of the magazine, for instance, was a 'woman's number' edited by Helen Hoyt, one of a number of special issues which aimed to present new ideas or to represent the experiences of distinct constituencies of people. The idea of having a 'woman's number' was unusual in this period, and Hoyt felt the need to defend the idea in her foreword. Answering the charge that 'Art is surely sexless', the foreword states: [E]veryone grants the convenience and justice of such categories as French Poetry, Spanish Poetry—Greek, German, Hindu Poetry—and is there not as great difference, in physical make-up, in psychology, custom and history, between the people called Men and the people called Women?'[6] In her attempt to describe 'the people called Women', she shifts into a rhetoric of sociological or anthropological study: the difference between men and women is analogous to the cultural and linguistic difference of nation-states, or linguistic groupings. And just as anthropologists aim to study other peoples in their natural habitats, so the magazine's woman's number wants to 'hear what woman will tell of herself'. Hoyt's cultural feminism, then, involves a belief in the cultural importance of the self-expression of a representative group of writers.

Loy, in her 'Feminist Manifesto', suggests similar ideas about the psychological and cultural gulfs separating men and women. Yet, despite her obvious feminist interest in ideas of sexual difference, she is notably absent from the women's issue. She would not be the first or the last poet to want to dissociate herself from the category of 'female poet'. Yet it is also possible that Hoyt did not want to hear what Loy had to tell of herself, as Loy's tendency to foreground the 'erotic garbage' of women's sexuality was in conflict with the rather prim contributions to the volume. The difference in style is mocked in the November 1916 issue of *Poetry* magazine, which published what it called 'an imaginary conversation between two lady poets':

> Said Mina Loy to Muna Lee,
> 'I wish your style appealed to me.'
> 'Yours gives me anything but joy!'
> Said Muna Lee to Mina Loy.'

Carolyn Burke discusses this portrayal of Loy in her biography, but fails to mention that Muna Lee was not simply an imaginary person, but a published poet and translator, whose work appeared in Hoyt's 'special issue'.[7]

In Chapter 1 we looked at how the discussion of women's sexuality split apart the women's movement in the pre-war period. As we saw, there was much at stake in the different attitudes to this issue, as

---

[6] Helen Hoyt, 'Foreword', *Others*, 3.3 (1916), 54.
[7] Carolyn Burke, *Becoming Modern: The Life of Mina Loy* (Berkeley: University of California Press, 1997), 6. See Muna Lee, *Sea-Change* (New York: Macmillan, 1923).

women's sexuality was seen to encompass other questions about the relationship between subjectivity and writing. The *Poetry* Conversation highlights the fundamental differences between the style of Loy's poems and the poems by Lee and Hoyt, which, despite their free verse, were sentimental and conventional in subject-matter. One of Hoyt's contributions to the 'woman's number', for instance, is a poem called 'To a Pregnant Woman'. The stability of selfhood is assumed in this poem, and its tone is sincere:

> This is possession!
> To own so surely, so completely;
> So absolutely to command,
> To serve, to keep.
> Knowing you hold the beating life of the beloved
> In the depths of your life.

Knowledge of the self is consonant with an unproblematic possession and command of the other.

Loy had addressed the same topic two years earlier in her poem 'Parturition', but she had specifically used the topic of giving birth to problematize such a stable idea of the self.[8] 'Parturition' adopts Bergsonian dichotomies in its description of the process of giving birth, in which categories of time, modelled on the 'logic of solids', are contrasted to images of intuitive becoming. Mechanistic, geometrical, and spatial models of time, measurement, and memory are contrasted with the female individual's experience of time, which is specifically non-spatial, in which 'the delirium of night-hours' blurs 'spatial contours'. The conscious mind is a site of 'the subliminal deposits of evolutionary processes'; and birth is compared to the evolutionary processes of moths, cats, and insects, in which, the poem declares in a Bergsonian flourish, 'I am knowing / All about / Unfolding.'[9] Loy's poem seems to ask what happens to Bergson's categories of creative evolution in the context of parturition, a moment in which a woman's innately creative biological body is literally split apart into her ego and the emerging baby. The emerging baby, then, is a literal instance of Bergsonian 'Unfolding', in which the 'past presses against the present', causing 'the upspringing of a new form of consciousness'. Yet the poem also describes a battle between the 'I' and its biological, or intuitive, body: the 'I', or ego, is described

---

[8] Mina Loy, 'Parturition', *Trend* (1914), repr. in Roger Conover, ed., *Lost Lunar Baedeker* (Manchester: Carcanet, 1997), 4–8.

[9] Ibid. 5, 6, 7.

as a 'false quantity', an idea which is somewhat similar to Bergson's description of the ego as 'an artificial bond' which unites the disparity between psychic states which we have artificially 'distinguished and separated' in order to conceptualize them. The ego keeps disintegrating in the poem: the 'I' is a 'circle of pain' which exceeds 'its boundaries in every direction', and this destabilization of self is consonant with a disruption of the boundaries which separate what is inside and what is outside the self:

> Locate an irritation   without
> It is   within
> Within
> It is without

Loy's questioning of what is inside and what is outside the self is central to the representational strategies of her writing practice more generally. She is often at her most powerful when she reveals the illusions which control our imaginative lives.

In an unpublished short story called 'Pazzerella', Loy jokingly suggests the limitations of female self-expression. At the end of the story Loy writes the following conclusive statement:

Note sent with MSS
Sympathetic Enemy.
One night I set to work and composed the gigantic opus for the vindication of feminine psychology with which I had threatened you. Whether it is that truth is more powerful than determination, or fantasy less fantastic than truth or that woman being incapable of thinking, reads the thoughts of others. However that may be, this is how it turned out.
Your affectionate.

At the top of this final page, in a space drawn between two lines, in both a written draft of the story and a typescript, Loy has written 'Mss long ago lost', making it ambiguous whether the 'this' which has 'turned out' is a long lost MS or the story called 'Pazzerella' itself.[10]

If the pronoun does refer to the text of 'Pazzerella', then Loy's vindication of feminine psychology is precisely one which 'reads the thoughts of others'. 'Pazzerella' is a story narrated by a male protagonist

---

[10] Mina Loy, 'Pazzerella', Beinecke Library, Mina Loy Papers, MS 6, Writings, fol. 171, 46. Although 'Pazzerella' is undated, it is likely that it was written during the latter part of Loy's stay in Florence, as it is a scathing satire of Giovanni Papini, the Italian poet.

called Geronimo, which ends with Geronimo stating that the secret of woman lies in himself: 'The secret of woman is that she does not yet exist. Being a creator I realized that I can create woman .... Until now she had nothing but her breath and the everlasting attraction toward man, lacking an axis about which to revolve. I am a man and I shall be her axis.'[11] Geronimo's concluding assertion of agamogenesis suggests that 'the vindication of feminine psychology' has 'turned out' to be the masculine fantasies of an Italian Futurist. Yet Loy's reference at the top of the page to the missing 'Mss', in both written and typescript drafts, insists that the referent of the vindication is ambiguous.

The ambiguity is perhaps one of Loy's jokes. The anticipation of 'the gigantic opus for the vindication of feminine psychology', however failed a project, is tantalizing. Perhaps Loy's joke is that the vindication which 'turned out' is both the male Futurist voiced text of 'Pazzerella' and a missing manuscript. Perhaps the wider joke is that they amount to the same thing: that both the material text and the imaginary text constitute a kind of missing 'Mss'.

The joke of the blank space, the lost manuscript which should perform the 'gigantic' 'vindication', suggestively encapsulates a trajectory in Loy's writing. Loy seems ideally positioned to fill in this blank page, but something fails her, whether it is the truth, her imagination, or her gender. Perhaps it is easier to 'read the thoughts of others' than to represent the truth of oneself or one's gender. Perhaps, more profoundly, the representation of feminine psychology is an impossibility, because it would be either too wedded to an inadequate present-tense materiality or too involved in an ideal, and therefore abstract, future. Her early writing suggests that the vindication of feminine psychology constitutes a central missing manuscript in literary modernism as a whole, that the liberated woman is the missing subject of modernism. Her writing describes women who imagine escaping from the structures of home, family, and outdated moral codes and confronting both the 'freedoms' and the economic realities of the modernized city. Her later writing thinks through another missing subject of modernism, concentrating attention on itinerant and homeless tramps, criminalized individuals who exist on the outermost boundaries of society. In 'Parturition' and 'Pazzerella' Loy undermines the idea that self-expression is 'revolutionary'. As I will

---

[11] Mina Loy, 'Pazzerella', 45.

suggest in this chapter, however, she is also deeply suspicious of the authoritarian fantasies of certain sections of the European avant-garde, particularly the Italian Futurists. Loy's politics and poetry cannot be aligned with either Pound's 'aristocracy' or Kreymborg's 'democracy'. Her writing is attuned to the artifice of selfhood and representation. Her 'psycho-democracy' is a challenge to authoritarian forms of power, while aware of the 'illusions' of conventional notions of democracy which rest on the ideas of representative government and political inclusiveness.

WOMEN OF THE FUTURE: LOY'S FEMINISM, 1910–1916

Loy's early writing emerged out of her encounters with the Italian Futurists. She had initially trained as a painter in Munich and Paris, and had moved to Florence with her first husband, Steven Haweis, in 1906. When Mabel Dodge took up residence in Florence in 1910, the two women read Bergson and Freud together, and Loy became acquainted with the expatriate Florentine artistic community, meeting amongst others the American Futurist painter Frances Simpson Stevens in 1911. She attended the Futurist exhibition at Ferrante Gonelli's gallery in Florence in 1913, and quickly became intimate with Marinetti, Carrà, Papini, and Palazzechi. In 1914 Loy had affairs with Papini and Marinetti, experiences she describes in an unfinished and unpublished satirical novel called 'Brontolivido'. Marinetti's personal impact on Loy was brief, but intense, succeeding in jolting her awake from what she later saw as a lethargic Florentine existence. Loy suggests that whilst Marinetti's destructive aesthetic and critique of liberalism appealed to her own attempts to escape from the strictures of the past, she never fully identified herself with the propositions of the Futurist programme.

Loy had a more significant affair with Giovanni Papini, nicknamed both the 'best-read' and the 'ugliest man in Italy', who had spearheaded Florentine cultural activity from the early 1900s. Papini's cultural perspective was a product of the particular combination of elements which created the Italian avant-garde in the early twentieth century. After its unification in 1861, Italy tried to modernize fast. However, unification had created a centralized state dependent on corrupt, localized patronage. From 1900, the Catholic and Socialist masses entered into the political equation, with the creation of a political system based on democratic parliamentary principles. Prime Minister Giovanni Giolitti, who dominated Italian politics in the decade and a half before the First World War, tried to establish the civil society and political mechanisms of a modern liberal state. In 1911–12, for example, he granted near-universal manhood suffrage. However, despite its parliamentary changes, economically and socially, Italy remained largely unchanged from the society that had existed for centuries, with an antiquated agricultural system and a large gap in economic prosperity between the North and South.

Italian avant-garde artists in the period 1900–14 saw themselves as leading the cultural modernization which would propel Italy into the modern world, with Florence as the centre of this activity. Papini launched the journal *Leonardo* in 1903, on a radical platform of philosophical idealism and artistic pagan individualism. Giuseppe Prezzolini, who would found *La Voce* in 1908 and edit it until 1916, argued in December 1903 that the writers of *Leonardo* were united by an 'enemy' which included 'Positivism, erudition, naturalist (*veristà*) art, historical method, materialism, bourgeois and collectivist varieties of democracy'.[12] Like their British counterparts, Papini and Prezzolini were critical of democracy, positivism, and materialism, the political and philosophical features of modernization, rather than modernization as such. And, like other avant-garde writers across Europe, they used Nietzsche's work to develop an alternative philosophical and artistic culture in which the intellectual would lead, rather than be enslaved by, the democratized masses. Artistically, despite the fact that their romantic predecessors had been similarly critical of materialism, they saw themselves as confronting a particularly post-romantic problem. Whereas, in the face of materialism, their romantic predecessors had embraced a return to the past, Papini believed that the modern artist must respond to the consequences of romantic nostalgia itself. He argued that the culture of romanticism had given us back the 'nudity of man' by stripping him of his religious and cultural beliefs. There were three possible ways of moving forward artistically. Artists could follow the romantics in their 'return to the human past' through neo-classicism or tradition. They

[12] Giuseppe Prezzolini, 'Alle sorgenti dello spirito', *Leonardo*, 19 Apr. 1903; quoted in Walter Adamson, *Avant-Garde Florence: From Modernism to Fascism* (Cambridge, Mass.: Harvard University Press, 1993), 66.

could create new rules and constraints. Or they could 'resolve to remain nude and to act more powerfully without the need for instruments and restraints'. Whereas Pound and Eliot forged an Anglo-American poetic modernism by embracing the authority and order of a reinvigorated classicism and literary tradition, Lawrence created a new English prose tradition by writing in the spirit of powerful nudity. Papini agreed with Lawrence that it was also only the last solution which offered 'the possibility of a real cultural renewal for only it would unleash the "subliminal self," the "power that is personal, secret, awe-inspiring, quick-moving, that resides in every person" '.[13]

The sexual politics of the group were fed through this understanding of the cultural and political past. Another important writer for the *Leonardo* and *La Voce* group was Otto Weininger, whose theories of the absolute difference between male and female and the inferiority of women were adopted enthusiastically by Papini. Papini's interest in Weininger formed part of a more general attempt to understand history, politics, and culture by means of the legislating categories of male and female. Giosuè Carduccio, one of the leading intellectual figures of the late nineteenth century, was important for Papini and his contemporaries, because he was an example of the ' "plebeian", "realist", and "masculine" tradition of Dante—as against the "elegant", "empty", and "feminine" tradition of Petrarch, most recently embodied in D'Annunzio and other "decadents" '.[14] Papini argued that Carduccio's mistake was to identify his interests with the 'democratic illusions of Mazzinian republicanism', but that this was because Carduccio pre-dated the historical revelation of these illusions. Papini aligned his masculine tradition with a literary classicism which must override the feminine romanticism of decadent art.

Papini's connection of D'Annunzio's decadence with an 'empty' femininity was the Italian counterpart to the Anglo-American rejection of decadent 'femininity'. It forms part of a battle over terminology central to the avant-garde rejection of symbolist and decadent art. D'Annunzio, after all, had also embraced Nietzsche's theory of the male 'superman' who is beyond moral categories.

In 'Lion's Jaws', Loy satirizes both Gabrunzio, as she nicknames D'Annunzio, and Raminetti, as she nicknames Marinetti, because they both ground their art in a 'disdain' for women. Gabrunzio's women are a kind of 'harem' of decadence, providing both sensual pleasure

[13] Adamson, *Avant-Garde Florence*, 81–2.   [14] Ibid. 27.

and the 'impotent' neurosis which is the subject-matter of his art. Raminetti's women are a barrier to the 'spiritual integrity' necessary for Futurist art, which is based on 'agamogenesis', the rejection of sensual distraction. Nevertheless, just to ram home his superiority to Gabrunzio, Raminetti 'possesses the women of two generations' anyway. In the shift from decadence to Futurism, then, femininity is a third term which both artistic movements try to supersede. Loy's poem highlights the structural similarities between D'Annunzio's, Papini's, and Marinetti's use of women to ground their aesthetic projects.

Yet, Loy does not simply satirize these Italian writers. The philosophical interests and artistic principles which informed the Futurist group were adopted by some feminist writers and used to further their own concerns. Sibilla Aleramo, for example, the feminist author of the extremely popular 1906 novel *Una donna*, who had an affair with Papini in 1912, also identified with aspects of Weininger's thought, although she 'separated herself sharply from Weininger's argument that women were intellectually and creatively inferior'.[15] The Futurist group also, perhaps surprisingly given Marinetti's shouted 'disdain' for women, opened up a space for a small number of women writers and artists. Women Futurists such as the French Valentine Saint-Point, Magamal, and Rosa Rosa share the style and humour of Futurist art, as well as the philosophical understanding of the Futurists and their *Leonardo* and *La Voce* predecessors.[16] This is because Marinetti was both disdainful of sentimental femininity and supportive of women's liberation as the only way of killing off Italian artistic 'amore'. Like those of women Futurists such as Valentine Saint-Point, Magamal, and Rosa Rosa, Loy's feminist statements are also disdainful of parasitic women and celebrate a libertarian feminist agenda.

Aesthetically, Marinetti embraced an artistic 'screeching of machines' which was the product of industrialized Milan, rather than the more mystical interests of the Florentine writers, Papini and Prezzolini.[17] The Futurists argued that the modern artwork should capture the moment by representing objects in motion: 'the dynamic sensation, that is to

---

[15] Adamson, *Avant-Garde Florence*, 123.

[16] For a discussion of the relationship between Futurism, feminism, and women artists, see Walter Adamson, 'Futurism, Mass Culture, and Women: The Reshaping of the Artistic Vocation, 1909–1920', *MODERNISM/Modernity*, 4.1 (1997), 102–6.

[17] F. T. Marinetti, 'The Founding and Manifesto of Futurism', repr. in *Let's Murder the Moonshine: Selected Writings* (Los Angeles: Sun & Moon Press, 1991), 47–52. (The 'Manifesto' was first published in *Le Figaro* in 1909.)

say, the particular rhythm of each object, its inclination, its movement, or to put it more exactly, its interior force'. Rather than standing back from the object in order to represent it, the artist's perspective should be part of the object's rhythm.

Given that Loy had initially trained as a painter rather than as a writer, and that she was introduced to Futurism through her contact with the Florentine painters Carlo Carrà and Ardengo Soffici, it is surprising that her first serious piece of writing, 'Aphorisms on Futurism', which she wrote during 1913, does not discuss Futurist theories of painting and sculpture. Instead, the aphorisms psychologize Futurist themes. This was because the real spur to these aphorisms was her relationship with Marinetti. He visited Florence in the autumn of 1913, and immediately began to try to seduce her. Through his theory of 'parole-in-libertà', Marinetti revealed how the principles of painterly composition also applied to writing. There were features of his theory of free verse which Loy seems to have adopted in this period, such as his claim that the dynamic sensation of the moment was best captured by the infinitive, which would continue to be a feature of her writing long after she had turned her back on the Futurists.

The aphorisms focus on the dynamics between self and world, 'IN pressing the material to derive its essence, matter becomes deformed'; the way in which Futurist art captures the minute particulars of life, 'LOVE the hideous to find the sublime core of it', and the psychological dimensions of Futurist art, 'HERE are the fallow-lands of mental spatiality that Futurism will clear'. Futurism, in these aphorisms, is a form of artistic freedom based on the wilful and risk-taking individual, embraced in Loy's description of leaping into the future, 'the Future is only dark from outside. / *Leap* into it—and it EXPLODES with *Light*', by adjusting 'activity to the peculiarity of your own will', and by clearing the sedimented forms of ideology which enslave the mind.[18] Above all, it is only by loving or recognizing other people or objects in their particularity, that individuals attain a kind of self-understanding: 'Love of others is the appreciation of one's self.' Self-understanding is the basis for freedom: 'MAY your egotism be so gigantic that you comprise mankind in your self-sympathy.'[19] Loy's description of an inflated egotist perhaps pokes a joking finger at Papini and Marinetti. However, the

[18] Mina Loy, 'Aphorisms on Futurism', repr. in *Lost Lunar Baedeker*, 149. (First published in *Camera Work*, 45 (Jan. 1914), 13–15.)
[19] Ibid. 150.

ego is also embraced sincerely here and is seen as the foundation for the destruction of prejudices handed down from the previous generation. She goes on to demand that the modern artist must confront this naked modern reality and legislate a new set of secular values:

To readjust activity to the peculiarity of your own will.
THESE are the primary tentatives towards independence.

These warnings and recommendations adopt a familiar 'egoist' language of will, independence, and strength, in which the Christian deity is discarded, and the new egotistical artist takes his place: 'TO your blushing we shout the obscenities, we scream the blasphemies, that you, being weak, whisper alone in the dark.'[20] Loy announces her intention to articulate the sexual obscenities and religious blasphemies which hold the key to the self's subconscious drives. She immediately fulfilled this intention in her 'Songs to Joannes'. It is only through this confrontation with the self's wilful desires that the modern moment can be fully embraced and the future imagined: 'THUS shall evolve the language of the Future.' In a stroke, Loy declares that the religion, morality, and tradition which stifle the mind can be wilfully smashed apart.

In some senses, Loy seems to sacrifice the political dimension of the Futurist manifestos, in which the institutions and beliefs of the bourgeois class are ridiculed and undermined, in favour of a focus on the relationship between Futurist themes and the individual's psychic reality. But was this interest in 'mental spatiality' and the subconscious an apolitical withdrawal into the self, or was Loy interested in developing a different kind of political aesthetic?

It is in her other manifesto of 1914, her 'Feminist Manifesto', that we can find some answers to this question. One of the striking differences between the two texts is the shift in tone of address. Unlike many Futurist manifestos, it is unclear who is the 'you' and who is the 'Us' in *Aphorisms on Futurism*. This may well have been because Loy, as an expatriate Englishwoman, could not simply see the Italian bourgeoisie as *her* enemy in the way that Marinetti and Papini did. In fact, at times the 'You' in aphorisms like 'OPEN your arms to the dilapidated' seems to amount to little more than the restrictive parts of the self. In her 'Feminist Manifesto', by contrast, the 'you' is a specific target, liberal rights feminists, who are angrily denounced. She begins by describing the 'inadequate' nature of the feminist movement: 'Women if you want to realise yourselves—you are on the eve of a devastating psychological upheaval—all your pet illusions must be unmasked—the lies of centuries have got to go—are you prepared for the Wrench—?' She insists that feminists are 'glossing over reality' in their focus on reform, economic legislation, vice-crusades, and uniform education.[21]

Like Nietzsche, Loy sees herself as confronting an ideology so entrenched that it has been in place for 'centuries'. The only way of escaping such sedimented values is through avant-garde shock. Demolition replaces reform; psychological upheaval replaces legislative amendment, and mental autonomy replaces economic autonomy. Rather than staring reality in the face, the dominant feminist groups are described as creating a different kind of 'gloss' on reality. In going on to attack what she calls 'that pathetic clap-trap war cry Woman is the equal of man', Loy completes her denunciation of liberal feminist principles. Marinetti, in 'Against *Amore* and Parliamentarianism', had 'scorned' the feminist focus on the 'legislative instrument' rather than the development of woman's intelligence.[22] Like the writers analysed in Chapter 1, as well as Marinetti, Loy advises women to stop searching for their liberation in the lawcourts, and instead 'seek within' for an understanding of their identity: 'Leave off looking to men to find out what you are not—seek within yourselves to find out what you are.'

In some senses, Loy's claim that women's liberation will happen on the level of the psyche and the body, rather than through legal reform, merely describes her own personal predilections. As she wrote to Mabel Dodge in 1914, 'Do tell me what you are making of Feminism ... Have you any idea in what direction the sex must be shoved—psychological I mean—bread and butter bores me rather.' Loy states, in a characteristically flippant tone, that she is simply bored by the mundane particulars of bread-and-butter feminism.[23] However, this flippancy disguises a more serious set of concerns. In fact, her feminist proclamations are consistent with her principles of composition in a way which suggests a sustained and intellectually coherent perspective.

Papini and Prezollini, in the early editions of *Leonardo* had argued that the modern artist should embrace the modern self which has been

[21] Mina Loy, 'Feminist Manifesto', repr. in *Lost Lunar Baedeker*, 153.
[22] F. T. Marinetti, 'Against *Amore* and Parliamentarianism' (1911–15), in *Let's Murder the Moonshine*, 81.
[23] Mina Loy, Letter to Mabel Dodge, Beinecke Library, Luhan Papers, MS Survey Za Luhan.

stripped of the moribund cultural and religious forms which obscure its real drives. Like them, Papini believed that Rousseau's democratic ideals had elevated man into a new deity, but that this new subject was peculiarly ill-equipped to be a source of collective beliefs.

Loy's focus on the naked psyche, the 'subconscious', or 'elements unconditionally primeval', should be read as part of this wider debate. It is not so much a withdrawal into a self-absorbed bourgeois self-interest, but more an attempt to engage with a modernity in which the individual is naked, stripped of meaningful religious, moral, or political categories of understanding. The key for Loy, as for the Italian avant-garde, was to engage with this modern reality, not to gloss over it. The conflict between a moral liberal rights feminism and Loy's poems, then, is not simply a difference in taste over whether one should or should not mention 'promiscuous lips', the 'mucous-membrane' of sex, or more generally to find 'the sublime' in the hideous. It was a more profound conflict over whether the language of religious morality and democratic rights could propel women forward into the future or would hold them fast in a static historical grip. Her poems are at their most powerful when they make for slightly uncomfortable reading—when they capture something of the raw mental spaces which one feels might be better left uncovered. Loy focuses on such spaces, it seems, because they tell us something about the clash between convention and those aspects of naked self-interest which constitute our drives and desires.

This stripping bare, for Loy, reveals the combative self-interested nature of men and women: 'Men & women are enemies, with the enmity of the exploited for the parasite, the parasite for the exploited.'[24]

Loy describes a sex war based on mutual exploitation. She repeats the terms of her address to a 'sympathetic enemy' in the conclusion to 'Pazzerella' and argues that it is up to women themselves to break free of their financial and psychological parasitism on men. The prime psychological barrier to women's freedom is the social belief in certain 'illusions', particularly the division of women into mistresses and mothers. The categories of mistress and mother enforce a sexual division of labour. The value of female virginity marks the female body as an intact, unused object of exchange:

'The fictitious value of woman as identified with her physical purity—is too easy a stand-by—rendering her lethargic in the acquisition of intrinsic

---

[24] Loy, 'Feminist Manifesto', 154.

merits of character by which she could obtain a concrete value—therefore, the first self-enforced law for the female sex, as protection against the manmade bogey of virtue—which is the principal instrument of her subjection—would be the <u>unconditional</u> surgical <u>destruction of virginity</u> throughout the female population at puberty—.'[25]

Loy's wry recommendation that pubescent girls be surgically divested of their assets irreverently dismantles the idea of feminine purity. The 'Manifesto' thereby deftly performs the values it espouses, and mocks the prim reader who would be shocked by Loy's immoral invective. The combative nature of Loy's focus on the body and the unconscious is also central to her poems.

VIRGINS AND EROTIC GARBAGE: LOY'S EARLY POEMS

In her earliest poems Loy separates women's desiring bodies from the 'illusion' of their social worth, in order to criticize the existing connection between moral and monetary notions of value. The terms 'parasitism' and 'prostitution', as they are used in Loy's 'Manifesto', incorporate ideas both of sex and of economics. Both senses of these words inform 'Virgins Plus Curtains Minus Dots', which was published in *Rogue* in 1915. The poem depicts the house as a specific structure of imprisonment, and the style is Futurist: The capitalized line 'VIRGINS FOR SALE' shouts out of the page like an advertising poster on the street. Quotation marks signal a shift of diction into the register of clichéd romance. Typographical spacing in the middle of lines cuts across the reading process. Loy also provides a footnote to the word 'dots', cutting across a linear reading of the poem. The idea that virgins might be advertised as objects for sale ironizes the ideology of love and virginity described in the poem.

The poem begins with the lines 'Houses hold virgins / The doors on the chain'.[26] The houses are described as 'holding' virgins, both in the sense of restraint, as though the virgins are literally on the end of a chain, and in the sense that virgins are the material contents of the house. The word 'property' also incorporates two meanings. Whilst

[25] Ibid. 154–5.

[26] Mina Loy, 'Virgins Plus Curtains Minus Dots', repr. in *Lost Lunar Baedeker*, 21. (First published in *Rogue*, 2 (15 Aug. 1915), 10.)

houses constitute the most important legal form of bourgeois property, the virgins are also a property, in the sense of a quality or characteristic, of the house. The image of houses 'holding' humans suggests both the idea of human enslavement to property and the particular position of women in a society in which they are treated and exchanged as objects. The object status of women is central to the poem: 'Men's eyes   look into things / Our eyes   look out.' Men's eyes look into houses and women, two 'things' which they own and exchange. The phrase 'look into' also suggests the process of scientific or philosophical inquiry, adding another dimension to the line. The value of objects, properties, and women is determined by male standards of surveillance and classification. Female value, in the existing classifications, is tied to the structures which 'hold' her, the houses, the dowry portion, or 'dots', which determine her value and a classificatory ideology which labels her as virgin or whore.

The sexual embrace is mediated by ideology and economics:

> Nobody shouts
> Virgins for sale
> Yet where are our coins
> For buying a purchaser
> Love is a god
> Marriage expensive.[27]

Love-deities obscure the economics of sexual relationships. In contrast to the male classificatory gaze, the gaze of the women is directed outwards, towards the prospective buyers outside the house and towards the love ideology which determines their imprisonment. The nature outside the house offers an alternative to these classifications: 'Nature's arms spread wide   Making room for us'.[28] Nature offers an alternative space to that of the house, and natural desires invade the stultifying interior:

> Fleshes like weeds
> Sprout in the light
> So much flesh in the world
>   Wanders at will
> Some   behind curtains
> Throb to the night
> Bait   to the stars [29]

---

[27] Loy, 'Virgins Plus Curtains Minus Dots', 22.   [28] Ibid.

The flesh is 'like weeds', in that the women's bodies are unwanted, ugly, and useless natural forms which grow and throb in the dark. However, the flesh presents itself as 'bait' to the stars, and thereby throbs to a different idea of love. The idea that women are like 'bait' is repeated in other poems of the period. 'Italian Pictures' and 'Café du Néant', two of Loy's first published poems, describe 'baited bodies' and 'Bits of bodies', phrases which describe the bodies as tempting pieces of flesh, suggesting both the physicality and destructiveness of desire.[30]

The female body is marked by the categories of property and economic value, and the exchange of women is dependent on an ideology of love: women 'have been taught / Love is a god / White with soft wings'.[31] In 'At the Door of the House', which was written in 1915, but not published until 1917, the house is again analogous to female imprisonment. The card-teller poses a choice between those who 'are going to make a journey' and those who wait 'at the door of the house' for the man with 'Intentions little honourable'.[32] Whilst the love-tale secures the women's imprisonment, the fantasy of a journey shakes the foundation of their passive relationship to men. In contrast to the physical freedoms of the strolling men, these women can only imagine the sexual 'journey' they might make. Yet Loy believes that these fantasies constitute potentially revolutionary ideals.

Loy presents a poetic counterpart to her domestic virgins in the *cocottes* (the French word for 'flirt') of 'Three Moments in Paris', a poem which was written in 1914 and published in 1915. Her advice to 'FORGET that you live in houses, that you may live in yourself—' connects the domestic space to conformity to a social ideal and links freedom to the individual ego. Loy's writing more generally ties freedom to the subject position of the tramp, the itinerant, the solitary, and property-less individual. Baudelaire's *flâneur*, Mallarmé's tramps, and Laforgue's lunar revellers all link modernity with the experience of solitary wandering. Loy's poems adopt the terms of this tradition. Her poems are peopled by itinerant subjects whose physicality is foregrounded: she depicts 'Some other tramp', 'the Clown of Fortune', 'shuffling shadow bodies', 'This

[29] Ibid. 20.

[30] Mina Loy, 'Italian Pictures' & 'Café Du Néant', repr. in *Lost Lunar Baedeker*, 9–14, 15–18. (First published in *International*, 8 (1914), 255, and *Trend*, 8 (1914), 220–2.)

[31] Loy, 'Virgins Plus Curtains Minus Dots', 22.

[32] Loy, 'At the Door of the House', repr. in *Lost Lunar Baedeker*, 34. (First published in *Others: An Anthology of the New Verse* (1917), 64–6.)

abbess prostitute', 'Misfortune's monsters', and 'An electric clown'.[33] Her poetic scenes tend to be urban spaces, rather than private interiors: she describes women and men who roam in the 'red-lit thoroughfare', 'the half-baked underworld' of Zelli's bar, 'a department store', and 'a lurid lane'.[34] Her characters are individuals who escape the solid structures of property and family, and experience physical and psychic freedom.

Whilst Loy reworks the French tradition of the poet-itinerant, she also twists it slightly by inserting women into the subject position of the *flâneur*. Baudelaire, Rimbaud, and Laforgue represent poet-wanderers who are specifically male. Baudelaire's *flâneur*, for instance, is a languid but desiring subject whose route through the city is created through chance responses to the seductions of both shop-windows and prostitutes. Loy's poem 'Three Moments in Paris', published in *International* in 1914 and in *Rogue* in 1915, presents women who are somewhat similar to *flâneurs*, but their roaming leads them to confront their own seductive performances.[35]

The poem describes a female subject who wanders the city like her male counterparts. It is composed of three scenes. The first takes place at one o'clock at night, the second takes place in a café, the third takes place in a shop. The poem refers to a *cocotte*, who 'wears a bowler hat'. It is ambiguous whether the 'cocotte' in Loy's poem is a prostitute or not, whether the 'eyes that are full of love' are for sale or not, whether she is a buyer or seller of commodities. This ambiguity pervades the poem as a whole. The difficulty of identifying the social position of the women in the café, and the ambiguity as to whether the love on offer is for sale or for free captures the uncertainty of the anonymous city itself.

The ambiguity of words and behavioural patterns is a corollary of the experience of being in a crowded city in which the relationships between individuals are mediated by surfaces. The poem describes city spaces which are determined by the play of 'artificial' surface forms. In the first section, the voices of the pugilist males are 'cerebral gymnastics'. In 'Café

[33] 'Ignoramus', 'On Third Avenue', 'Lady Laura in Bohemia', 'Hot Cross Bum', 'The Widow's Jazz', repr. in *Lost Lunar Baedeker*, 44, 109, 98, 133, 95.

[34] 'On Third Avenue', 'Lady Laura in Bohemia', 'Chiffon Velours', 'Hot Cross Bum', repr. in *Lost Lunar Baedeker*, 109, 98, 119, 133.

[35] 'Three Moments in Paris', repr. in *Lost Lunar Baedeker*, 15–18. (First published as 'Café du Néant' in *International*, 8 (1914), 255, and as a whole in *Rogue*, 1 (1915), 10–11.)

du Néant' the bodies swathed in kohl, blue powder, and yellow dust obscure the natural body. In 'Magasin du Louvre' both the commodities in the *magasin* and the *cocottes* are dolls with glass eyes. The glass eyes of the cocottes are cultivated in order to reflect back the existing world, rather than to offer up the particularities of individuality.

Yet the poem describes how irrepressible natural reflexes underpin these synthetic forms. In 'One O'Clock at Night' the male voice 'roars' across a 'thousand miles' and a 'thousand years' from 'the beginning of time', allowing the woman to be momentarily 'the animal woman'. In 'Café du Néant' the eyes of the women in the café trail 'the rest of the animal behind them'. And in 'Magasin du Louvre' the eyes of the *cocottes* 'flicker' with 'elements unconditionally primeval'. The synthetic 'perfections' of swathed bodies fail to control physical and sexual impulses. Despite the cultivated artifice of individuals in the modern city, the animal body continues to reveal itself.

Whilst 'Three Moments in Paris' depicts women who are free to roam in the city, then, these women continue to be defined in relation to objects and money. Whereas 'Virgins Plus Curtains Minus Dots' criticizes the property relations which hold women as objects, 'Three Moments in Paris' represents women who are free of the conventions of traditional Italian society. Rather than being free of gendered property relations, however, women in the public spaces of the city confront a different exchange process. In 'Three Moments in Paris' the women consciously fashion nature in order to make it publicly saleable and desirable. The *cocottes* in 'Magasin du Louvre' accentuate their relation to the exchange process. In contrast to the controlling ideologies of marriage, domesticity, and love of the 'Italian poems', the women in 'Magasin du Louvre' interiorize ideas of gender difference through the performative artifice of synthetic beauty and fashion.

Loy's other publication of 1915, in which her mature poetic style is revealed, focuses exclusively on the body, and disregards any social or economic register. The first four poems of what were subsequently called 'Love Songs' were published in *Others* magazine, and they created an instant scandal. Kreymborg describes the stir caused by Loy's poetic style: 'Detractors shuddered at Mina Loy's subject-matter and derided her elimination of punctuation marks and the audacious spacing of her lines.' Loy's demand in her 'Feminist Manifesto' for the 'surgical destruction of virginity' satirizes the ideology of femininity and romantic love by focusing on biology. Her 'Love Songs' also foreground biological rather than romantic bodies. 'Love Song I' opens with the following stanza:

> Spawn of Fantasies
> Silting the appraisable
> Pig Cupid
> His rosy snout
> Rooting erotic
> garbage
> 'Once upon a time'
> Pulls a weed
> White star-topped
> Among wild-oats
> Sown in
> mucous-membrane[36]

This poem has moved away from the more literal references of her other 'Italian poems'. While the punctuation and typographical spacing have obvious affinities with Futurist poetry, the perspective and tone of these lines are more difficult to identify. The opening 'Pig Cupid' creates a joke about the sordid sexual appetites of the gods which informs the rest of the poem: lofty fantasies are fertilized by spawn; Cupid is actually interested in erotic garbage; and the celestial, sentimental stories of 'once upon a time' are really grounded in membrane fluid. The rather violent juxtaposition of gods and bodily fluids, written in a pseudo-scientific vocabulary, serves to ridicule both discourses as explanations of sexual behaviour. The poem's serious point seems to be that we need a third language, that of art, to account for the dynamic dimensions of love.

This combination of humorous and serious registers informs Loy's poetry in general, and is central to the rest of the 'Love Songs': 'I would / An eye in a Bengal light / Eternity in a skyrocket.' These lines announce a different, yet equally characteristic, 'Loy' tone. A Bengal light is a kind of firework which produces a steady and vivid blue and coloured light, and is used for signals. A skyrocket is a rocket which ascends high into the sky before exploding. Both the Bengal light and the skyrocket are linked to more abstract ideas of force or duration. The 'eye' obviously suggests sight, but it could also be a reference to the 'eye', or central calm area of a cyclone. 'Eye' also echoes the 'I' of the previous line. The

---

[36] Mina Loy, 'Songs to Joannes', repr. in *Lost Lunar Baedeker*, 53. (First published as 'Love Songs I–IV', *Others: A Magazine of the New Verse*, 1.1 (1915), 6–8, and as the complete 'Love Songs', *Others*, 3.6 (1917), 3–20.)

line creates a flash of identity between the subjective 'I' and the object. The phrase 'Eternity in a skyrocket' also connects distinct ideas to create a sensual image of soaring visual pleasure. The exuberant sensuality of these images, the reference to 'lunar' landscapes to denote psychic and sensual pleasures, and the overriding joke of the bathetic 'Pig Cupid' introduces a mixture of elements which are distinctive of Loy's poetry. The irony and the focus on the night-sky recall Laforgue, as Eliot points out, but the considered tastelessness of Loy's images and the abstruse vocabulary are less easy to trace. These poems look forward to the artful constructions of Dada.

'Love Songs' as a complete sequence continues to manipulate the idiosyncratic tone and subject-matter of 'Love Song I'. They bring to light the biological and sensual processes of both female and male sexual bodies through a clash of scientific and religious registers. Loy manipulates biological terms such as 'spawn', 'mucous-membrane', 'Birdlike abortions', 'spermatozoa', 'cymophanous sweat', 'Etiolate body', 'dorsal vertebrae', 'Éclosion', and 'Proto-plasm'.[37] The transportation of scientific terminology into these love poems ironizes, through sordid somatic nature, the celestial ideas of love.

At times, the sexual act is described as a depersonalized and genderless 'clash': it is 'humid carnage', 'lighted bodies / Knocking sparks off each other', and bodies 'Bouncing / Off one another'.[38] At other moments, she addresses the significance of sexual difference. In 'Love Song XII' and 'Love Song XIII' she describes gender enmity and the 'point at which the interests of the sexes merge'. Both of these things had been central to her 'Feminist Manifesto'. 'Love Song XII' begins:

> Voices break on the confines of passion
> Desire   Suspicion   Man   Woman
> Solve in the humid carnage[39]

Man and woman are spaced apart and suspicious; but the 'De' of 'Desire' and 'Solve' of the next line combine to 'dissolve' the gendered hostility in a damp sexual embrace. 'Love Song XIII' continues the theme of enmity, but begins by envisaging a utopian love union by describing a 'new illusion' of love.[40]

As with Loy's faith, in her 'Feminist Manifesto', in the future, 'Love Song XIII' declares her hope in a new illusion of love. This is where

---

[37] Ibid. 53, 54, 56, 64, 65, 67.   [38] Ibid. 57, 59, 61.   [39] Ibid. 57.
[40] Ibid. 57–8.

Loy's writing is at its most powerful. In the 'Love Songs' as a whole, she dismantles the sentimental and biological discourses of sex. Both are inadequate, because they either idealize love or reduce love to a set of materialistic impulses. The future, she declares, will require a new 'illusion', which the avant-garde artists, the unacknowledged legislators of the modern world, must provide. Yet, this is no easy task, as it relies on a series of haphazard personal relationships. The poem continues by describing the other's refusal of her offerings: 'Oh that's right/Keep away from me   Please give me a push/Don't let me understand you Don't realize me.' The result is a 'depersonalized' 'tumble together' in which 'Me' and 'you' are impossible to distinguish.[41] This mingling is the opposite of the egoistic individuation needed for a futuristic love of mutual realization and understanding.

The importance of recognition is also addressed in 'Love Song XXIX', which explores the link between sexuality, language, and sexual equality: 'Evolution fall foul of / Sexual equality'.[42] Things are ironically off-course in this poem. The mathematical languages of equality and calculation fail to recognize and understand human entities who are fundamentally idiosyncratic. The imposition of these categories onto humans creates a series of biological and linguistic distortions: men and women jibber or speak only senseless words. The second stanza announces the evolution of a new language to aid these unnatural couplings: 'Give them some way of braying brassily / For caressive calling / Or to homophonous hiccoughs.[43]

The alliteration in the opening three lines is insistent, creating connections which are somewhat similar to 'homophonous hiccoughs'. Loy's hint that her alliterative connections are involuntary linguistic spasms humorously satirizes the pseudo-scientific language she includes in her poems. The poem concludes with the lines:

> Let them clash together
> From their incognitos
> In seismic orgasm
> For far further
> Differentiation
> Rather than watch
> Own-self distortion
> Wince in the alien ego [44]

---

[41] Loy, 'Songs to Joannes', 58.   [42] Ibid. 65.   [43] Ibid.

The physical 'clash together' takes place between 'incognitos', repeating the 'depersonalized' contact of 'Love Song XIII'. In contrast to this alienating physical clash in which men and women remain as strangers to each other, the gaze of conscious identity is described as a painful 'Wince' of recognition. The self, then, is distorted in the gaze of a separated 'alien ego'. This excruciating confrontation with the other is in some sense necessary, the kind of psychological 'wrench' that Loy identifies as crucial to modern women in her 'Feminist Manifesto'.

Like Papini, Loy captures the shock of being stripped bare of cultural accoutrements. In 'Love Song XXX', however, she explores the ethical codes which mediate the relationships between naked individuals: 'the proto-form / We fumble / Our souvenir ethics to'.[45] 'Love Song XXX' repeats the idea that procreation is a blind natural impulse. Fertilization, we are told, is in the hands of 'Foetal buffoons'. In the final stanza, Loy asks the key question: what kind of ethics could be attached to the blind, immature, and depersonalized natural impulses depicted in these poems?

Loy's concern with ethics suggests that these witty but somewhat dispersed lyrics have a more serious aim. Her satire of the love lyric strips bodies down 'To Nature/that irate pornographist'.[46] But she also asks about the ethical consequences of the anarchic nature she describes. Loy's early writing advocates the destruction of the false Victorian morality of her upbringing, and celebrates the nature of women's, and men's, sexual liberation. Yet what takes the place of this morality once it has been dismantled? If there is no ethical frame by which to recognize the connections between individuals, as well as their differences, then there are only 'blind' and sensual relations between individuals. Chapter 1 suggested that Marsden failed to get beyond this question, that her writing remains caught in an egoism which celebrates the fact that each individual is 'cut off from and different' from others. Loy became increasingly interested in how art could capture the self-knowledge produced through a recognition of the other's reality. At the same time, she distanced herself from the Futurists after her arrival in New York in 1916.

[44] Ibid. 66.   [45] Ibid. 66–7.   [46] Ibid. 63.

LOY'S PSYCHO-DEMOCRACY

Loy participated in the avant-garde Bergson vogue in the years leading up to the outbreak of the war. There were a number of reasons for this interest, but Bergson's vitalist philosophy is best seen as part of a more general philosophical critique of positivism, a critique which was embraced by thinkers from across the political spectrum. However, a number of writers accused Bergson of equating reason with positivism, and of thereby embracing what he saw as the progressive and liberatory qualities of intuition and irrationality. As Sanford Schwartz has shown, thinkers from both the radical right, such as Maritain, and the radical left, such as Lukács, attacked Bergson for his account of reason: 'The notable similarity of their approach to Bergson reveals the longstanding kinship between reactionary and radical attacks on the particular form of rationality encouraged by the Enlightenment.'[47]

Loy discusses her interest in Bergson in her 1924 essay on Stein, in which she describes the moment in 1911 when she 'left Gertrude Stein's Villino in Fiesole with a manuscript'. She goes on: 'This was when Bergson was in the air, and his beads of Time strung on the continuous flux of Being, seemed to have found a literary conclusion in the austere verity of Gertrude Stein's theme— "Being" as the absolute occupation.'[48] Loy argues that Stein's Bergsonian notion of 'flux of Being' is ultimately a theory of 'the individual' which involves a foregrounding of the biological and instinctual self, and a scepticism about mechanistic understandings of the individual.

This interest in the intuitive self leads to the representation of particular ideas of time and space in 'Parturition', as we saw at the beginning of this chapter. It also, however, produces particular poetic principles of composition which are important for Loy's work as a whole. For Loy, these questions about composition involve a meditation on the ideas of authority and democracy: 'Modernism has democratized the subject matter and *la belle matière* of art; through cubism the newspaper has assumed an aesthetic quality, through Cezanne a plate

---

[47] Sanford Schwartz, 'Bergson and the Politics of Vitalism', in Frederick Burwick and Paul Douglas, eds., *The Crisis in Modernism: Bergson and the Vitalist Controversy* (Cambridge: Cambridge University Press, 1992), 290.

[48] Mina Loy, 'Gertrude Stein', repr. in Roger Conover, ed., *Last Lunar Baedeker*, (Manchester: Carcanet, 1982), 289. (First published as a two-part letter to Ford Madox Ford, editor of the *Transatlantic Review* (1929)).

has become more than something to put an apple upon, Brancusi has given an evangelistic import to eggs, and Gertrude Stein has given us the Word, in and for itself.'[49] Democratization is consonant with a dadaist levelling of effect, in which the most advanced art techniques create a shift in the layout of the newspaper, and plates become objects of aesthetic contemplation. Stein, the only writer mentioned here, has democratized language by dislodging words from their habitual contexts and giving them to us anew: she has liberated words from 'some sort of frame or glass case or tradition'. For Loy, this is a form of cultural democratization, because it destabilizes hierarchies of language and art and traces 'intellection back to the embryo'.

This is a rather different kind of democracy from that discussed in the *Others* editorial at the beginning of this chapter, less a 'democracy of feeling', more a democracy of form in which the artifice of the language of the self, as well as emotions, is accentuated. Here, she identifies democratization with the formal properties of the work, rather than with a series of questions about the identity of the writer who is expressed through the work. It is important that Loy sees the democratization process as flowing from the art object to life, rather than the other way round: it is Cubism that has changed the aesthetic nature of the newspapers, not the newspaper that has changed the aesthetic properties of painting.

As I discussed in Chapter 2, Wyndham Lewis, in *Time and Western Man* (1927), describes Stein's early writing in similar terms, but argues that she produces a false literary democratization: it is 'undoubtedly intended as an epic contribution to the present mass-democracy'.[50] He describes *Three Lives* as an artistic primitivism, in both a political and a psychological sense: it employs a 'plainmanism' which tries to represent 'primitive mass-life', and it is part of the modern 'child-cult', which tries to reproduce the 'mental habits of childhood'.[51] Stein is fed through Lewis's particular ideological frame in *Time and Western Man*, which sees Bergson's time philosophy as a form of belated romanticism. Stein's writing, we are told, is actually a form of modernist romanticism, as it is organized by 'the metre' of an 'obsessing' and personalized Bergsonian time: 'Bergsonian durée, or psychological time, is essentially the "time"

[49] Ibid. 298.
[50] Wyndham Lewis, *Time and Western Man*, ed. Paul Edwards (Santa Rosa, Calif.: Black Sparrow Press, 1993), 60.
[51] Ibid. 60.

of the true romantic.' For Lewis, this psychologism is based on sensation, and is both politically and artistically solipsistic.[52]

Both Lewis and Loy argue that by stripping away the 'glass-case' structures of tradition and authority, Stein has democratized writing. Lewis, however, suggests that she replaces tradition and authority with a subjective rhythm. Her writing, then, whilst stripping language down to its bare essentials, can also be seen to flip over into a kind of abstraction. Lewis argues that her writing is fundamentally unreal, dead, and doll-like. Stein's writing is a 'contribution to the present mass-democracy', because he thinks that mass democracy is grounded in individuals, who can be 'hypnotized' by external cultural and political forms as effectively as Stein's prose song hypnotizes its reader. Lewis argues, then, that her literary solipsism is similar to a political solipsism, in which the individual is separated off from the political or ethical beliefs which would create meaningful democracy.

Lewis was not the only writer to connect such literary or philosophical questions to political claims. Like Maritain and Lukács, as well as Eliot and Babbitt, he equates Bergson's philosophy with a debased romanticism and liberalism. Loy's attitude to these ideas is complex, and shifting. Her claim that Stein's writing is Bergsonian, democratic, and rhythmical is remarkably similar to Lewis's, but she has a rather different understanding both of 'democratization' and of reason. In *Time and Western Man*, Lewis jumps around between the romantic, Rousseauistic democratic subject of Hulme's, Eliot's, and Babbitt's writing and mass democracy. He is explicitly hostile to both, seeing art as a timeless language which resists these transitory political forms. Loy, by contrast, explicitly identifies herself with artistic and political democratization. Her description of Stein's writing is helpful for an understanding of the way in which Loy connects poetry to authority, and it also helps explain some of the formal dimensions of her work. Like Stein, her Futurist writing dislodges words from their 'glass cases' and gives them to us anew: her 'Pig Cupid', for instance, gives us a new, pink, animalistic Cupid, stripped of his classical rhetoric; and her 'Love Songs' as a whole depict what she calls a 'new illusion' of love. Like Stein, she also seems to trace 'intellection back to the embryo', less in a linguistic sense and more in a literal focus on the 'animal woman', or the biological body.

---

[52] Lewis, *Time and Western Man*, 8.

Loy's poems avoid the rhythmical formalism which Lewis sees as dead and abstract; instead, her poems often focus on moments in time which gesture towards the canvas or the photographic snapshot. The titles of her poems signal this interest in the moment: 'Three Moments in Paris', 'Sketch of a Man on a Platform', 'At the Door of the House'. Nevertheless, as with Lewis's attack on Stein, the main criticisms of her work were aimed at what other writers saw as the abstract nature of her writing. Both Eliot and Pound reviewed the *Others, 1917* anthology, which included Loy's 'At the Door of the House', 'The Effectual Marriage', and 'Human Cylinders'. It is unclear whether they had also read her earlier *Others* contributions, 'Love Songs, I–IV', 'To You', and the complete 'Songs to Joannes', although Pound claimed that he had previously 'seen a deal of rubbish' by her. Both picked out Loy's poems for comment, and both accused her of creating linguistic abstraction through dissociation: Pound that her poems are a form of 'logopoeia', which he defines as 'poetry that is akin to nothing but language', though severed from the emotion which accompanies Laforgue's logopoetical poetry; and Eliot that 'Human Cylinders' is 'abstract', because 'she needs the support of the image', and without it, 'the word separates from the thing'.[53]

Eliot's accusation of abstraction relates to Loy's creation of a poetic language which does not foreground the image, or the 'world of objects', which, for him, is the basis of good poetry. Pound's insistence that her work is a 'mind cry, more than a heart cry' accuses her of remaining coldly suspended above her own writing. The accusation of abstraction is important, because it was an issue that Pound and Eliot were intensely focused on in 1917. Yet, as I suggested in my reading of 'Pazzerrella', the question of abstraction was also something with which Loy was concerned, but specifically with reference to how the self, or femininity, is constructed in language. Both Eliot and Pound avoid abstraction, or formalism, by finding order in literary or mythical traditions which make meaningful the disparate particulars of modern life. Stein and Loy specifically discard such 'glass-case' traditions, and instead focus on capturing the constructions of the present-tense self from different angles. Importantly, both can also be seen specifically to block the relationship between word and Eliot's 'world of objects', and instead to focus on the artifice of language and the self.

---

[53] T. S. Apteryx, 'Observations', *Egoist*, 5.5 (1918), 70. T. S. Apteryx was one of Eliot's pseudonyms.

Eliot, in this logic, can be seen to miss the point of 'Human Cylinders'. The poem can be seen to ridicule, through mimicry, Futurist abstraction, which involves precisely the separation of the word from the thing with which Eliot is concerned. The poem captures the potential destructiveness of this aesthetic:

> Or which of us
> Would not
> Receiving the holy-ghost
> Catch it and caging
> Lose it
> Or in the problematic
> Destroy the Universe
> With a solution[54]

Here, Loy suggests that metaphysics catches, cages, solves, and thereby destroys the spiritual universe. Loy's writing is partly an attempt to express the ephemeral without caging, and thereby destroying, it. Importantly, Loy is also mimicking the linguistic flourishes, precisely the metaphysical abstractions, of a heavily masculine avant-garde.

Loy's attack on abstraction is directed at the masculine posturings of the Futurists. Her early satirical poems mock the arrogant assertions of masculine cultural and political authority. In 'The Effectual Marriage', Gina is scared to peep inside Miovanni's study, because she fears that the 'shining' light of his mind might either 'blind her', or 'that she should see Nothing at all'. The idea that male intellectual endeavour is a form of posturing which asserts power but masks an intellectual absence recurs in other poems of this period: in 'Three Moments in Paris' an 'indisputable male voice roared / through my brain and body', and whilst the pugilists of 'the intellect' roar, boom, and 'thunder', the 'animal woman' understands 'nothing of man / But mastery'. In 'Sketch of a Man on a Platform', the man's genius is 'So much less in your brain / Than in your body', and involves the pointless pursuit of 'pushing / THINGS / In the opposite direction / To that which they are lethargically willing to go'. In 'Giovanni Franchi', Giovanni's 'eyes were intrepid with phantom secrets'.[55] Here, Loy ridicules the male avant-garde writer, with his booming, aggressive attempt to revolutionize the arts by violently seizing the existing components of the art object or

---

[54] Mina Loy, 'Human Cylinders', repr. in *Last Lunar Baedeker*, 41.
[55] Mina Loy, 'Sketch of a Man on a Platform' and 'Giovanni Franchi', repr. in *Lost Lunar Baedeker*, 19, 20, 31.

text and forcing them into a different mould. Such a criticism could, however, be extended beyond the Italian Futurists to Anglo-American modernist writers such as Lewis, Eliot, Pound, and Lawrence, who also wanted to mould things, through either the blinding light of their intellects or a chaos they inflected as 'female'. Loy absorbs these desires into her poems by creating images of men with an unfortunate excess of energy, which involves them in the explosive, but rather pointless, pursuit of pushing things around.

At the same time, however, Loy does not construct a stable female voice with which to authorize her satire of male egoism. In 'Parturition', she suggests that a knowledge of male egoism can imprison women in a static idea of women's difference: 'The irresponsibility of the male / Leaves woman her superior Inferiority.'[56] The phrase 'superior Inferiority', is seemingly contradictory, but it makes sense in relation to the attempt, by political feminists as well as writers, simply to reverse the value attached to gender categories, to inject value into existing ideas of women's difference. The idea of women's moral superiority can, in this logic, actually serve to perpetuate women's enslavement to men after their economic dependence has ceased.

The fact that an idea of women's difference can function as a form of repressive legislation, both of other women and of the self, importantly structures the content of her texts. Loy's poems always turn the satire back on to the women who ridicule male egoism: in 'The Effectual Marriage', Gina, whilst serving as a vantage-point from which to ridicule Miovanni, is also depicted as dependent on him for her humour: echoing 'Pazzerella', the poem has the lines

> 'If he had become anything else
> Gina's world would have been at an end
> Gina with no axis to revolve on
> Must have dwindled to a full stop'.[57]

In 'Lion's Jaws', Loy ridicules both Raminetti and 'the erudite Bapini' who experiment 'in auto-hypnotic God-head', but also describes her anagrammatic self as a 'secret service buffoon to the Woman's Cause'.

Whilst Loy's satirical poems joyfully ridicule male assertions of intellectual mastery, then, the idea that forms of artifice mask a kind of interior absence applies to women as well as men. Gina's dwindling

---

[56] Mina Loy, 'Parturition', 5.
[57] Mina Loy, 'The Effectual Marriage', repr. in *Lost Lunar Baedeker*, 39.

identity and Imna Oly's jesting mask an emptiness, captured in 'Three Moments in Paris', in the lines, 'virgin eyes' 'Stare through the human soul / Seeing nothing'. Where the male is defined by the gap separating his godhead from the empty light of his intellect, women tend to be split apart by forms of self-surveillance.

Loy's depiction of gender difference offers a rather different way of considering the relationship between poetry and authority, for these poems connect avant-garde metaphysical abstraction to a pugilistic and war-like mastery which could easily be extended to political authoritarianism. In fact, this is precisely the move that Loy makes in her pamphlet 'International Psycho-Democracy', which she first published in 1920.[58] In this she criticizes what she calls 'the **Heroic Personification of Man as Dominator of the Elements** until those elements are at the disposal of every man'. As she states, psycho-democracy is 'Democracy of The Spirit, government by creative imagination, participation in essential wisdom—Fraternity of Intuition, the Intellect and Mother Wit. (The Creator, the Scholar, the Natural Man)'. Here, Rousseau, Dada, psychology, and feminism meet in an idiosyncratic politics. Just as Dada creates newspapers which are art objects, so everyone, both men and women, has a 'natural' creative impulse and therefore a right, she implies, to be an artist. This creative democracy is specifically opposed to the cultural 'hypnotism' of 'Education' and a press which is 'financed by the Capitalist'. The press creates the abstract category of the 'Dummy Public' in order to justify military aggression, political legislation, and religion. The 'Dummy Public' is actually a mask for the 'self-conscious minority of *Power*' which controls society. The public, then, is a fiction used to hide the real workings of power, which are obscured from view. Loy argues that psycho-democracy recognizes the need to counter the natural impulse towards war, as well as the 'psychically magnetic' rhythms of militarism. Instead, she wants to 'present intellectual heroism as a popular ideal in place of physical heroism encouraging the expression of individual psychology in place of mob-psychology'. In the pamphlet, then, intellectual autonomy is fundamental for resisting identification with Italian fascistic forms of military authority and charisma. Art is crucial for resisting the hypnotism of the press. Her psychologism in this pamphlet is a kind of radical individualism in which the form and content of politics is fused on the level of the individual.

---

[58] Mina Loy, 'International Psycho-Democracy', repr. in *Lost Lunar Baedeker*, 276–82.

Loy's psycho-democrats are sceptical about a new mass democracy in which individuals can be controlled by the hypnotic power of a capitalist media. She argues that the categories of both the mass and the public are political constructions which mask the authoritarian mastery of a minority of power. There is a dangerous illusion of inclusion in this politics. She attacks the formalism of this politics, the way in which the political language is language about language.

This chapter has suggested that Loy constructs a rather different understanding of the relationship between poetry and democratization than that presupposed in either the *Others* editorials or Pound's 'aristocracy of the arts'. She is far removed from the authoritarian male modernist positions which have 'presented sympathetic critics with insuperable problems of explanation', as North puts it.[59] Like Lawrence, Lewis, Pound, and Eliot, Loy is critical of aspects of liberal democracy. Yet, the vantage from which this criticism comes is not one which conforms to Huyssen's divides. Loy's work gives expression to a newly 'democratized' world, but it is not a vision of democracy which accords with Huyssen's categories. She depicts, for instance, the new subject positions of the 1910s and 1920s: the itinerant movie star and the vampish 'flappers of the millionaires'. But her writing is distinctive for its attempt, through satirical power, wit, intellectualism, vulgarity, sexual explicitness, and violence, to destabilize the 'democratic' illusions of mass politics and mass culture.

---

[59] Michael North, *The Political Aesthetic of Modernism: Yeats, Eliot and Pound* (Cambridge: Cambridge University Press, 1991), 1.

Conclusion

Henri Bergson declared in his *Introduction to Metaphysics* that 'The essential fact of modern times is the advent of democracy.'[1] The avant-garde attack on liberalism and democracy was fundamental to the form and content of modernist texts. Across Europe, from Italy's pre-war liberal regime to the dominance of the Liberal Party in British politics before the war, artists believed that politics was in the grip of liberal values. The European avant-garde declared its 'revolutionary' credentials by attacking this political target. Claims about the subject went hand in hand with this political vision: in the place of the moral and rational citizen-subject of liberal ideology, avant-garde writers declared the reign of the new poetic legislators, defined by the wilful, egoist, or 'unconscious' drives of the individual artist.

The creation and interpretation of Anglo-American modernist writing, then, involved a number of key oppositions: élitist versus inclusive, classical versus romantic, authoritarian versus democratic, impersonal versus introspective, and male versus female. Pound's 'aristocracy of the arts' and the inclusive editorial policy of *Others* magazine seem to offer suggestive images of two different models of poetic authority. Images of sexual difference are consolidated by means of these oppositions. Hulme, Eliot, and Lewis oppose a literary romanticism they associate with democracy and introspection. The political and the cultural meet in these terms. The aesthetic decadence against which modernist writers react, and the political and cultural shifts towards mass democracy, are linked and construed as 'feminine' by a number of writers in the period. The modern poet confronts these symptoms and signs of modernity in a number of ways: at moments he is figured as a heroic subject whose task is to mould the modern into a meaningful shape; in other texts, the modern poet is associated with techniques of irony and

[1] Henri Bergson, *Introduction to Metaphysics*, authorized translation by T.E. Hulme (London: Macmillan & Co., 1913), 24.

detachment which hold the ego at a firm distance from the object of contemplation.

Perversely, this construction of the artist as a kind of legislator is partly a response to the perception of the writer's circumscribed role in modern society. As we saw in Chapter 2, the new century was marked by artistic declarations that the world is chaotic, secular, and amoral; 'too large to be seen whole', as Ford put it.[2] The new writing, then, aims to confront what is knowable about this modern landscape. The result is the creation and defence of a new kind of realism, in which the self is figured as a refuge of sense certainty or ironic detachment. In a bold move, however, the modernist legislator sees art as providing the formal authority with which to make sense of this debased, chaotic, and mimetic modernity.

Ideas of sexual difference are essential to these visions of the modern. Eliot, as we saw in Chapter 4, tends to figure women as signs of the contemporary moment, encompassing both an unexamined verisimilitude and a linguistic abstraction. Both are forms of democratization which threaten to tear apart the cultural sphere and the art object. Despite the shifting nature of his object of attack, from the liberal democratic ideology of the 1910s to the mass democracy of the 1920s and 1930s, Eliot sustains the vision of a feminized democracy against which a masculine poetry is defined. Lawrence, in contrast, puts his faith in the union of male and female. For example, Birkin, in a discussion with Gerald in *Women in Love*, argues that in the absence of the 'old ideals', there is nothing to 'centre' life apart from the 'perfect union with a woman'. Birkin's faith in love is partly a realism in the face of a world that 'doesn't centre', and partly an idealistic vision of the balance between polarized male and female principles. While Gudrun, who represents the figure of the modern woman most forcefully in the book, is critical of democracy, she also blocks Birkin's 'perfect union' by insisting on her own freedom: 'One must be free, above all, one must be free .... No man will be sufficient to make that good.'[3] In the end, Gudrun's demand for a freedom of isolation is one of the most potent expressions of the arid democratic forces elsewhere criticized in the book.

The connections between Anglo-American modernist writing, democracy, and sexual difference, then, are never straightforward. This is

---

[2] Ford Madox Ford, *The Critical Attitude* (London: Duckworth, 1911), 28.

[3] D. H. Lawrence, *Women in Love*, ed. David Farmer, Lindeth Vasey, John Worthen (Cambridge: Cambridge University Press, 1987), 58, 374.

particularly true of texts by women writers, who struggle to represent the role of the female artist in the modern world by negotiating the relationship between cultural inclusion and ideas of artistic legislation. Ideas of democracy, as a result, are split apart. There is an attempt, by a number of women writers, to challenge the identifications of women with aspects of modern democracy. In Chapter 1 I discussed the way in which a number of feminist thinkers believed that the task of modern feminism was to sever women's connection to democratic ideals of equality, legality, and altruism. Such ideas are central to the work of a number of literary writers in the period. H.D. and Loy embrace a literary egoism specifically at odds with ideas of cultural inclusion, romanticism, democratic equality, and introspection.

H.D. writes poetry which is hostile to the modernity of the commodity, the crowd, standardization, and industrial warfare. Instead, she embraces a literary egoism in which art is defined by its ability to stand outside these signs of the modern. In the process she develops an idiosyncratic 'ego-centric' vision of historical interpretation. The artistic egoist is figured as a bulwark against the modernity of industrialization and the machine. Unlike her male contemporaries, however, she links the female artist to this ahistorical egoism. This is revealed most forcefully in her construction of poetry's relationship to the past. Many modernist writers see themselves as confronting an unhallowed modernity which can be made meaningful through aesthetic form. This secular vision seems to contrast with H.D.'s creation of a poetic language connected to its pre-modern, sacred origins. It is as though she wants the past, along with its occult significance, to be blasted into the present. Rather than seeing the fragments of the past as sources of aesthetic authority, however, these mythical and literary fragments seem to invade the self. In the process, the writer is construed less as a source of heroic authority, and more as someone who is haunted and split apart by the past. Texts and words are figured as impersonal and inescapable ghosts which haunt the present. Out of this understanding of the poet's relationship to his or her linguistic past, H.D. creates a subtle account of the relationship between self and word. The subject is never straightforwardly in control of the language with which he or she works. H.D. creates what she calls an 'ego-centric' vision of interpretation and poetic creation which is distinct from poetic introspection. This egocentric art is defined through its difference from the modern.

Mina Loy insists that the female artist must confront the modern world in all its guises, however sordid. She sees the artist as penetrating to the innermost core of language by tearing down the psychological veils which mask us from the world, and from ourselves. This involves a heroic effort of will, a 'wrench', in which women face a modernity emptied of sacred and sentimental values. In the process, the modern woman confronts a female self bereft of familiar feminine attributes. The shock of this laying bare lies at the heart of her writing, informing the iconoclastic language and radically dispersed formal experimentation.

H.D. and Loy, then, like the anarchistic feminists analysed in Chapter 1, are ambivalent about modern democracy. Before the war, Loy attacked liberal feminism, seeing the ideas of rights and equality as damaging illusions which keep women in chains. After the war, she was critical of what she saw as the new political illusions of democratization. She was particularly worried about the dominance of the category of the 'Man in the Street', and the way it is used to justify the political interests of those who are hidden from view. At the same time, she is both a feminist and a democrat: it is no accident that her two manifestos are defences of these two positions. Her politics makes sense only in the context of a historical understanding of the period.

H.D.'s and Loy's poems, then, complicate the 'divides' of Huyssen's analysis. Both H.D. and Loy figure women as split apart by what they see as a conflict between democratic ideals and art. Huyssen's theory of post-modernism and modernism is destabilized by this dislocation of 'female' modernism from democratic ideals. This alters our reading of the gender of modernism more generally. The analysis of previously marginalized women modernist writers such as Loy and H.D. was, and is, energized by recent feminist and democratizing politics, which specifically aimed to undermine the authority of the male literary canon. Yet, the political impulses behind the recovery of previously marginalized writers may, at times, have distorted our understanding of their work. As we have seen, Loy and H.D. believed that the modern female artist must confront the modern by revealing the wilful, egoistic, and amoral drives of the modern woman. In the 1910s and early 1920s, this was to position themselves against the prevailing liberal values of the main feminist groups. They saw the female artist as a kind of 'unacknowledged legislator'. In doing so, their work is important to our understanding of the period, as well as to our interpretation of both male and female modernist texts.

Bibliography

ADAMSON, WALTER, *Avant-Garde Florence: From Modernism to Fascism* (Cambridge, Mass.: Harvard University Press, 1993).

—— 'Futurism, Mass Culture, and Women: The Reshaping of the Artistic Vocation, 1909–1920', *MODERNISM/Modernity*, 4.1 (1997), 89–114.

ALEXANDER, MICHAEL, *The Poetic Achievement of Ezra Pound* (Edinburgh: Edinburgh University Press, 1998).

ARMSTRONG, TIM, *Modernism, Technology, and the Body: A Cultural History* (Cambridge: Cambridge University Press, 1998).

ASHER, KENNETH, *T. S. Eliot and Ideology* (Cambridge: Cambridge University Press, 1995).

BABBITT, IRVING, *Democracy and Leadership* (Boston: Houghton Mifflin, 1924).

—— *The Masters of Modern French Criticism* (London: Constable, 1913).

—— *Rousseau and Romanticism* (Boston: Houghton Mifflin, 1919).

BARNES, DJUNA, *The Book of Repulsive Women* (1915; New York: The Lincoln Press, 1948).

BENSTOCK, SHARI, *Women of the Left Bank: Paris, 1900–1940* (London: Virago Press, 1987).

BERGSON, HENRI, *An Introduction to Metaphysics*, trans. T. E. Hulme (London: Macmillan, 1913).

—— *Creative Evolution*, trans. Arthur Mitchell (London: Macmillan, 1911).

BUCK, CLAIRE, *H.D. and Freud: Bisexuality and a Feminine Discourse* (London: Harvester Wheatsheaf, 1991).

BURKE, CAROLYN, *Becoming Modern: The Life of Mina Loy* (Berkeley: University of California Press, 1997).

—— ed., *T. S. Eliot: The Modernist in History* (Cambridge: Cambridge University Press, 1991).

BUSH, RONALD, *T. S. Eliot: A Study in Character and Style* (Oxford: Oxford University Press, 1983).

CHRIST, CAROL, 'Gender, Voice and Figuration in Eliot's Early Poetry', in Ronald Bush, ed., *T. S. Eliot: The Modernist in History* (Cambridge: Cambridge University Press, 1991).

CLARK, BRUCE, 'Dora Marsden and Ezra Pound: The New Freewoman and "The Serious Artist"', *Contemporary Literature*, 33.1 (1992).

CLARK, SUZANNE, *Sentimental Modernism: Women Writers and the Revolution of the Word* (Bloomington, Ind.: Indiana University Press, 1991).

COLLECOTT, DIANA, *H.D. and Sapphic Modernism, 1910–1950* (Cambridge: Cambridge University Press, 1999).

COLLINI, STEFAN, *Liberalism and Sociology: L. T. Hobhouse and Political Argument in England, 1880–1914* (Cambridge: Cambridge University Press, 1979).

DEKOVEN, MARIANNE, *Rich and Strange: Gender, History, Modernism* (Princeton: Princeton University Press, 1991).

DOGGETT, MAEVE E., *Marriage, Wife-Beating and the Law in Victorian Britain 'Sub Virga Viri'* (London: Weidenfeld & Nicolson, 1992).

DOOLITTLE, HILDA, *Between History and Poetry, The Letters of H.D. and Norman Holmes Pearson*, ed. Donna Krolik Hollenberg (Iowa City: University of Iowa Press, 1997).

—— *Bid Me To Live* (London: Virago Press, 1984).

—— *Collected Poems: 1912–1944*, ed. Louis Martz (New York: New Directions, 1983).

—— *End to Torment: A Memoir of Ezra Pound by H.D.* (Manchester: Carcanet New Press, 1982).

—— 'The Ghost' (1941), H.D. Writings, Beinecke Library, Yale University, New Haven, Conn., folder 1004.

—— *Her [HERmione]* (New York: New Directions, 1981).

—— *Notes on Thought and Vision & The Wise Sappho* (San Francisco: City Lights, 1982).

—— *Richard Aldington & H.D.: The Early Years in Letters*, ed. Caroline Zilboorg (Bloomington, Ind.: Indiana University Press, 1992).

—— 'Selected Letters from H.D. to F. S. Flint: A Commentary on the Imagist Period', ed. Cyrena N. Pondrom, *Contemporary Literature*, 10.4 (1969), 557–86.

—— 'The Suffragette' (n.d.), Beinecke Library, H.D. Papers, MS 24, Writings, folder 952.

—— *Trilogy* (Cheadle, Cheshire: Carcanet, 1973).

DOUGLAS, MAJOR C. H., *Economic Democracy* (London: Cecil Palmer, 1920).

DOWSON, JUNE, *Women, Modernism and British Poetry, 1910–1939: Resisting Femininity* (Aldershot: Ashgate, 2002).

DUPLESSIS, RACHEL BLAU, *H.D.: The Career of that Struggle* (Bloomington, Ind.: Indiana University Press, 1986).

—— and FRIEDMAN, SUSAN STANFORD, eds., *Signets: Reading H.D.* (Madison: University of Wisconsin Press, 1990).

EDMUNDS, SUSAN, *Out of Line: History, Psychoanalysis, and Montage in H.D.'s Long Poems* (Cambridge: Cambridge University Press, 1994).

ELIOT, T. S., *After Strange Gods: A Primer of Modern Heresy* (New York: Harcourt, Brace and Co., 1959).

—— *T. S. Eliot: The Complete Poems and Plays* (London: Faber & Faber, 1969).

—— *Selected Prose of T. S. Eliot*, ed. Frank Kermode (London: Faber & Faber, 1975).

Eliot, Valerie, ed., *The Letters of T. S. Eliot i: 1898–1922* (San Diego: Harcourt Brace Jovanich, 1988).

Ford, Ford Madox, *The Critical Attitude* (London: Duckworth, 1911).

—— *Memories and Impressions: A Study in Atmospheres* (London: Harper & Brothers, 1911).

—— *Parade's End* (Harmondsworth: Penguin Books, 1982).

—— *The Soul of London: A Survey of a Modern City*, ed. Alan G. Hill (London: J. M. Dent, 1995).

—— *Women and Men* (Paris: Contact Editions, 1923).

Foster, John Burt, *Heirs to Dionysus: A Nietzschean Current in Literary Modernism* (Princeton: Princeton University Press, 1981).

Friedman, Susan Stanford, ' "I Go Where I Love": An Intertextual Study of H.D. and Adrienne Rich', *Signs*, 9.2 (1983).

—— *Penelope's Web: Gender, Modernity, H.D.'s Fiction* (Cambridge: Cambridge University Press, 1990).

—— *Psyche Reborn: The Emergence of H.D.* (Bloomington, Ind.: Indiana University Press, 1981).

Garner, Les, *A Brave and Beautiful Spirit: Dora Marsden, 1882–1960* (Aldershot: Avebury, 1990).

Garnett, Edward, 'Nietzsche', *Outlook*, 3 (8 July, 1899), 747.

Gelpi, Albert, *A Coherent Splendor: The American Poetic Renaissance, 1910–50* (Cambridge: Cambridge University Press, 1987).

Goldman, Emma, *Anarchism and Other Essays* (New York: Mother Earth Publishing Association, 1910).

—— *Red Emma Speaks: The Selected Speeches and Writings of the Anarchist Emma Goldman*, ed. Alix Kates Shulman (London: Wildwood House, 1972).

Gooding-Williams, Robert, *Zarathustra's Dionysian Modernism* (Stanford, Calif.: Stanford University Press, 2001).

Gordon, Lyndall, *T. S. Eliot: An Imperfect Life* (London: Vintage, 1998).

Gray, John, *Liberalism* (Milton Keynes: Open University Press, 1986).

Gregory, Eileen, *H.D. and Hellenism: Classic Lines* (Cambridge: Cambridge University Press, 1997).

Guest, Barbara, *Herself Defined: The Poet H.D. and her World* (New York: Doubleday, 1984).

Henderson, Alice Corbin, 'Our Contemporaries: A New School of Poetry', *Poetry*, 3.2 (1916), 103.

Hobhouse, L. T., *Liberalism* (London: Williams & Norgate, 1911).

Hoffman, Frederick J., Allen, Charles, and Ulrich, Carolyn F., *The Little Magazine: A History and Bibliography* (Princeton: Princeton University Press, 1946).

Holcombe, Lee, *Wives and Property: Reform of the Married Women's Property Law in Nineteenth Century England* (Toronto: University of Toronto Press, 1983).

HOYT, HELEN, 'Foreword', *Others*, 3.3 (1916).

HULME, T. E., *Speculations: Essays on Humanism and the Philosophy of Art*, ed. Herbert Read (London: Routledge & Kegan Paul, 1960).

HUMM, MAGGIE, 'Landscape for a Literary Feminism: British Women Writers 1900 to the Present', in Helena Forsäs-Scott, ed., *Textual Liberation: European Feminist Writing in the Twentieth Century* (London: Routledge, 1991).

HUNEKER, JAMES, *Egoists: A Book of Supermen* (London: T. Werner Laurie, 1909).

HUYSSEN, ANDREAS, *After the Great Divide: Modernism, Mass Culture, and Postmodernism* (Bloomington, Ind.: Indiana University Press, 1986).

KERFOOT, J. B., *How to Read* (Boston and New York: Houghton Mifflin, 1916).

KINNAHAN, LINDA, *Poetics of the Feminine: Authority and Literary Tradition in William Carlos Williams, Mina Loy, Denise Levertov and Kathleen Fraser* (Cambridge: Cambridge University Press, 1994).

KREYMBORG, ALFRED, *Edna: The Girl of the Street* (New York: Guido Bruno, 1919).

LAFORGUE, JULES, *Selected Poems*, trans. Graham Dunstan Martin (Harmondsworth: Penguin Books, 1998).

LAITY, CASSANDRA, *H.D. and the Victorian fin de siècle: Gender, Modernism, Decadence* (Cambridge: Cambridge University Press, 1996).

LAWRENCE, D. H., *The Cambridge Edition of the Works of D. H. Lawrence: Study of Thomas Hardy and Other Essays*, ed. Bruce Steele (Cambridge: Cambridge University Press, 1985).

—— *The Complete Poems* (Harmondsworth: Penguin Books, 1993).

—— *The Letters of D. H. Lawrence*, i, ed. Harry T. Moore (London: Heinemann, 1962).

—— *The Letters of D. H. Lawrence*, iii, ed. James T. Boulton and Andrew Robertson (Cambridge: Cambridge University Press, 1984).

—— *New Poems* (London: Martin Secker, 1918).

—— *Phoenix: The Posthumous Papers, 1936*, i and ii (Harmondsworth: Penguin Books, 1978).

—— *The Rainbow* (London: Penguin Books, 1981).

—— *Women in Love*, ed. David Farmer, Lindeth Vasey, and John Worthen (Cambridge: Cambridge University Press, 1987).

LEE, MUNA, *Sea-Change* (New York: Macmillan, 1923).

LEVENSON, MICHAEL, *A Genealogy of Modernism: A Study of English Literary Doctrine 1908–1922* (Cambridge: Cambridge University Press, 1984).

LEWIS, WYNDHAM, ed., *Blast*, 1 (1914).

—— 'Imaginary Letters', *Little Review*, 4.12 (1918), 52.

—— *Tarr: The 1918 Version*, ed. Paul O'Keefe (Santa Rosa, Calif.: Black Sparrow Press, 1996).

—— *Time and Western Man*, ed. Paul Edwards (Santa Rosa, Calif.: Black Sparrow Press, 1993).

LIDDERDALE, JANE, and NICHOLSON, MARY, *Dear Miss Weaver, 1876–1961* (New York: Viking, 1970).

LOY, MINA, *The Last Lunar Baedeker*, ed. Roger Conover (Manchester: Carcanet, 1982).

—— *The Lost Lunar Baedeker*, ed. Roger Conover (Manchester: Carcanet, 1997).

—— 'Pazzerella', Beinecke Library, Mina Loy Papers, MS 6, Writings, fol. 171.

LUDOVICI, ANTHONY M., *The False Assumptions of "Democracy"* (London: Heath Cranton, 1921).

—— *Who is to be Master of the World? An Introduction to the Philosophy of Friedrich Nietzsche* (London: T. N. Foulis, 1909).

MARINETTI, F. T., *Let's Murder the Moonshine: Selected Writings* (Los Angeles: Sun & Moon Press, 1991).

MARX, KARL, *Capital: A Critique of Political Economy*, i, trans. Ben Fowkes (Harmondsworth: Penguin Books Ltd., 1976).

—— and ENGELS, FREDERICK, *The German Ideology*, trans. S. Ryazanskaya (London: Lawrence & Wishart, 1965).

MILLER, CRISTANNE, *Cultures of Modernism: Marianne Moore, Mina Loy, and Else Lasker-Schuler, Gender and Literary Community in New York and Berlin* (Ann Arbor: University of Michigan Press, 2005).

MILLER, JANE ELDRIDGE, *Rebel Women: Feminism, Modernism and the Edwardian Novel* (London: Virago, 1994).

MILLER, NINA, *Making Love Modern: The Intimate Public of New York's Literary Women* (Oxford: Oxford University Press, 1999).

MOODY, DAVID, *Thomas Stearns Eliot, Poet* (Cambridge: Cambridge University Press, 1979).

NICHOLLS, PETER, *Ezra Pound: Politics, Economics and Writing: A Study of the Cantos* (London: Macmillan, 1984).

—— *Modernisms: A Literary Guide* (Basingstoke: Macmillan, 1995).

NIETZSCHE, FRIEDRICH, *Human, All Too Human: A Book for Free Spirits*, trans. R. J. Hollingdale (Cambridge: Cambridge University Press, 1986).

—— *On the Genealogy of Morals: A Polemic*, trans. Douglas Smith (Oxford: Oxford University Press, 1996).

—— *Selected Letters of Friedrich Nietzsche*, trans. Christopher Middleton (Indianapolis: Hackett, 1996).

—— *The Will to Power*, trans. Walter Kaufmann and R. J. Hollingdale (New York: Vintage Books, 1968).

NORTH, MICHAEL, *The Political Aesthetic of Modernism: Yeats, Eliot and Pound* (Cambridge: Cambridge University Press, 1991).

—— *Reading 1922: A Return to the Scene of the Modern* (Oxford: Oxford University Press, 1999).

ORAGE, A. R., *Friedrich Nietzsche: The Dionysian Spirit of the Age* (London: T. N. Foulis, 1906).

PATMORE, BRIGIT, *No Tomorrow* (London: Century Co., 1929).

POUND, EZRA, *Literary Essays of Ezra Pound*, ed. T. S. Eliot (London: Faber & Faber, 1968).

—— *Selected Poems, 1908–1969* (London: Faber & Faber, 1975).

—— *Selected Prose: 1909–1965*, ed. William Cookson (London: Faber & Faber, 1973).

RUSSELL, MRS BERTRAND, *Hypatia: Or Woman and Knowledge* (London: Kegan Paul, Trench, Trubner & Co., 1925).

SCHWARTZ, SANFORD, 'Bergson and the Politics of Vitalism', in Frederick Burwick and Paul Douglas, eds., *The Crisis in Modernism: Bergson and the Vitalist Controversy* (Cambridge: Cambridge University Press, 1992).

—— *The Matrix of Modernism: Pound, Eliot, and Early Twentieth-Century Thought* (Princeton: Princeton University Press, 1985).

SCOTT, BONNIE KIME, *Refiguring Modernism: The Women of 1928*, 2 vols. (Bloomington, Ind.: Indiana University Press, 1995).

SEARLE, GEORGE, *The Liberal Party: Triumph and Disintegration 1886–1929* (Basingstoke: Palgrave, 2001).

SHERRY, VINCENT, *Ezra Pound, Wyndham Lewis, and Radical Modernism* (Oxford: Oxford University Press, 1993).

SHIACH, MORAG, *Modernism, Labour, and Selfhood in British Literature and Culture, 1890–1930* (Cambridge: Cambridge University Press, 2003).

SHULMAN, ALIX KATES, ed., *Red Emma Speaks: The Selected Speeches and Writings of the Anarchist and Feminist Emma Goldman* (London: Wildwood House, 1972).

SMITH, HAROLD L., *The British Women's Suffrage Campaign, 1866–1928* (London: Longman, 1998).

STEIN, GERTRUDE, *The Making of Americans, Being a History of a Family's Progress* (Paris: Contact Editions, Three Mountains Press, 1925).

STIRNER, MAX, *The Ego and its Own*, ed. D. Leopold, trans. S. T. Byington (Cambridge: Cambridge University Press, 1995).

STRACHEY, RAY, *The Cause* (London: G. Bell & Sons Ltd., 1928).

—— *Millicent Garrett Fawcett* (London: John Murray, 1931).

STRYCHACZ, THOMAS, *Modernism, Mass Culture, and Professionalism* (Cambridge: Cambridge University Press, 1993).

SWORD, HELEN, *Ghosthunting Modernism* (Ithaca, NY: Cornell University Press, 2002).

—— 'Orpheus and Eurydice in the Twentieth Century: Lawrence, H.D., and the Poetics of the Turn', *Twentieth Century Literature*, 35.4 (1989).

THATCHER, DAVID, *Nietzsche in England, 1890–1914* (Toronto: University of Toronto Press, 1970).

TILLE, ALEXANDER, 'Introduction', in Nietzsche, *A Genealogy of Morals*, trans. W. Housmann (London: Unwin, 1899).

TRATNER, MICHAEL, *Modernism and Mass Politics: Joyce, Woolf, Eliot, Yeats* (Stanford, Calif.: Stanford University Press, 1995).

TRILLING, LIONEL, *The Liberal Imagination: Essays on Literature and Society* (Harmondsworth: Penguin Books, 1970).

WEIGALL, ARTHUR, *The Paganism in our Christianity* (London: Hutchinson, 1928).

WHITMAN, WALT, *Leaves of Grass*, ed. Jerome Loving (Oxford: Oxford University Press, 1990).

Index